We started the New Year by mentioning the fact that God has given us so many great and wonderful gifts at the moment that we choose to start a spiritual life with Christ. The trouble is, some folks never open the user's guide or owner's manual for their lives to find out. Don't waste a minute of your new birth! Open the manual!

ADORATION/EXPLANATION

God's desire for us is to spend time daily in the Bible. It is in this inspired Word of God that we find a daily road map for living. In reading we will find some simple, obvious ways to live but also some more difficult commands that take years of trust and obedience to carry out. It is never with our own strength, but in the trusting of His power that we are capable of obeying these commands. The beauty of this is that we have our whole lifetime to read, study, and learn.

This is love; not that we loved God, but that he loved us and sent his Son as an atoning sacrifice for our sins. Dear friends, since God so loved us, we ought to love one another. No one has ever seen God; but if we love one another, God lives in us and his love is made complete in us. 1 John 4:10-12 (NIV)

We know that we have come to know him if we obey his commands. The man who says, "I know him," but does not do what he commands is a liar, and the truth is not in him. But if anyone obeys his word, God's love is truly made complete in him. This is how we know we are in him: Whoever claims to live in him must walk as Jesus did. 1 John 2:3-6 (NIV)

WORSHIP/OBEDIENCE

Whoa…if I am capable of obeying God's commands, then I need to make it a priority to do so! If I am claiming to believe in Him…how am I walking?

Dear God, help me to read, study, and live each day as a faithful follower of You. Teach me your ways and precepts and give me your energy and strength to carry them out. Help me to live as Jesus did. Amen.

One of the biggest issues in the life of a believer is doubt. You know, that all too irritating "not sure" feeling? Do you ever find yourself doubting that God is at work, doubting what God tells you, or even sometimes doubting His existence? These thoughts are normal, but do not let your mind reside here! Do not camp on these thoughts!

ADORATION/EXPLANATION

Faith is not necessarily the absence of all inklings of doubt. Rather, it is an assurance or hope that even if these feeling may come, we can choose to believe what God has said. We can choose to rest our trust and life on the Bible and its guidance for our lives. We can choose to accept that we have a heavenly Father who loves and cares about our existence.

"Come," he said. Then Peter got down out of the boat, walked on water and came toward Jesus. But when he saw the wind, he was afraid and, beginning to sink, cried out, "Lord, save me!" Immediately Jesus reached out his hand and caught him, "You of little faith," he said, "why did you doubt?" Matthew 14:29-31 (NIV)

Jesus replied, "I tell you the truth, if you have faith and do not doubt, not only can you do what was done to the fig tree, but also you can say to this mountain, 'Go throw yourself into the sea,' and it will be done." Matthew 21:21 (NIV)

If any of you lacks wisdom, he should ask God, who gives generously to all without finding fault, and it will be given to him. But when he asks, he must believe and not doubt, because he who doubts is like a wave of the sea, blown and tossed by the wind. James 1:5-6 (NIV)

WORSHIP/OBEDIENCE

I have lived and swam in the ocean most of my life. I love it and I am not afraid of it! But sometimes there's a rip current or a storm that brings in huge waves, and at times like this, you can be swept away if you are not careful. God uses this picture in the Bible to help us NOT get swept away by doubt. Do not allow your mind to stay in a constant state of doubting. It is a dangerous place to be. The lifeguard's sign says…Stay out of the water! Rip Currents! Do not even dip your toe in!

January 4

If doubt is one of the greatest deterrents to a strong Christian life, then faith is the most important asset! Faith is a trait that Jesus talks so much about in the Bible, and it is described as being more valuable than silver or gold, stronger than any weapon, and able to leap tall buildings in a single bound. Oh wait, that's Superman! But faith can still help each of us to leap tall obstacles in life!

ADORATION/EXPLANATION

Faith means giving up all trust in our own reasoning, resources, and abilities (things we can actually see). Notice that I didn't say giving up all reasoning, resources or abilities—it is giving up the TRUST in these things. Faith is relying instead on things we cannot see: God, and His reasoning, resources, and abilities. No worries, though! He will equip us for everything that we need.

***

Now faith is being sure of what we hope for and certain of what we do not see. Hebrews 11:1 (NIV)

Let us fix our eyes on Jesus, the author and perfecter of our faith, who for the joy set before him endured the cross, scorning its shame, and sat down at the right hand of the throne of God. Hebrews 12:2 (NIV)

We live by faith, not by sight. Examine yourselves to see whether you are in the faith; test yourselves. Do you not realize that Christ Jesus is in you—unless, of course, you fail the test? 2 Corinthians 5:7; 13:5 (NIV)

WORSHIP/OBEDIENCE

An inner belief alone should not be the only representation of our faith. For genuine faith to be present, action is required. Faith is proven in the steadfastness of our obedience to the Lord. How steadfast are you? Is there enough evidence in your daily life of your beliefs, to convict you in a court of law? Would there be any witnesses?

***

If faith is the most important asset of the Christian, then humility is the vehicle that provides the transport to this genuine asset! We only trust in God's absolute sovereignty if we fully understand and accept that we have NO sovereignty at all. Therefore, any act, talent, or behavior that would deserve applause or praise is credited directly to God.

ADORATION/EXPLANATION

The attribute of being humble is NOT being a doormat or walking around with a "poor pitiful me" persona. It is not being insecure or having low self-esteem. A truly humble person is quietly confident in all the talents and skills that God has given them. They understand that they can be and do wonderful things by the grace of God, and it is He that they are striving to please!

"When someone invites you to a wedding feast, do not take the place of honor, for a person more distinguished than you may have been invited. If so, the host who invited both of you will come and say to you, 'Give this man your seat.' Then, humiliated, you will have to take the least important place. But when you are invited, take the lowest place, so that when your host comes, he will say to you, 'Friend, move up to a better place.' Then you will be honored in the presence of all your fellow guests. For everyone who exalts himself will be humbled, and he who humbles himself will be exalted." Luke 14:8-11 (NIV)

When pride comes, then comes disgrace, but with humility comes wisdom. Proverbs 11:2 (NIV)

Be completely humble and gentle; be patient, bearing with one another in love. Ephesians 4:2 (NIV)

WORSHIP/OBEDIENCE

There is a major difference between the way the world will honor you and the way God does. Cultivate humility and seek to put others first, for this does not come naturally to us. It is a difficult garment to wear…but with practice we can model it well.

When God sees your genuine, humble character, He will exalt you!

Humility versus humiliation—what is the difference? They are spelled almost the same, yet they are so far apart in meaning and definition. Humility is not being proud or haughty, arrogant, or thinking higher of yourself then you ought. Humiliation is being reduced to a lower position in someone's eyes, lowering your self-respect or dignity, or being mortified in front of others.

ADORATION/EXPLANATION
Whenever the Bible addresses the problem of humiliation, it is always in a scenario where someone had already assumed that they were better than others. They thought more highly of themselves to begin with and therefore, were humiliated when they were asked to move seats, step down, or give another their spot. They were served a big slice of humble pie!

Do not exalt yourself in the king's presence, and do not claim a place among great men; it is better for him to say to you, "Come up here," than for him to humiliate you before a nobleman. Proverbs 25:6-7 (NIV)

Young men, in the same way be submissive to those who are older. All of you, clothe yourselves with humility toward one another, because, "God opposes the proud but gives grace to the humble." Humble yourselves, therefore, under God's mighty hand, that he may lift you up in due time. 1 Peter 5:5-6 (NIV)

WORSHIP/OBEDIENCE
Humiliation—how do we avoid it? In yesterday's devotional, we talked about being humble. This trait is not only the vehicle that moves us toward a greater faith, it will also keep us from ever being humiliated. If we keep a right perspective on what our position is, who we are, and what Christ has done for us, we need not worry about humiliation. Not that we won't ever face humiliating circumstances, but that God will allow us to learn and grow in these situations with joy; not humiliation! Another beautifully learned lesson. I never want to taste a piece of humble pie again.

If given the choice, would you choose to live or die? Dumb question, right? Yet Jesus asked people that very question, and then He actually gave them the answer to the question—His life as sacrifice! And yet many people are still choosing the wrong answer for their lives. What do you choose? Does anyone around you know what your answer is?

ADORATION/EXPLANATION

Jesus puts forth this choice in scripture because He already knows that many people will make the wrong choice. He calls their attention to something so obvious as life and death, and then follows up with the correct answer to this multiple-choice question.

This day I call heaven and earth as witnesses against you that I have set before you life and death, blessings and curses. Now choose life, so that you and your children may live and that you may love the Lord your God, listen to his voice, and hold fast to him. For the Lord is your life, and he will give you many years in the land he swore to give to your fathers, Abraham, Isaac and Jacob. Deuteronomy 30:19-20 (NIV)

"But if serving the Lord seems undesirable to you, then choose for yourselves this day whom you will serve, whether the gods your forefathers served beyond the River, or the gods of the Amorites, in whose land you are living. But as for me and my household, we will serve the Lord." Joshua 24:15 (NIV)

WORSHIP/OBEDIENCE

The only reason that anyone would NOT listen to God's words would be the very fact that they do NOT believe that He is God. It doesn't matter what we may say; what do our actions show to be true? What do you choose? Choose life! Choose the God who sent His only Son to die on the cross for your sins. Today, choose to listen to His voice and hold fast to His life-giving words. Allow others to see and know about your choice.

Whatever you need, God is! What if you need clothes, food, drink, or shelter? What if you need comfort? What if you need peace, calm, or rest? What if you need love? What if you need strength to carry on, or courage, or a friend who is faithful and loyal? What if you need help with mean people, fear, or frustration?

ADORATION/EXPLANATION

Whatever you need, God is! There are no "What about...?" There are no ifs, ands, or buts! There are no exceptions, whatsoever.

So do not worry, saying, "What shall we eat?' or 'What shall we drink?' or 'What shall we wear?' But seek first his kingdom and his righteousness, and all these things will be given to you as well." Matthew 6:31, 33 (NIV)

I said to the Lord, "You are my Lord; apart from you I have no good thing." Psalm 16:2 (NIV)

The Lord is my light and my salvation—whom shall I fear? The Lord is the stronghold of my life—of whom shall I be afraid? Psalm 27:1-2 (NIV)

My slanderers pursue me all day long; many are attacking me in their pride. When I am afraid, I will trust in you. Psalm 56:2-3 (NIV)

My soul finds rest in God alone; my salvation comes from him. Psalm 62:1 (NIV)

For the Lord is a sun and shield; the Lord bestows favor and honor; no good thing does he withhold from those whose walk is blameless. O Lord Almighty, blessed is the man who trusts in you. Psalm 84:11 (NIV)

WORSHIP/OBEDIENCE

Whatever you need, God already is!!

Today an acquaintance of mine passed away suddenly. They just did not wake up from sleep. They were not very old, and not known to be ill. They went to work yesterday, went home, went about their evening, and yet this morning it was all over. Why? How could this happen?

ADORATION/EXPLANATION

God tells us, shows us, beseeches us, and warns us in scripture that our lives are like a vapor. A vapor? This is really only seconds long! He compares our earthly lives to a mist and warns that they can be over when we least expect it.

"Show me, O Lord, my life's end and the number of my days; let me know how fleeting is my life. You have made my days a mere handbreadth; the span of my years is as nothing before you. Each man's life is but a breath. Man is a mere phantom as he goes to and fro: He bustles about, but only in vain; he heaps up wealth, not knowing who will get it." "But now, Lord, what do I look for? My hope is in you." Psalm 39:4-7 (NIV)

Now listen, you who say, "Tomorrow we will go to this or that city, and spend a year there, carry on business and make money." Why, you do not even know what will happen tomorrow. What is your life? You are a mist that appears for a little while and then vanishes. Instead, you ought to say, "If it is the Lord's will, we will live and do this or that." James 4:13-15 (NIV)

WORSHIP/OBEDIENCE

Does this scare you? God is not in the business of trying to scare us, but if we let it, the future and the unknown can be a little daunting. But it DOES NOT have to be! Realize that God loves you so much that He wants to prepare you for the future. He wants to give you a chance to seek His guidance for each new day and help you not take any moment for granted.

How are you spending your time?

When I am an old woman, I will have time to sit and watch the birds. When I am old, I will have time to "stop and smell the roses," as they say. In my seventies, I will definitely have more time for my children. When I get a bit older, I will finally...

ADORATION/EXPLANATION

I used to have so many plans for my golden years. For too long I thought I was too busy to read the Bible each morning and told myself I'd make up for it once life slowed down. I decided that I couldn't just waste an evening sitting and watching the stars. Too much housework to go to the beach and no time to take care of the garden I've always wanted. But then I woke up and realized that I have no guarantee of making it to my golden years. For some of us, old age may NOT come. It isn't promised to us at all! So we need to do things we've set aside for later right NOW, and improve our relationships (with God and others) TODAY!

The righteous will flourish like a palm tree, they will grow like a cedar of Lebanon; planted in the house of the Lord, they will flourish in the courts of our God. They will still bear fruit in old age, they will stay fresh and green. Psalm 92:12-14 (NIV)

As long as it is day, we must do the work of him who sent me. Night is coming, when no one can work. John 9:4 (NIV)

As for man, his days are like grass, he flourishes like a flower of the field; the wind blows over it and it is gone, and its place remembers it no more. Psalm 103:15 (NIV)

WORSHIP/OBEDIENCE

If we live to be very old in age, it will only be because of God's grace in our lives. Understanding that our lives may be shorter than our plans helps us take hold of every day and live for Christ. By knowing this, we gain a better appreciation for each new morning and every passing sunset. We will not postpone studying God's word, loving people, or enjoying and cultivating relationships until a later date.

Night may be coming. Today is the day!

We have all heard the phrase, "You can't take it with you." Yet so many people still seem to live and act like they can. Why is this? Money and the pursuit of things take precedence over relationships with God and people. If we really believed that we can't take anything with us when we die, it would result in a changed life where our material possessions are concerned. Unselfish people would be the norm, not the exception.

ADORATION/EXPLANATION

Working hard and earning an honest living are admirable. God speaks of working, saving, and being a good steward of our "stuff." It's good to desire to be a faithful worker at our jobs, but we must also keep God's perspective on our money and time. We must realize that everything we have is His provision for us, and no amount can ever buy us eternal life. No amount can make us better or worse than others. No amount should render a selfish or hoarding spirit within us!

No man can redeem the life of another or give God a ransom for him—the ransom for a life is costly, no payment is ever enough—that he should live on forever and not see decay. For all can see that wise men die; the foolish and the senseless alike perish and leave their wealth to others. Psalm 49:7-10, 16-17, 20 (NIV)

Do not be overawed when a man grows rich, when the splendor of his house increases; for he will take nothing with him when he dies, his splendor will not descend with him.

A man who has riches without understanding is like the beasts that perish.

Whoever trusts in his riches will fall, but the righteous will thrive like a green leaf. Proverbs 11:28 (NIV)

WORSHIP/OBEDIENCE

Do we want to thrive or fall? That should be the question that we ask ourselves every time that we are tempted to make monetary or material things overly important.

Lord, help me to work hard and save while also keeping a godly perspective on my money.

Even in the cold of winter, we can see God's creation all around us. Sometimes we take it for granted. Other times we just forget to look and see that the Lord is good. Today we should choose to look, really look, at God's marvelous works all around us.

ADORATION/EXPLANATION

Our awesome God never turns a cold shoulder towards us. His love is constant, even in the frigid seasons and times of our lives.

Dear God, open my eyes that I may see. Open my mind that I may appreciate. Open my heart and soul that I may give you praise for this wonderfully created world that You have placed me in, even in the dead cold of winter!

Let the heavens rejoice, let the earth be glad; let the sea resound, and all that is in it; let the fields be jubilant, and everything them. Then all the trees of the forest will sing for joy; Psalm 96:11-12 (NIV)

The Lord reigns, let the earth be glad; let the distant shores rejoice. His lightning lights up the world; the earth sees and trembles. The mountains melt like wax before the Lord, before the Lord of all the earth. The heavens proclaim his righteousness, and all the peoples see his glory. Psalm 97:1, 4-6 (NIV)

Praise him, sun and moon, praise him, all you shining stars. Praise him, you highest heavens and you waters above the skies. Praise the Lord from the earth, you great sea creatures and all ocean depths, lightning and hail, snow and clouds, stormy winds that do his bidding, you mountains and all hills, fruit trees and all cedars, wild animals and all cattle, small creatures and flying birds, Psalm 148:3-4, 7-10 (NIV)

WORSHIP/OBEDIENCE

Let's be faithful followers of God today. If all of creation rises up to praise God each day, then how much more should we rise up to praise Him? Part of having a heart of worship and obedience is to have an attitude of gratitude. Look around! Trees, mountains, rain, snow, oceans, rocks or plains—whatever terrain you live in, look around and give thanks!

Do you ever just mumble a silent prayer under your breath? I do very often.

Open my heart, Lord. I want to see Jesus. I want to feel God's presence and be moved to follow His example for my life. I want a transformed, obedient, and pliant heart. I choose today to listen to the Spirit as it moves me to be a faithful follower of Jesus in my comings and goings, during my errands and appointments, and all throughout this day.

ADORATION/EXPLANATION

In the Old Testament book of Ezekiel, we see that God would rather forgive us than condemn us. He always remains faithful and can use even our troubles for His greater good. Ezekiel was just one priest, but he was used by God to let people know that their hearts could be radically changed. If the people let Him, God could accomplish a transformation from hearts of cold stone to those that were warm and thriving. It was good advice, but not everyone followed it.

I will give you a new heart and put a new spirit in you; I will remove from you your heart of stone and give you a heart of flesh. And I will put my Spirit in you and move you to follow my decrees and be careful to keep my laws. Ezekiel 36:26-27 (NIV)

But if from there you seek the Lord you God, you will find him if you look for him with all your heart and with all your soul. When you are in distress and all these things have happened to you, then in later days you will return to the Lord your God and obey him. Deuteronomy 4:29-30 (NIV)

"You will seek me and find me when you seek me with all your heart." Jeremiah 29:13 (NIV)

WORSHIP/OBEDIENCE

What is the obvious path to worship and obedience? Seek God with all of your heart! Seek Him in every circumstance throughout your day. Today, seek Him with the intention of finding Him.

Open my heart Lord! I want to see Jesus!

January 14

When you open your heart to people, whether that be family or friends you also run the risk of getting wounded. Hurt feelings, insults, disappointment, sadness, and strife are just a few of the wounds that could result from opening your heart. Letting someone in to your deepest thoughts and emotions is risky, but it can also provide the greatest joy and comfort for you.

ADORATION/EXPLANATION

We cannot and should not avoid opening our lives for fear of a broken heart. The fact is that most of us will have our hearts broken or saddened at some point in our lives. But if we try to avoid sadness and disappointment in relationships, we will never have any relationships at all. This has never been God's plan for us. We desperately crave closeness to other human beings, just as God craves closeness with us.

I sought the Lord, and he answered me; he delivered me from all my fears. The Lord is close to the brokenhearted and saves those who are crushed in spirit. Psalm 34:4, 18 (NIV)

I will praise the Lord, who counsels me; even at night my heart instructs me. I have set the Lord always before me. Because he is at my right hand, I will not be shaken. Therefore my heart is glad and my tongue rejoices; my body will also rest secure, Psalm 16:7-9 (NIV)

Therefore we do not lose heart. Though outwardly we are wasting away, yet inwardly we are being renewed day by day. For our light and momentary troubles are achieving for us an eternal glory that far outweighs them all. 2 Corinthians 4:16-17 (NIV)

WORSHIP/OBEDIENCE

Go ahead and let others in. Open your heart and emotions to potentially beautiful and stimulating relationships. Don't miss out. Love, give, and share your heart freely. Trust God and He will take care of the rest!

Have you ever blurted out this directive to someone:, "Open your eyes! It's right in front of you!" Or how about this: "It's as plain as the nose on your face!" My parents said these things to me many times as I was growing up and I in turn repeated them to my children. Why? Well it wasn't to be mean or critical or to point out the fact that they couldn't see something. In fact it was just the opposite!

ADORATION/EXPLANATION
Most of the time, parents, teachers, and friends make these statements not to be critical, but to be helpful. Sometimes the answers or solutions to our problems are right in front of our faces and we do not see it, not because we are physically blind, but because we are so distracted or in a hurry that we can't seem to see clearly. We may be looking right past what we need to find.

This happened to many people who encountered Jesus during his ministry on earth. Their vision was blurred.

When Jesus had finished these parables, he moved on from there. Coming to his hometown, he began teaching the people in their synagogue, and they were amazed. "Where did this man get this wisdom and these miraculous powers?" they asked. "Isn't this the carpenter's son? Isn't his mother's name Mary, and aren't his brothers James, Joseph, Simon and Judas? Aren't all his sisters with us? Where then did this man get all these things?" And they took offense at him.

But Jesus said to them, "Only in his hometown and in his own house is a prophet without honor." And he did not do many miracles there because of their lack of faith. Matthew 13:53-58 (NIV)

WORSHIP/OBEDIENCE
God has unlimited power but He does not force us to see it. He desires our faithfulness and clear eyesight when looking for Him. In Scripture, the people of Jesus's hometown had already made their minds up about him. Their eyes and ears did not recognize who was right in front of them.

They missed it. Are you missing it?

Lord, today I will choose to look carefully around me!

"Trust and obey" is a common buzz phrase in the Christian world, yet God also directs us in scripture to test everything. If I am puzzled by what is going on in the world and not sure what God would have me do, I need to check that it lines up with His instructions in the Bible. After careful searching, praying, and mature godly counsel, I can then go about the business of trusting and obeying in confidence.

ADORATION/EXPLANATION

God does not want me to become so skeptical that I view everything with contempt, nor does He want me to indiscriminately accept every word or message that appears to come from God. As a prudent and faithful follower of Christ, I will confidently take the time to search the Bible for answers and guidance.

Do not conform any longer to the pattern of this world, but be transformed by the renewing of your mind. Then you will be able to test and approve what God's will is—his good, pleasing and perfect will. Romans 12:2 (NIV)

For no one can lay any foundation other than the one already laid, which is Jesus Christ. If any man builds on this foundation using gold, silver, costly stones, wood, hay or straw, his work will be shown for what it is, because the Day will bring it to light. It will be revealed with fire, and the fire will test the quality of each man's work. 1 Corinthians 3:11-13 (NIV)

Test everything. Hold on to the good. Avoid every kind of evil. 1 Thessalonians 5:21-22 (NIV)

WORSHIP/OBEDIENCE

The obvious act of worship and obedience on our part requires making time to read God's word daily. The more that we familiarize ourselves with Scripture and apply it to our everyday lives, the more we will understand how to confidently trust and obey. Any time that we have a decision to make, we should automatically and habitually test it against what we know to be good and true.

Read, pray, trust, and obey!

We are representatives of God here on earth. God has entrusted us to this business of being His ambassadors in our daily environments where we live, work and play. What a privilege and what confidence this should give us all!

ADORATION/EXPLANATION

God encourages us to take a bold approach to problem solving and decision making in our daily schedules. Each time that we trust Him and act decisively, we build up our confidence in Him. On the flip side, there will be days when we second-guess our decisions and wonder where our boldness has gone. Those are the times that we need to pray a little more and rely on God a lot more.

In him and through faith in him we may approach God with freedom and confidence. Ephesians 3:12 (NIV)

The wicked man flees though no one pursues, but the righteous are as bold as a lion. Proverbs 28:1 (NIV)

See to it, brothers, that none of you has a sinful, unbelieving heart that turns away from the living God. But encourage one another daily, as long as it is called Today, so that none of you may be hardened by sin's deceitfulness. We have come to share in Christ if we hold firmly till the end the confidence we had at first. Hebrews 3:12-14 (NIV)

WORSHIP/OBEDIENCE

In times of uncertainty, my obvious act of obedience to God will be to run to Him in simple prayer.

Dear God, help me not to worry when my confidence starts to waver and my boldness seems to have disappeared. I need to see these times as a warning that I am starting to trust myself more than I trust you. I want others to see me acting with a boldness and confidence that can only come from you. Please help me recognize the difference! Amen

In the New Testament account of Peter and the disciples in the boat on the Sea of Galilee, we see boldness and faith in God demonstrated. In the midst of a violent storm, believing that they were seeing a ghost coming toward them across the water, they cried out in fear. Out from the pelting rain and swirling clouds came Jesus, walking on water and assuring them who He was. They had nothing to fear, yet it was only Peter who trusted.

ADORATION/EXPLANATION

In Matthew 14 we read that Peter alone seemed to be the only one who believed Him, yet he still boldly asks Jesus to prove himself. Jesus does this by commanding Peter to come to Him on the water. And just because Christ said he could, full of confidence Peter steps out of the boat and starts walking on water!

"Lord, if it's you," Peter replied, "tell me to come to you on the water."

"Come," he said. Then Peter got down out of the boat, walked on the water and came toward Jesus. But when he saw the wind, he was afraid and, beginning to sink, cried out, "Lord, save me!" Immediately Jesus reached out his hand and caught him. "You of little faith," he said, "why did you doubt?" And when they climbed into the boat, the wind died down. Matthew 14:28-32 (NIV)

Be strong and take heart, all you who hope in the Lord. Psalm 31:24 (NIV)

WORSHIP/OBEDIENCE

As soon as the howling wind and the raging sea distracts Peter, his fear overtakes him. His boldness and faith (that moments before let him walk on waves, no less!) gives way, and Peter begins to sink. The beauty of this story is that Peter calls out, and Jesus saves him. The lesson for us is clear: once we take our eyes off of Jesus and get distracted by the storms of our everyday lives, we will lose confidence and begin to sink.

Call out today and ask the Lord to rescue you from your storms!

January 19

Tomorrow my son and daughter-in-law are coming for lunch. I am excited and pleased that they are coming, so today I am shopping and preparing the food that I am going to serve them. I will not wait until the last minute to get ready. Because I love them and am excited for their visit, I am going about all the chores and preparation today so that I will be able to enjoy their company tomorrow.

ADORATION/EXPLANATION

Too often we wait to get prepared. We say to ourselves, "No rush, I have plenty of time." This is called procrastination, putting off what we should and could do now until later. Imagine if God did this. Aren't you glad He doesn't?

However, as it is written: "No eye has seen, no ear has heard, no mind has conceived what God has prepared for those who love him"—but God has revealed it to us by his Spirit. 1 Corinthians 2:9-10 (NIV)

"Do not let your hearts be troubled. Trust in God, trust also in me. In my Father's house are many rooms; if it were not so, I would have told you. I am going there to prepare a place for you. John 14:1-2 (NIV)

"Then the King will say to those on his right, 'Come, you who are blessed by my Father; take your inheritance, the kingdom prepared for you since the creation of the world. For I was hungry and you gave me something to eat, I was thirsty and you gave me something to drink, I was a stranger and you invited me in…" Matthew 25:34-35 (NIV)

WORSHIP/OBEDIENCE

Just as I am preparing ahead of time for my son to visit, God has already prepared a life for me here on earth and a wonderful home in heaven. I am preparing in advance so that I will not be too busy to enjoy my family's conversation and, because of this, they will know that they are special to me! What a joy it is to be assured by God's word that He has already prepared a place for you and me! We are special to the Most High God!

January 20

Sometimes we feel that we have the right to say whatever we want. _I am angry and someone needs to know this!_ The cashier is moving too slowly, the bank teller is wrong, the teacher is mean, the coach is unfair, or the boss is downright dumb. We have the right to speak out! Don't we?

ADORATION/EXPLANATION
As a Christian, I may have to give up my "rights" in favor of acting the way Jesus would want me to act. The cashier may indeed be too slow, the coach unfair, and the boss downright dumb, but if speaking up or yelling harsh words or arguing will ensue, then our "rights" must take a back seat. Many people will be watching your character and behavior in these situations, and your actions will speak volumes.

I said, "I will watch my ways and keep my tongue from sin; I will put a muzzle on my mouth as long as the wicked are in my presence." Psalm 39:1 (NIV)

Consider the blameless, observe the upright; there is a future for the man of peace. Psalm 37:37 (NIV)

Don't have anything to do with foolish and stupid arguments, because you know they produce quarrels. Those who oppose him he must gently instruct, in the hope that God will grant them repentance leading them to a knowledge of the truth, 2 Timothy 2:23, 25 (NIV)

WORSHIP/OBEDIENCE
So, do I mean that we can never stand up for ourselves again? Of course not, and God is not suggesting that either! Speaking up truthfully and peaceably is wonderful, but there will be many times when we _could_ say something but _should_ muzzle our mouths instead. Our "right" to speak will be traded for the fruit of self-control, patience, and kindness. A fabulous swap, if you ask me!

I have a choice to give up some of my rights; I have a choice to muzzle my mouth; and I have a choice to believe God when He gives me advice, commands, and promises in the Bible. I know what I am choosing. What about you?

ADORATION/EXPLANATION

Sometimes this free will thing that God has given us is not so much fun. It would be easier if the correct choice was made for us and we didn't have to worry about the outcome of our decisions. Right move, wrong move…just give me a push! But God desires our actions to be motivated by our faith in Him, our faith in His word, and our relationship with Him. Therefore, He cannot make our choices, but He will give us guidance and direction if only I study, ask, and persevere.

Blessed is the man who perseveres under trial, because when he has stood the test, he will receive the crown of life that God has promised to those who love him. James 1:12 (NIV)

For this very reason, make every effort to add to your faith goodness; and to goodness, knowledge; and to knowledge, self-control; and to self-control, perseverance; and to perseverance, godliness; and to godliness, brotherly kindness; and to brotherly kindness, love. For if you possess these qualities in increasing measure, they will keep you from being ineffective and unproductive in your knowledge of our Lord Jesus Christ. 2 Peter 1:5-8 (NIV)

You have persevered and have endured hardships for my name, and have not grown weary. Revelation 2:3 (NIV)

WORSHIP/OBEDIENCE

Our minds cannot conceive of what God has prepared for us, and therefore we will have to step out in faith. Choose today to persevere in your choices, to persevere in giving up your rights if need be, and to persevere in your trust of God's perfect guidance in His word.

Do not be ineffective and unproductive today!

January 22

We have all heard the saying, "You are what you eat." Basically that is the health experts and nutritionists trying to tell us that our diet is very important. Sometimes our appetites can get the best of us and even the most disciplined person will on occasion be tempted to over-indulge in candy, cake, chips, ice cream, or whatever their pleasure may be. God tells us that what we hunger for is going to change us, for good or bad!

ADORATION/EXPLANATION

When my boys were growing up, I regularly fed them a wide variety of sautéed vegetables for dinner. Yes, the things that most kids will not eat! Onions, squash, zucchini, turnips, beets, beans, broccoli, cauliflower, spinach, and a salad were the standard at my house. Whether they liked it or not, they had to eat a little every day because it was good for their nutrition. As they grew into men, they would tell me that now they crave those vegetables and salads. Why? Because the result of eating that way as a child had become a habit and so much a part of their daily diet.

Blessed are those who hunger and thirst for righteousness, for they will be filled. Matthew 5:6 (NIV)

Let them give thanks to the Lord for his unfailing love and his wonderful deeds for men, for he satisfies the thirsty and fills the hungry with good things. Psalm 107:8-9 (NIV)

For the kingdom of God is not a matter of eating and drinking, but of righteousness, peace and joy in the Holy Spirit, because anyone who serves Christ in this way is pleasing to god and approved by men. Romans 14:17-18 (NIV)

WORSHIP/OBEDIENCE

We really are what we eat, especially when it comes to our spiritual lives! We need to hunger for the traits, actions, and behaviors that will make us more like Christ. Do you want to be like Jesus? Hunger and thirst for His character and lifestyle today!

Don't delay in making it a habit!

January 23

So many young folks today just want to fit in. Actually, so many young *and* old folks today just want to fit in! Let's rephrase that thought once again: so many young *and* old folks have *always* wanted to fit in, not just in today's times, but long ago too! Sadly, many people will do whatever it takes to fit into society, even if fitting in calls for them to go against their beliefs, morals, or God.

ADORATION/EXPLANATION

God has NOT called you to fit in. As a matter of fact, it is just the opposite! God has called you to stand up, stand apart, and stand firm against the things of this world. This is not always an easy task, but when we look to the Bible for advice and guidance, we are sure to be on the right path.

But you are a chosen people, a royal priesthood, a holy nation, a people belonging to God, that you may declare the praises of him who called you out of darkness into his wonderful light. Once you were not a people, but now you are the people of God; once you had not received mercy, but now you have received mercy.

Dear friends, I urge you as aliens and strangers in the world, to abstain from sinful desires, which war against your soul. Live such good lives among the pagans that, though they accuse you of doing wrong, they may see your good deeds and glorify God on the day he visits us. For it is God's will that by doing good you should silence the ignorant talk of foolish men. Live as free men, but do not use your freedom as a cover-up for evil; live as servants of God. 1 Peter 2:9-12, 15-16 (NIV)

WORSHIP/OBEDIENCE

"So, you are telling me that I am supposed to stand out and be strange?" Well, not exactly! Our goal is not to *try* to be strange, but to realize that we *are* strangers to this world's way of thinking. We are to stand out and stand apart, not with protests, soapboxes, or fights, but with good deeds and right behavior. To abstain from certain sinful behaviors may not allow us to fit in with our peers sometimes, but if this is lived out in a loving, non-judgmental way, it will take the limelight off of us and point others to God.

Our daily act of worship should be to STAND apart!

"What in the world is going on?" I have heard people ask this and have also asked this question myself! In the Old Testament book of Habakkuk, there was a Jewish prophet by the same name. Habakkuk lived about 600 B.C. at a time when the nation of Judah was in rapid decline. Injustice, violence, and immorality of all kinds were reigning supreme over the land. Sounds kind of like the world in which we are living today, doesn't it?

ADORATION/EXPLANATION

The name "Habakkuk" means "to grab hold of, embrace, or to wrestle." What a cool name! Habakkuk took to heart some of the serious problems of his day and certainly wrestled with the Lord about them. I am in awe over the fact that God does not mind us wrestling with Him about the things of this world. God knows that we can become confused, scared, and worried, so He welcomes the chance for us to search for His meaning and wrestle with His concepts.

How long, O Lord, must I call for help, but you do not listen? Or cry out to you, "Violence!" but you do not save? Why do you make me look at injustice? Why do you tolerate wrong? Destruction and violence are before me; there is strife, and conflict abounds. Therefore the law is paralyzed, and justice never prevails. The wicked hem in the righteous, so that justice is perverted.

The Lord's Answer

"Look at the nations and watch—and be utterly amazed. For I am going to do something in your days that you would not believe, even if you were told." Habakkuk 1:2-5

WORSHIP/OBEDIENCE

Sometimes I think, "Why isn't God doing something?" This is the same problem Habakkuk faced, and he may have prayed as long as twelve years for these issues without any response! During our waiting times, we may be learning something about God's timing. He is always working behind the scenes, even if we cannot see Him. He loves the fact that we obey and worship Him even though we continue to wrestle with what is going on.

True obedience and worship does not need all the answers!

Yesterday we ended with the thought that true obedience and worship does not need all the answers. The prophet Habakkuk was down in the dumps about this. He was way down in a valley, at a low point mentally and spiritually. He believed that God was inactive and inconsistent because He was not getting answers to his prayers.

ADORATION/EXPLANATION

Before we criticize Habakkuk, I must confess that sometimes I have asked these same things of God. Why? Where? When? This is my fragile human mind getting in on the action. But pure adoration and awe of God requires us to trust Him even when things are still going badly; even when we have yet to be delivered from our troubles.

O Lord, are you not from everlasting? My God, my Holy One, we will not die. O Lord, you have appointed them to execute judgment; O Rock, you have ordained them to punish. Your eyes are too pure to look on evil; you cannot tolerate wrong. Why then do you tolerate the treacherous? Why are you silent while the wicked swallow up those more righteous than themselves? Habakkuk 1:12-13 (NIV)

Since ancient times no one has heard, no ear has perceived, no eye has seen any God besides you, who acts on behalf of those who wait for him.

You come to the help of those who gladly do right, who remember your ways. Isaiah 64:4-5a (NIV)

WORSHIP/OBEDIENCE

When I read the morning paper or watch the news on television, I think to myself, "Why doesn't God stop this?" Just when I let it begin to depress me, I hear God's voice whisper, "I AM doing something. Keep waiting and be patient. Even though you can't see it, trust me, continue to live by faith and not by sight."

Then we may not be sure, but if we listen closely we can also hear, "Close your mouth and keep quiet!" Remember, Psalms 46:10a tells us to "be still, and know that I am God!"

Have you ever prayed fervently for help and it appeared as though God was not hearing? Even Jesus' disciples had a problem like that. In the book of Mark they said, "Lord, don't you care that we are perishing?" Of course they knew He cared, but when times got tough, they questioned Him instead of looking at their own lack of faith.

ADORATION/EXPLANATION

Jesus never said that we would not face fearful circumstances. Instead, we are taught all throughout Scripture that God is greater than whatever we are facing. Genuine faith means trusting that we never face our problems alone.

"But the Lord is in his holy temple; let all the earth be silent before him." Habakkuk 2:20 (NIV)

Lord, I have heard of your fame; I stand in awe of your deeds, O Lord. Renew them in our day, in our time make them known; in wrath remember mercy. Habakkuk 3:2 (NIV)

A furious squall came up, and the waves broke over the boat, so that it was nearly swamped. Jesus was in the stern, sleeping on a cushion. The disciples woke him and said to him, "Teacher, don't you care if we drown?" He got up, rebuked the wind and said to the waves, "Quiet, be still!" Then the wind died down and it was completely calm. He said to the disciples, "Why are you so afraid? Do you still have no faith?" Mark 4:37- 40 (NIV)

WORSHIP/OBEDIENCE

Do you notice that Jesus didn't answer their question of, "Teacher, don't you care if we drown?" Why? Because Jesus knew that the issue was not their possible drowning, it was their lack of faith in times of stress and hardship. As Habakkuk says, "Lord, I have heard of your fame; I stand in awe of your deeds." What a reminder for us all!

Lord, please be with me today. I don't know why I am so afraid sometimes, but I DO have faith. Help me to live this way.

Can sickness, disease, terminal illness, or even death bring glory to God? Don't feel guilty if you answered, "NO!" This may be a scary proposition for many readers. It is sometimes frightful for me to even think about. The point is that, it is not the ordeal itself that brings glory, but rather the end result of God's power through the disease.

ADORATION/EXPLANATION

God chooses to conquer and heal some illnesses and in other cases, He gives us a strong spiritual strength to live above our physical limitations.

Now a man named Lazarus was sick. He was from Bethany, the village of Mary and her sister Martha. This Mary, whose brother Lazarus now lay sick, was the same one who poured perfume on the lord and wiped his feet with her hair. So the sisters sent word to Jesus, "Lord, the one you love is sick." When he heard this, Jesus said, "This sickness will not end in death. No, it is for God's glory so that God's Son may be glorified through it." Jesus loved Martha and her sister and Lazarus. Yet when he heard that Lazarus was sick, he stayed where he was two more days. Then he said to his disciples, "Let us go back to Judea." John 11:1-7 (NIV)

After he had said this, he went on to tell them, "Our friend Lazarus has fallen asleep; but I am going there to wake him up." His disciples replied, "Lord, if he sleeps, he will get better." Jesus had been speaking of his death, but his disciples thought he meant natural sleep. So then he told them plainly, "Lazarus is dead, and for your sake I am glad I was not there, so that you may believe. But let us go to him." John 11:11-14 (NIV)

WORSHIP/OBEDIENCE

The obvious question in my mind is, "What in the world was Jesus waiting for? Why wait two more days? Why not rush quickly to the scene?"

God has a plan. God has THE plan! For every prayer request for healing, strength, lessened pain, and discomfort, God knows our situation and hears us when we call.

\Worship and trust Him during your time of waiting!

January 28

Does God really care? Does He actually hear us when we call out in prayer? Did Jesus actually understand the message from Mary and Martha, that Lazarus was really terminally ill? Was there a communication problem?

ADORATION/EXPLANATION

Of course He did, and now I realize that my doubt was rooted in that fact that I didn't see the big picture myself! And if I'm being really transparent and honest, isn't that arrogance on my part? Why do I think that my decision could be better than God's? We think that God must not really be "getting" the seriousness of our situation. We say, "Come on God, what are You waiting for?"

On his arrival, Jesus found that Lazarus had already been in the tomb for four days. When Martha heard that Jesus was coming, she went out to meet him, but Mary stayed at home. "Lord," Martha said to Jesus, "if you had been here, my brother would not have died. But I know that even now God will give you whatever you ask." Jesus said to her, "Your brother will rise again." Martha answered, "I know he will rise again in the resurrection at the last day." Jesus said to her, "I am the resurrection and the life. He who believes in me will live, even though he dies; and whoever lives and believes in me will never die. Do you believe this?"

"Yes, Lord," she told him, "I believe that you are the Christ, the Son of God, who was to come into the world." John 11:17, 20-27 (NIV)

WORSHIP/OBEDIENCE

Martha's reaction is amazing. She didn't go out screaming and yelling and accusing Jesus. She makes a statement. Actually a real, genuine statement of belief: "Lord, if you had been here my brother would not have died. But I know that even now God will do whatever you ask." Not "Why? Where? How come?" But a calm, assured comment! She kept her faith and belief in Jesus, even in extreme grief. She trusted His plan, not her own!

Dear God, give me the heart of Martha today!

January 29

In John's Gospel, we read that Jesus wept when He saw others grieving over the death of Lazarus. Why would Jesus cry if He knew that Lazarus was going to be raised from the dead? Does God grieve? Could God in the human form of Jesus feel Mary and Martha's pain at the loss of their brother?

ADORATION/EXPLANATION

Wow…what a concept! Jesus is our intercessor, our advocate, and direct link to God the Father, who can and does feel our pain and grief along with us. He did it then and He is still doing it now!

When the Jews who had been with Mary in the house, comforting her, noticed how quickly she got up and went out, they followed her, supposing she was going to the tomb to mourn there. When Mary reached the place where Jesus was and saw him, she fell at his feet and said, "Lord, if you had been here, my brother would not have died." When Jesus saw her weeping, he was deeply moved in spirit and troubled. "Where have you laid him?" he asked. "Come and see, Lord," they replied. Jesus wept. Then the Jews said, "See how he loved him!" But some of them said, "Could not he who opened the eyes of the blind man have kept this man from dying?" John 11:31-37 (NIV)

For we do not have a high priest who is unable to sympathize with our weaknesses, but we have one who has been tempted in every way, just as we are—yet was without sin. Let us approach the throne of grace with confidence, so that we may receive mercy and find grace to help us in our time of need. Hebrews 4:15-16 (NIV)

WORSHIP/OBEDIENCE

Customary Jewish mourners always wailed loudly. As was their custom, the mourners and friends wailed and grieved for days on end. The fact that Jesus's spirit was troubled and Scripture says that He wept conveys a quiet, sad, grieving of the heart in the shedding of tears. Even though Jesus knew that the Father could heal Lazarus, He cried because of the agonizing impact that His friend's death had on family and friends.

We cannot help but worship a mighty God who sympathizes with us in sorrow!

If you look closely in the story of Lazarus, there were optimists and pessimists on the scene. Optimists always anticipate the best possible outcome, while pessimists expect the worst. Is it acceptable to have an attitude of pessimism where God is concerned? Can an attitude of pessimism even exist with God? With genuine faith, can we even allow it to be a characteristic of our daily life??

ADORATION/EXPLANATION

Some of you may be thinking, "Well, I'm just a realist. I tend to see things as they really are, good or bad. I don't want to get too excited about a good outcome when something bad, sad, or frightening may happen. I am just preparing myself!" Maybe so…but couldn't it also be that you might be allowing the devil to get a foothold in your mind?

Then the Jews said, "See how he loved him?" But some of them said, "Could not he who opened the eyes of the blind man have kept this man from dying?" John 11:36-37 (NIV)

And this is my prayer: that your love may abound more and more in knowledge and depth of insight, so that you may be able to discern what is best and may be pure and blameless until the day of Christ, Philippians 1:9-10 (NIV)

Jesus, once more deeply moved, came to the tomb. It was a cave with a stone laid across the entrance. "Take away the stone," he said. "But, Lord," said Martha, the sister of the dead man, "by this time there is a bad odor, for he has been there four days." John 11:38-40 (NIV)

WORSHIP/OBEDIENCE

Some of the Jews in this story noticed how Jesus loved Lazarus. Others questioned His delay in coming and His ability. It's amazing that they DO acknowledge that Jesus made the blind to see, yet still question His motives in this situation. Did they really believe? Do we really believe?

Doubting and pessimistic thoughts come from Satan.

Genuine worship requires fewer questions and more obedience!

Is it okay to ask questions of God? Can we wonder about what He is doing in our lives or the lives of others? Sure! We would all be lying if we said that we never, ever had a question or concern about what takes place sometimes.

ADORATION/EXPLANATION

Martha and Mary, the sisters of Lazarus, had questions, but they also had faith in Jesus. Their faith allowed them to ask human questions of the one whom they believed was the Savior of the world. Do you see the difference? The others asked among themselves or mumbled under their breath the very questions that they should have asked Christ himself.

They did not see that He was the author of life.

At this the Jews began to grumble about him because he said, "I am the bread that came down from heaven." They said, "Is this not Jesus, the son of Joseph, whose father and mother we know? How can he now say, "I came down from heaven?" "Stop grumbling among yourselves," Jesus answered. John 6:41-43 (NIV)

Then Jesus said, "Did I not tell you that if you believed, you would see the glory of God?" So they took away the stone. Then Jesus looked up and said, "Father, I thank you that you have heard me. I knew that you always hear me, but I said this for the benefit of the people standing here, that they may believe that you sent me." When he had said this, Jesus called in a loud voice, "Lazarus, come out!" The dead man came out, his hands and feet wrapped with strips of linen, and a cloth around his face. John 11:40-44 (NIV)

WORSHIP/OBEDIENCE

Dear God, I promise today, as my daily act of worship, that if I have any questions about Your plan for my life I will just ask YOU. I believe that You already know my mind and soul and the questions or concerns that linger there. You never get upset or mad when I ask. I choose not to grumble and mumble to others but to trust You! You are the author and finisher of my faith. Your ways are perfect!

February 1

Why doesn't God send a fire from heaven and destroy all the evil people in this world? At least reform all of the murderers and child abusers, drug dealers and terrorists, thieves and criminals? Because even though it might be a temporary fix, it would not heal the world. We don't need for people to be reformed, we all need regeneration!

ADORATION/EXPLANATION

Hearts have to be changed! Regeneration means to rebuild, reestablish, or reconstruct. Until hearts are changed by His grace, society and people will not change at all. Without His healing, society will only continue to follow the same dark pattern. It is sad sometimes…

"Woe to him who piles up stolen goods and makes himself wealthy by extortion! How long must this go on?" Habakkuk 2:6b, 9, 12 (NIV)

"Woe to him who builds his realm by unjust gain to set his nest on high, to escape the clutches of ruin!"

"Woe to him who builds a city with bloodshed and establishes a town by crime!

Unless the Lord builds the house, its builders labor in vain. Unless the Lord watches over the city, the watchmen stand guard in vain. Psalm 127:1 (NIV)

But God demonstrates his own love for us in this: While we were still sinners, Christ died for us.

Since we have now been justified by his blood, how much more shall we be saved from God's wrath through him! Romans 5:8-9 (NIV)

WORSHIP/OBEDIENCE

Woe to us if we do not accept God's wonderful free gift of His son, Jesus. The very meaning of the word "woe" is summed up as "sorrow, disaster, trouble, suffering, sadness and grief." Our world cannot be reformed by its own power. It needs to have regenerated, rebuilt, and newly reestablished hearts for God.

Lord, help me to faithfully live today as a REGENERATED child!

February 2

Sometimes God lets us get exactly what we deserve. Sound good? Not always. In general, people want God to step in and do something in their lives, but they do not want to faithfully follow Him.

ADORATION/EXPLANATION
People don't want to read the Bible, they don't want standards, they don't want absolutes, and they don't feel like going to church. They don't want rules or regulations or anything that goes against their personal comfort. And to that God says, fine. He isn't going to force Himself on anyone.

My son, do not forget my teaching, but keep my commands in your heart, for they will prolong your life for many years and bring you prosperity. Let love and faithfulness never leave you, bind them around your neck, write them on the tablet of your heart. Then you will win favor and a good name in the sight of God and man. Trust in the Lord with all your heart and lean not on your own understanding; in all your ways acknowledge him, and he will make your paths straight. Proverbs 3:1-6 (NIV)

My son, pay attention to what I say; listen closely to my words. Do not let them out of your sight, keep them within your heart; for they are life to those who find them and health to a man's whole body. Proverbs 4:20-22 (NIV)

"The fear of the Lord is the beginning of wisdom, and knowledge of the Holy One is understanding. For through me your days will be many, and years will be added to your life. Proverbs 9:10 (NIV)

WORSHIP/OBEDIENCE
We can live exactly as we please in this life and God will let us reap the consequences of the life that we choose to live. What I find to be so wonderful and fantastic is the fact that God provides terrific advice for us in the Bible. He doesn't force it upon us, but it is there for the taking.

We need to take our daily dose of His vitamins!

"I need help! I cannot do this on my own!" How often have we uttered these phrases, either in our heads or out loud? Well the truth is we all need help! Some admit it, some do not! As Christians, we have a Helper who has been given to us for our everyday lives yet we do not always use Him! When Jesus left this earth, He told His disciples and followers that, though He was leaving, He would leave them a Helper!

ADORATION/EXPLANATION

The moment that we accept Christ as our personal Savior, we have access to a wonderful spiritual guide: the Holy Spirit! So if He is available to us, then why don't we call on Him? We might be missing out on so many wonderful blessings because we are trying to do this thing called "life" on our own.

On one occasion, while he was eating with them, he gave them this command: "Do not leave Jerusalem, but wait for the gift my Father promised, which you have heard me speak about. For John baptized with water, but in a few days you will be baptized with the Holy Spirit." Acts 1:4 (NIV)

"But the counselor, the Holy Spirit, whom the Father will send in my name, will teach you all things and will remind you of everything I have said to you." John 14:26 (NIV)

"But I tell you the truth: It is for your good that I am going away. Unless I go away, the Counselor will not come to you; but if I go, I will send him to you."

"I have much more to say to you, more than you can now bear. But when he, the Spirit of truth, comes, he will guide you into all truth. He will not speak on his own; he will speak only what he hears, and he will tell you what is yet to come." John 16:7, 12-13 (NIV)

WORSHIP/OBEDIENCE

I don't know about you, but I need help in my daily life!

Thank you, God, for giving me an inner spiritual guide that helps me understand Your ways and to obey them.

Most people do not like to wait. No one wants to wait for food, love, money, purchases, time, grades, laundry to dry, or anything else for that matter. But waiting on God is a beautiful characteristic of the Christian that needs to be developed. To wait on God is a sign that we trust Him and continue to be faithful even when things are not panning out as quickly as we may have wanted.

ADORATION/EXPLANATION

"Now hold on there, do you mean to tell me that God may not answer or intervene in my life when I ask? Why? Doesn't He want me to be happy?"

Well maybe, just maybe, God knows more about what waiting will produce in our lives than we do! Have I got you thinking?

Yet the Lord longs to be gracious to you; he rises to show you compassion. For the Lord is a god of justice. Blessed are all who wait for him! Isaiah 30:18 (NIV)

Since ancient times no one has heard, no ear has perceived, no eye has seen any God besides you, who acts on behalf of those who wait for him. Isaiah 64:4 (NIV)

O Lord, hear my voice. Let your ears be attentive to my cry for mercy. I wait for the Lord, my soul waits, and in his word I put my hope. My soul waits for the Lord more than watchmen wait for the morning, more than watchmen wait for the morning. Psalm 130:2, 5-6 (NIV)

WORSHIP/OBEDIENCE

Even if we do not like to wait, the Bible is clear that we are supposed to wait on God and His perfect timing for things in our lives. In Psalms, the writer repeats the last phrase to show that he understood God's timing. A night watchman knows that morning will eventually come, so he keeps watch and waits on the dawn's first light. Obviously our daily worship to God is seen in how we handle our "waiting" times! A new morning is coming soon!

February 5

Does God want sacrifices, rituals, and ceremonies from us? Does He even care about rote prayers, recitations, and lukewarm church attendance? Some folks think so. They continue to do these behaviors out of obligation rather than from a sincere heart full of awe and adoration for God.

ADORATION/EXPLANATION

The prophet Micah writes and uses poetry at times to encourage the few godly people in the land of Judah. Micah knew that God desired sincere worship and growth in the people of Judah and in our lives today!

With what shall I come before the Lord and bow down before the exalted God? Shall I come before him with burnt offerings, with calves a year old? Will the Lord be pleased with thousands of rams, with ten thousand rivers of oil? Shall I offer my firstborn for my transgression, the fruit of my body for the sin of my soul? He has showed you, O man, what is good. And what does the Lord require of you? To act justly and to love mercy and to walk humbly with your God. Micah 6:6-8 (NIV)

But Samuel replied: "Does the Lord delight in burnt offerings and sacrifices as much as in obeying the voice of the Lord? To obey is better than sacrifice, and to heed is better than the fat of rams. 1 Samuel 15:22 (NIV)

WORSHIP/OBEDIENCE

Micah and Samuel were both trying to make the point that true obedience comes from the heart. Burnt offerings, gifts, traditions, and rituals are not usually done with a contrite, humble heart. They were and still are sometimes done today out of habit and repetition. God desires our obedience to His word in our daily living. Isn't that an awesome concept?

God does not desire our "stuff," instead He just wants us!

February 6

Did you ever notice in the Bible how many times God tells us how to walk? He's not being literal here—it's not like God cares how we saunter! Rather, God is directing us in the path we choose and the manner of how we conduct our daily lives.

ADORATION/EXPLANATION

If I take a walk around my neighborhood, I can easily get distracted by everything that I see. I look one way and I see someone's gardens, dogs, or cats; look another way and I may see kids in their pool. On some occasions I see people out in their front yard that call for me to stop and chat. But if I want to finish my walk, I need to fix my eyes straight ahead and basically act like I have blinders on. It all depends on how well I want my walk to go.

So be careful to do what the Lord your God has commanded you; do not turn aside to the right or to the left. Walk in all the way that the Lord your God has commanded you, so that you may live and prosper and prolong your days in the land that you will possess. Deuteronomy 5:32-33 (NIV)

Observe the commands of the Lord your God, walking in his ways and revering him. Deuteronomy 8:6 (NIV)

Fix these words of mine in your hearts and minds; tie them as symbols on your hands and bind them on your foreheads. Teach them to your children, talking about them when you sit at home and when you walk along the road, when you lie down and when you get up. Deuteronomy 11:18-19 (NIV)

WORSHIP/OBEDIENCE

Look before you leap? Pray before you walk!

Lord, I want a good walk. I want a long walk worthy of my relationship with You.
I want those that see my walking patterns to be able to recognize who is my life coach.
I want my life to be lived in accordance with Your words today!
Help me to be a faithful walker!
Amen

I am convinced that God puts "metal testers" in our lives. A metal tester in the old days was someone who took samples of silver and gold (and various other ores) and melted them in a fire in order to burn off the impurities. In this way, the less valuable metal was separated from the genuine or truly valuable.

ADORATION/EXPLANATION
God puts people in our paths, lives, jobs, and circumstances in order to find and discover our true worth for Him. Some improve us and burn off the impurities; others can dull us and keep our value down. We can choose to harden our hearts at life's hardships and the people that God puts there, or we can realize that these very events are burning and melting off the impurities that are keeping us from truly shining.

"I have made you a tester of metals and my people the ore, that you may observe and test their ways. They are all hardened rebels, going about to slander. They are bronze and iron; they all act corruptly. The bellow blow fiercely to burn away the lead with fire, but the refining goes on in vain; the wicked are not purged out. They are called rejected silver, because the Lord has rejected them." Jeremiah 6:27-30 (NIV)

But he knows the way that I take; when he has tested me, I will come forth as gold. Job 23:10 (NIV)

He must become greater; I must become less. John 3:30 (NIV)

WORSHIP/OBEDIENCE
We should shine like a precious metal in our daily existence. Then we need to embrace and welcome the various "metal testers" that may come into our lives during work, school, car-pool, yoga, or whatever our plans are today.

Genuine faith is always <u>strengthened</u> by opposition,
while false self-confidence is <u>discouraged</u> by it.

Obviously we need to be tested, examined, and even tried by fire sometimes to prove our faith. Why? "I do not like tests," you may be thinking? But the Bible teaches us that we WILL go through much testing in our daily lives and this is what confirms our faith to be genuine. We can learn to welcome it!

ADORATION/EXPLANATION

Learn to welcome tests of our faith? No way! But the Bible tells us that we can learn to welcome and learn from these tests if we can just realize what they are producing in us for the long-term! Wow!

In this you greatly rejoice, though now for a little while you may have had to suffer grief in all kinds of trials. These have come so that your faith—of greater worth than gold, which perishes even though refined by fire-may be proved genuine and may result in praise, glory and honor when Jesus Christ is revealed. 1 Peter 1:6-7 (NIV)

If you are insulted because of the name of Christ, you are blessed, for the Spirit of glory and of God rests on you. If you suffer, it should not be as a murderer or thief or any other kind of criminal, or even a meddler. However, if you suffer as a Christian, do not be ashamed, but praise God that you bear that name.

So then, those who suffer according to God's will should commit themselves to their faithful Creator and continue to do good. 1 Peter 4:14-16, 19 (NIV)

WORSHIP/OBEDIENCE

We can learn to accept tests, but now the Bible is telling us to praise God through them? Our daily worship to God reveals itself in how we handle the hardships and trials. We should choose to "rejoice in the Lord always, and again I say, REJOICE!"

We often come across Christians who are smart and clever, and strong and righteous. In fact, they may be a little too annoyingly smart and clever. Maybe there seems to be a lot of "self" in their strength and righteousness, which renders them severe and critical. They have everything to make them look like perfect saints on the outside, except that they don't crucify themselves and rely on Christ's crucifixion on the cross at Calvary to change their lives.

ADORATION/EXPLANATION

What an awesome God! He did the finish work for us when He was hung on a cross for our sins. When we get this—really GET this fact—then we do not have to rely on being smart and clever, or strong and righteous. This belief will result in supernatural concern, genuine rightness, and limitless love for others. So cool to see…

May I never boast except in the cross of our Lord Jesus Christ, through which the world has been crucified to me, and I to the world. Galatians 6:14 (NIV)

"I have been crucified with Christ and I no longer live, but Christ lives in me. The life I live in the body, I live by faith in the Son of God, who loved me and gave himself for me. Galatians 2:20 (NIV)

For Christ's love compels us, because we are convinced that one died for all, that those who live should no longer live for themselves but for him who died for them and was raised again. Therefore, if anyone is in Christ, he is a new creation; the old has gone, the new has come! 2 Corinthians 5:14-15, 17 (NIV)

WORSHIP/OBEDIENCE

Today we need to remember that not only was Jesus hung on a cross, but that we must also daily remember to die to our SELVES—our hang-ups, our selfishness, our pride, our cleverness, our smarts, our strengths and self-righteousness. We ARE a new creation!!

In this still, deep chilly month of winter, I want to produce a crop. No, not actual plantings… but a harvest of growth in my life that comes from God. I want to make the sower thankful for the fact that He planted seeds in my life and they have been fertilized, diligently cultivated, and are presently producing a good crop.

ADORATION/EXPLANATION

As I am writing today's inspirational thought, I glance out of the window at the frozen ground. Frigid temperatures are hovering at twenty-one degrees! This in NO way inspires me to even think of gardening, but I realize that it is in these frigid times that fertilizing and cultivating of the soil should be going on. It is in the hidden, underground composting and percolating of the soil that something is happening. Persevering through the winter brings soil ready for spring.

"This is the meaning of the parable: The seed is the word of God. Those along the path are the ones who hear, and then the devil comes and takes away the word from their hearts, so that they may not believe and be saved. Those on the rock are the ones who receive the word with joy when they hear it, but they have no root. They believe for a while, but in the time of testing they fall away. The seed that fell among thorns stands for those who hear, but as they go on their way they are choked by life's worries, riches and pleasures, and they do not mature. But the seed on good soil stands for those with a noble and good heart, who hear the word, retain it, and by persevering produce a crop. Luke 8:11-15 (NIV)

"No good tree bears bad fruit, nor does a bad tree bear good fruit. Each tree is recognized by its own fruit. People do not pick figs from thorn- bushes, or grapes from briers." Luke 6:43-44 (NIV)

WORSHIP/OBEDIENCE

If our lives are a garden, then our hearts are the soil. A productive garden must have good soil. Simple as that! So how can we improve our soil?

We can choose to worship, obey, fertilize our minds and souls by reading God's Word and meditating daily on it, praying for guidance, and seeking correct, godly advice for our garden. The ground outside might still be frozen, but something warm can begin to germinate in our hearts.

Lord, help my soul be good soil today!

February 11

As a parent, teacher, employer, etc., can you imagine having people obey your orders immediately without question? People jumping to attention? Wow! Obviously that would make life so much easier, wouldn't it?

ADORATION/EXPLANATION

Obedience makes life so much easier, efficient, and effective. Yet as Christians, we still seem to have a difficult time following God, even though the very name of "Christian" means to be a "Christ follower."

Our adoration of God needs to be so strong that it compels us to be grateful followers. Immediately!

Do not let this Book of the Law depart from your mouth; meditate on it day and night, so that you may be careful everything written in it. Then you will be prosperous and successful."

Then they answered Joshua, "Whatever you have commanded us we will do, and wherever you send us we will go." Joshua 1:8, 16 (NIV)

""Still other seed fell on good soil. It came up, grew and produced a crop, multiplying thirty, sixty, or even a hundred times." Then Jesus said, "He who has ears to hear, let him hear."

"Consider carefully what you hear," he continued. "With the measure you use, it will be measured to you—and even more." Mark 4:8-9, 24 (NIV)

WORSHIP/OBEDIENCE

In the Bible, it seems so clear that God is warning us to hear and obey. Hearing alone is NOT obeying. Obedience requires hearing, accepting, and then action on our part. We should desire to be effective, efficient, and productive followers of Christ in our daily lives. We know that we have ears, but are they hearing and obeying God?

Are your ears turned on?

February 12

One of the many things—or should I say, one of the only things—that I look forward to in February is Valentine's Day. I just love the idea of heart-shaped cards, candy, donuts, flowers, and proclamations of love! Yet for many, this is not a fun day at all! In a couple of days, many folks will be proclaiming their love for each other; yet others will be saddened at the absence of love in their lives.

ADORATION/EXPLANATION

Earthly love and relationships can be fleeting, yet God tells us of His beautiful love that never leaves, fails, fades, or gives out. Awesome!

So whether we have an earthly love with someone or are alone, we can still count on God's love every day of the year.

Teach me your way, O Lord, and I will walk in your truth; give me an undivided heart, that I may fear your name. I will praise you, O Lord my God, with all my heart; I will glorify your name forever. Psalm 86:11-12 (NIV)

"I will give them an undivided heart and put a new spirit in them; I will remove from them their heart of stone and give them a heart of flesh. Then they will follow my decrees and be careful to keep my laws. They will be my people, and I will be their God." Ezekiel 11:19-20 (NIV)

WORSHIP/OBEDIENCE

Our hearts are the center of our human soul. God wants our total devotion, commitment, and faithfulness, even if we do or do not have an earthly love affair with someone. God wants an undivided heart that is pure and unselfish in emotions, thoughts, and attitudes. Can we do this? Do we exude this kind of heart attitude to friends, family, and God? Only God can give us an undivided heart, but we must really want it. Pursue it!

Search and examine me, dear Lord,
and give my soul a singleness of action and devotion to you!
This in turn will flow out to others.
I want one big, beautiful HEART!

February 13

God speaks so much about our heart in His word. I can't help but think of all the things that we also say concerning the heart: "Her heart is cold as ice." "He has a heart that is hard as stone." "She has a heart of gold." "He has a soft heart when it comes to his children." "I sent my heart-felt sympathies in a card." "Turn on your heart light."

"That comment shot me straight through the heart!"

ADORATION/EXPLANATION
God knows what He is doing when He teaches us over and over again in the Bible about guarding our heart. He also reminds us to open our hearts, follow with our hearts, and apply our hearts to His wisdom. Much more than just pumping blood and oxygen through our physical bodies, our hearts are the most important aspect to our spiritual beings. It is the wellspring of our lives!

"I will give them a heart to know me, that I am the Lord. They will be my people, and I will be their God, for they will return to me with all their heart." Jeremiah 24:7 (NIV)

"They will be my people, and I will be their God. I will give them singleness of heart, and action, so that they will always fear me for their own good and the good of their children after them." Jeremiah 32:38-39 (NIV)

The goal of this command is love, which comes from a pure heart and a good conscience and a sincere faith. Some have wandered away from these and turned to meaningless talk. 1Timothy 1:5-6 (NIV)

WORSHIP/OBEDIENCE
We need a pure heart! Just as we would not want a filthy heart pumping unclean blood and oxygen through our bodies, we want our hearts to be so in tune with God that it spews out His pure love to others.

Dear God, help my heart not wander away from Your goals for me today!

February 14

Happy Valentine's Day! The ultimate act of the truest form of selfless LOVE was Jesus dying on the cross for our sins—yours and mine! As we ponder about the significance of Valentine's Day to the world and the commercial aspect of the card companies, we realize that nothing can ever compare to the sacrifice that Christ made for us. No cards, no flowers, no candy or gifts can ever equal the love that was and still is being lavished upon us by our Heavenly Father.

ADORATION/EXPLANATION

Make no mistake, I love my husband with all my soul and he will always be my "forever sweetheart!" I even love when he gives me cards that tell of his love and devotion. But my ultimate security is the fact of God's love for His children. The Bible speaks volumes about this marvelous, glorious devotion that God feels for us. Even if you have no earthly sweetheart at this time, God sent His only son as the perfect valentine for all of us. He adores us!

"A new command I give you: Love one another. As I have loved you, so you must love one another. By this all men will know that you are my disciples, if you love one another." John 13:34-35 (NIV)

You see, at just the right time, when we were still powerless, Christ died for the ungodly. Very rarely will anyone die for a righteous man, though for a good man someone might possibly dare to die. But God demonstrates his own love for us in this: While we were still sinners, Christ died for us. Romans 5:6-8 (NIV)

WORSHIP/OBEDIENCE

No boyfriend? No girlfriend? No husband, wife, or special someone at this time in your life? What's the big deal…? Christ gave His life up for you and me. He didn't wait for us to be perfect, but loved us in spite of ourselves. Forget cards and candy—we need to carry this love to all that we meet today. Now that is a big deal!

February 15

Where do we get the power we need to live the Christian life? Through much study, learning, and living, we eventually realize that the power comes from God. God did not ask us to be <u>associates</u> with Jesus Christ, but privileged us into a <u>union</u> with Him. We are fellow heirs with Jesus in a relationship that includes an actual sharing of His life and power for living. Who wouldn't want this kind of relationship?

ADORATION/EXPLANATION

We can be strong in the Lord! It may take us many years after becoming a Christian to understand our union with Christ and experience the benefit in our daily lives. Most people view having the power of God to live the Christian life like a timid worker asking for a raise. We might get it and we might not! So most of the time we never even ask…

See that what you have heard from the beginning remains in you. If it does, you also will remain in the Son and in the Father. And this is what he promised us—even eternal life.

And now, dear children, continue in him, so that when he appears we may be confident and unashamed before him at his coming. 1 John 2:24-25, 28 (NIV)

So then, just as you received Christ Jesus as Lord, continue to live in him, rooted and built up in him, strengthened in the faith as you were taught, and overflowing with thankfulness. See to it that no one takes you captive through hollow and deceptive philosophy, which depends on human tradition and the basic principles of this world rather than on Christ. Colossians 2:6-8 (NIV)

WORSHIP/OBEDIENCE

When we finally grasp the significance of what the Apostle Paul meant when he said that we are <u>in Christ</u>, it will drastically change the way that we relate to people. We will begin to see ourselves as a branch that is vitally and personally joined to the vine of Jesus. We are not just glued or taped on. We are actually a part of that vine. Just as the life of that vine flows naturally into the branch so that it can bear fruit, so too does the power from Christ flow naturally into you and me, giving us power to get through our daily journey!

February 16

Do you realize that every expression of God in and through your life is the result of your union with Christ? Every desire to read the Bible, use a daily devotional book, or pray and do God's will, be it ever so small, is the living, breathing result of you being IN Christ. Merely looking to God, as opposed to living attached to Him like a branch to a vine, are not the same action.

ADORATION/EXPLANATION

Looking to God can mean that we are just casually gazing in His direction while trying to maneuver through daily life by our own strength and craftiness. Anyone can look to God! As a matter of fact, many people occasionally do. But just looking, compared to remaining attached or abiding IN Christ, are two very different things.

"Remain in me, and I will remain in you. No branch can bear fruit by itself; it must remain in the vine. Neither can you bear fruit unless you remain in me. I am the vine; you are the branches. If a man remains in me and I in him, he will bear much fruit; apart from me you can do nothing." John 15:4-5 (NIV)

Then he said to them all: "If anyone would come after me, he must deny himself and take up his cross daily and follow me." Luke 9:23 (NIV)

"I have been crucified with Christ and I no longer live, but Christ lives in me. The life I live in the body, I live by faith in the Son of God, who loved me and gave himself for me." Galatians 2:20 (NIV)

WORSHIP/OBEDIENCE

Choose today to really get to know God. God is saying…look, touch, taste and see that I am good. Choose to be more than a window shopper!

Dear God, help me today to not only LOOK to you in times of trouble,
but to look to you during every decision, every moment of my day.
I am choosing to stay yoked to YOU in all things and acknowledge
that YOU are where my strength comes from.

Do you want to be a sheep or a goat? Today's thoughts are relatively simple in concept. Do you want to be a sheep or a goat? I repeat the question so that it gives you time to mull it over in your head. Now I am sure that you are thinking, "Why exactly would I want to be either one of those animals?" Sheep or goat…..why care?

ADORATION/EXPLANATION
In the New Testament book of Matthew, Jesus tells a story about sheep and goats. Back in those times, sheep and goats did not mix well in the flock and were never raised together. After reading this parable, you will understand the earlier question. God has brought us into a vital relationship with Christ. We need our personal ties to Him to be so strong that we can't help being a sheep.

"When the Son of Man comes in his glory, and all the angels with him, he will sit on his throne in heavenly glory. All the nations will be gathered before him, and he will separate the people one from another as a shepherd separates the sheep from the goats. He will put the sheep on his right and the goats on his left. Then the King will say to those on his right, 'Come, you who are blessed by my Father; take your inheritance, the kingdom prepared for you since the creation of the world. For I was hungry and you gave me something to eat, I was thirsty and you gave me something to drink, I was a stranger and you invited me in, I needed clothes and you clothed me, I was sick and you looked after me, I was in prison and you came to visit me.'

"Then the righteous will answer him, 'Lord, when did we see you hungry and feed you, or thirsty and give you something to drink? When did we see you a stranger and invite you in, or needing clothes and clothe you? When did we see you sick or in prison and go to visit you?'

"The King will reply, 'I tell you the truth, whatever you did for one of the least of these brothers of mine, you did for me." Matthew 25:31-40 (NIV)

WORSHIP/OBEDIENCE
The right hand side of a king was always reserved for royalty or special people. Jesus is now sitting at the right hand of God. If sheep are the ones following God's will, then that is what we should desire to be.

Sheep or goat—it's your choice!

In yesterday's Bible passage of Matthew, the people asked Jesus, "When did we see you hungry, thirsty, in prison, etc.?" The question is even more compelling nowadays. When have you or I seen Jesus hungry, thirsty, or anywhere else for that matter?

ADORATION/EXPLANATION

We don't physically see Jesus, but Jesus was trying to urge us to minister, reach out, help, and be concerned for those that cannot help themselves. If Jesus was physically present with us now, everyone would come running to wait on him, worship Him, and gain His favor. God wants us to know that it is not to be done for applause or approval in men's eyes. We are really supposed to do it for Christ, because we are doing His work when we care for the least, lowest, and most downtrodden of people (even when no one is looking)!

Remember this: Whoever sows sparingly will also reap sparingly, and whoever sows generously will also rep generously. Each man should give what he has decided in his heart to give, not reluctantly or under compulsion, for God loves a cheerful giver. And God is able to make all grace abound to you, so that in all things at all times, having all that you need, you will abound in every good work.

Because of the service by which you have proved yourselves, men will praise God for the obedience that accompanies your confession of the gospel of Christ, and for your generosity in sharing with them and with everyone else. 2 Corinthians 9:6-8, 13 (NIV)

WORSHIP/OBEDIENCE

We can see Jesus. We can see Him in the faces, the eyes, and the lives of those seemingly insignificant folks that need help. The old man at the bank that needs help, the lady at the store that could use a hand with her packages, the people in prison, the young single mom that needs groceries, the young guy that needs a ride to work… the list goes on! It is not how much that we give or do, it is the fact that Jesus tells us that whatever we do for these people, we are doing for Him!

TODAY I want to give to Jesus!

February 19

Can you be interrupted without getting angry? How do you react if a child, a friend, family member, or even a phone call interrupts your time? When we read the Bible, we see that the life of Jesus was full of interruptions by random people. We may want to believe that His teaching was the most important part of His life on earth, but the interruptions actually accomplished just as much!

ADORATION/EXPLANATION

I am in awe of the fact that Jesus dealt so well with interruptions to His daily life. He never got angry or pushed people away because He was in a rush to get to His own agenda. Jesus taught that real significance is not a matter of power, fame, or greatness. True significance is found in service to others and taking the time to be patient with interruptions.

When he came down from the mountainside, large crowds followed him. A man with leprosy came and knelt before him and said, "Lord, if you are willing, you can make me clean." Jesus reached out his hand and touched the man. "I am willing," he said. "Be clean!" Immediately he was cured of his leprosy.

When Jesus had entered Capernaum, a centurion came to him, asking for help.

When Jesus came into Peter's house, he saw Peter's mother-in-law lying in bed with a fever. He touched her hand and the fever left her, and she got up and began to wait on him. Matthew 8:1-3, 5, 14 (NIV)

While he was saying this, a ruler came and knelt before him and said, "My daughter has just died. But come and put your hand on her, and she will live."

As Jesus went on from there, two blind men followed him, calling out, "Have mercy on us, Son of David!" Matthew 9:18, 27 (NIV)

WORSHIP/OBEDIENCE

Today I am choosing to see interruption as a potential blessing! What I may view as a disturbance or disruption to my agenda may be the very thing that God will use to teach me a valuable lesson.

February 20

Let's face it: doing things, speaking to people, or conducting ourselves the way Jesus did is difficult. It will definitely make you different. You may even have to do the opposite of everyone else at times. When it comes to speaking truthfully, the Bible mentions that we must do it in love if we want to effect change. If we have to talk to someone about a difficult subject, lovingly doing so is the best method to be used!

ADORATION/EXPLANATION
Speaking up and being different can cause its own problems. What if people think you are self-righteous? What if they think you are too good for them? The Apostle Paul realized this when he spoke up to the people of the church in the city of Corinth. But no need to worry! The God that he adored caused the correct changes to occur in the hearts of the listeners.

Even if I cause you sorrow by my letter, I do not regret it. Though I did regret it—I see that my letter hurt you, but only for a little while—yet now I am happy, not because you were made sorry, but because your sorrow led you to repentance. For you became sorrowful as God intended and so were not harmed in any way by us. Godly sorrow brings repentance that leads to salvation and leaves no regret, but worldly sorrow brings death. See what this godly sorrow has produced in you: what earnestness, what eagerness to clear yourselves, what indignation, what alarm, what longing, what concern, what readiness to see justice done. At every point you have proved yourselves to be innocent in this matter. 2 Corinthians 7:8-10 (NIV)

Instead, speaking the truth in love, we will in all things grow up into him who is the Head, that is, Christ. Ephesians 4:15 (NIV)

WORSHIP/OBEDIENCE
Paul realized that God directed him to say things that were hard to hear, but the end result was that it caused wonderful change in their lives. Pray and ask God for guidance if you need to talk to someone. Proceed gently.

If being truthful offends others but pleases God,
tread lightly and lovingly, but do not compromise!

When God says it, I should believe it! When God says it, I should do it! Can you say this is true of your life? Many people nowadays seem to have the audacity to think that the Bible is not relevant anymore. It's out of date, out of style, and underrated. It seems that a lot of folks want to pick and choose what parts to obey and what sections they want to ignore. This arrogance has pervaded the media and our culture. It is on just about every television channel and in almost every magazine. You are reading this devotional book, and the Bible verses daily. Is it causing any spiritual and mental changes in your life? When we give our will over to God's control, we know that whatever He asks will be in our best interest. But what if he asked us to dip? What exactly do you mean by dipping? Why dip? Who else is dipping? What kind of daily devotional book is this anyway??

ADORATION/EXPLANATION
In the Old Testament, there was a man who needed healing from leprosy and was told to go dip in the Jordan River. He thought that this was a ridiculous order so he didn't obey at first. He questioned!

Now Naaman was commander of the army of the king of Aram. He was a great man in the sight of his master and highly regarded, because through him the Lord had given victory to Aram. He was a valiant soldier, but he had leprosy.

Now bands from Aram had gone out and had taken captive a young girl from Israel, and she served Namaan's wife. She said to her mistress, "If only my master would see the prophet who is in Samaria! He would cure him of his leprosy." 2 Kings 5:1-3 (NIV)

So Namaan went with his horses and chariots and stopped at the door of Elisha's house. Elisha sent a messenger to say to him, "Go, (dip) wash yourself seven times in the Jordan, and your flesh will be restored and you will be cleansed." But Namaan went away angry and said, "I thought that he would surely come out to me and stand and call on the name of the Lord his God, wave his hand over the spot and cure me of my leprosy. Are not Abana and Pharpar, the rivers of Damascus, better than any of the waters of Israel? Couldn't I wash in them and be cleansed?" So he turned and went off in a rage. 2 Kings 5:9-12 (NIV)

WORSHIP/OBEDIENCE
Was it the dipping or washing in the Jordan River that Namaan was actually questioning? Or were God's methods just not exactly the way he pictured they should be? Many of us do this daily in our own lives. We need to worship God by obeying His Word, even if it doesn't always make sense to us!

If God says, "dip"…you dip!

Sometimes our suffering or disobedience leads to a dramatic encounter with the power of God. Let's be clear here—it is we who choose disobedience and very often, we bring our suffering upon ourselves. God does not strike us down with trials but He allows them in our lives to teach us some very important lessons about His divine ability.

ADORATION/EXPLANATION

Yesterday we read in the book of 2 Kings about Namaan and his inability to obey the prophet for his healing. It wasn't that he didn't want to be healed. After all, he came all that way with his horses, chariots, and entourage! So he must have believed that he could be healed, but the method that God chose to work with just didn't seem fantastic enough. Our faith in God requires us to trust in His ways!

Namaan's servants went to him and said, "My father, if the prophet had told you to do some great thing, would you have not done it? How much more, then, when he tells you, 'Wash and be cleansed'!" So he went down and dipped himself in the Jordan seven times, as the man of God had told him, and his flesh was restored and became clean like that of a young boy. Then Namaan and all his attendants went back to the man of God. He stood before him and said, "Now I know that there is no God in all the world except in Israel. Please now accept a gift from your servant."

"Go in peace," Elisha said. 2 kings 5:13-15, 19 (NIV)

"For my thoughts are not your thoughts, neither are your ways my ways," declares the Lord. Isaiah 55:8 (NIV)

WORSHIP/OBEDIENCE

We love to worship a strong, powerful, all-knowing God, but isn't it funny how we try to bring Him down to our level of thinking, especially if His plans and directives don't jive with how we think that they should go? True worship requires obedience to His way, even if it seems strange to us.

Who do we think we are?

More importantly, who do we think He is?

I love singing. I'm not saying that I'm particularly good at it, but I love to sing. I sing when I am doing chores, when I am walking, in the shower, and especially when I am driving in my car!

ADORATION/EXPLANATION
There are sad songs, happy songs, up-beat, swing-beat, jazz, blues, rock and roll, pop, rap, country, and love songs. If God made our lives one big song, what kind of music would represent you? What would your verse be? What would you contribute? Would it be the cheery stanza, the sad stanza, the depressing, monotonous verse, the giggly sing-a-long verse, or the roaring chorus?

***

He put a new song in my mouth, a hymn of praise to our God. Psalm 40:3a (NIV)

Shout for joy to the Lord, all the earth, burst into jubilant song with music; make music to the Lord with the harp, with the harp and the sound of singing, with trumpets and the blast of the ram's horn—shout for joy before the Lord, the King. Let the sea resound, and everything in it, the world, and all who live in it. Let the rivers clap their hands, let the mountains sing together for joy. Psalm 98:4-8 (NIV)

Is any one of you in trouble? He should pray. Is anyone happy? Let him sing songs of praise. James 5:13 (NIV)

Speak to one another with psalms, hymns and spiritual songs. Sing and make music in your heart to the Lord, Ephesians 5:1 (NIV)

WORSHIP/OBEDIENCE
God tells us, compels us—even exhorts us!—to sing our song in praise! If life is one big song to God, what will your verse be? Sing out loud…sing out strong!

Sing!

***

February 24

Extravagance is the opposite of greediness. Extravagant generosity is an attitude of the heart, not the pocketbook! In the same vein, greed is also an attitude of the heart. When we go above and beyond in extravagant love for God's people, we push all notions of selfish greed out of our lives.

ADORATION/EXPLANATION

The Bible shows us many examples of extravagant, loving hearts versus greedy hearts. This attitude is not necessarily born from great financial or material means, but instead is an attitude of understanding that all we have is God's to begin with. We should not hold onto anything so tightly that God needs to pry our hands loose!

❦

While Jesus was in Bethany in the home of a man known as Simon the Leper, a woman came to him with an alabaster jar of very expensive perfume, which she poured on his head as he was reclining at the table. When the disciples saw this, they were indignant. "Why this waste?" they asked. "This perfume could have been sold at a high price and the money given to the poor." Aware of this, Jesus said to them, "Why are you bothering this woman? She has done a beautiful thing to me. The poor you will always have with you, but you will not always have me. When she poured this perfume on my body, she did it to prepare me for burial. I tell you the truth, wherever this gospel is preached throughout the world, what she has done will also be told, in memory of her." Matthew 26:6-13 (NIV)

Then one of the twelve—the one called Judas Iscariot—went to the chief priests and asked, "What are you willing to give me if I hand him over to you?" So they counted out for him thirty silver coins. From then on Judas watched for an opportunity to hand him over. Matthew 26:14-16 (NIV)

WORSHIP/OBEDIENCE

We see two extreme examples from the Gospel of Matthew. One person willingly dumped, poured, and totally gave up a very expensive bottle of perfume without a second thought, even though this may have been worth a marriage dowry or life savings in those days. Another person was willing to betray Jesus Christ for a paltry sum of thirty coins.

True worship requires our hands to be open, not clenched tight!

❦

February 25

To hesitate is sometimes a good thing, but when it comes to obeying God, there should never be any stalling on our part. When we stall or hesitate, it gives our feeble human minds time to take over and try to out-think God's plan. We try to make sense of our wonderful Creator's divine purpose. How can this be? How is God going to work this one out? I don't think that I can do this!

ADORATION/EXPLANATION

In the story of David and Goliath, we notice that every time David is told to do something, he runs quickly to the job. Imagine how much we could accomplish for God's purposes if we would just move quickly to the task. Today we will start this story, and in tomorrow's reading we will be in awe of God's finish.

The Philistines occupied one hill and the Israelites another, with the valley between them. A champion named Goliath, who was from Gath, came out of the Philistine camp. He was over nine feet tall.

Goliath stood and shouted to the ranks of Israel, "Why do you come out and line up for battle? Am I not a Philistine, and are you not the servants of Saul? Choose a man and have him come down to me. On hearing the Philistine's words, Saul and all the Israelites were dismayed and terrified.

David left his things with the keeper of supplies, ran to the battle lines and greeted his brothers. As he was talking with them, Goliath, the Philistine champion from Gath, stepped out from his lines and shouted his usual defiance, and David heard it. When the Israelites saw the man, they all ran from him in great fear.

David said to Saul, "Let no one lose heart on account of this Philistine; your servant will go and fight him." Saul replied, "You are not able to go out against this Philistine and fight him; you are only a boy, and he has been a fighting man from his youth." 1 Samuel 17:3-4, 8, 11, 22-24, 32-33 (NIV)

WORSHIP/OBEDIENCE

Who, why, when, where and how—are all questions that can stop us in our tracks from fulfilling God's purposes in our life, especially if we don't like the answers we get. Saul did not believe that David could defeat Goliath because of the obvious amount of physical evidence to the contrary. David trusted and believed the Lord!

God's power is best shown when all the human evidence is stacked against it!

In today's reading, we continue to look at David's experiences when he faced Goliath. He did not hesitate. When his father asked him to go somewhere or do something, the Bible tells us that he got up and went. When he saw and heard Goliath challenging God's men, he started asking questions in order to find answers. When others turned and ran in terror, David stayed and volunteered to fight.

ADORATION/EXPLANATION

David volunteered to take on a literal giant. Why would he do that, since he could obviously see the size and strength of the man? Didn't he understand the implications of losing this fight? Couldn't he see that the odds of winning the battle were not in his favor? I don't believe that he even really thought about these things. David was so in awe of what his God could do that he refused to take time to look at the possible problems of failing! Wow!

"The Lord who has delivered me from the paw of the lion and the paw of the bear will deliver me from the hand of the Philistine." Saul said to David, "Go, and the Lord be with you." Then Saul dressed David in his own tunic. He put a coat of armor on him and a bronze helmet on his head. David fastened on his sword over the tunic and tried walking around, because he was not used to them. "I cannot go in these," he said to Saul, "because I am not used to them." So he took them off. Then he took his staff in his hand, chose five smooth stones from the stream, put them in the pouch of his shepherd's bag, and, with his sling in his hand, approached the Philistine.

He said to David, "Am I a dog that you come at me with sticks?" And the Philistine cursed David by his gods. David said to the Philistine, "You come against me with sword and spear and javelin, but I come against you in the name of the Lord Almighty, the God of the armies of Israel, whom you have defied." 1 Samuel 17:37-40, 43, 45 (NIV)

WORSHIP/OBEDIENCE

God never asks us to foolishly rush into situations with our own ideas and strength. As a matter of fact, when King Saul put his armor on David, it was not even useful. David remembered that his other battles against lions, bears, and other foes were won with the power of God working through him. He didn't trust or even try to use the conventional methods of battle. Today we may face many giants in our lives.

Lord, remind me that if You are on my side, then nothing else matters!

Whether it is car racing, marathon running, boating, horses or any other race or competition, the finish is the most important aspect. Every task we set out to do is judged upon its completion and finishing well. Our goal as Christians should be to finish our lives in the same way! But we must begin by trusting God with each new day.

ADORATION/EXPLANATION

We have been reading about David and Goliath in the Old Testament book of 1 Samuel. David's adoration of God gave him the courage and determination to go forward and face a giant, but his finish and unexplainable victory over Goliath was what gave God the glory.

This day the Lord will hand you over to me, and I'll strike you down and cut off your head. Today I will give the carcasses of the Philistine army to the birds of the air and the beasts of the earth, and the whole world will know that there is a God in Israel. All those gathered here will know that it is not by sword or spear that the Lord saves; for the battle is the Lord's, and he will give all of you into our hands." As the Philistine moved closer to attack him, David ran quickly toward the battle line to meet him. Reaching into his bag and taking out a stone, he slung it and struck the Philistine on the forehead. The stone sank into his forehead, and he fell facedown on the ground. So David triumphed over the Philistine with a sling and a stone; without a sword in his hand he struck down the Philistine and killed him. 1 Samuel 17:46-50 (NIV)

WORSHIP/OBEDIENCE

David finished well!

Dear God, every day you give me new opportunities to live for you. Help me to view each new morning as an opportunity to finish the day well and give You the glory for my successes; to finish the day with a heart full of praise and thanksgiving. Most of all, help me to finish the day with a hope in You that I will have another chance to finish well tomorrow!

Limitations—we've all got 'em! Sometimes the word refers to a physical handicap or a possible mental slowness, but it can also describe a height or weight disability, or maybe even a lack of education or knowledge in an area. Whatever the case, we can rest assured that everyone suffers from a limitation in some area in their life.

ADORATION/EXPLANATION

We tend to run to God in prayer more often when we realize that we have limitations in certain areas. We may try and try and try again to do something our way, and all of a sudden, come to the realization that we are desperate. We need help because we are limited by our own efforts! We rely on ourselves and run out of our own strength and resources. But our wonderful God never runs out and He is never desperate! He is limitless!

Give us aid against the enemy, for the help of man is worthless. With God we will gain the victory, and he will trample down our enemies. Psalm 60:11-12 (NIV)

But thanks be to God! He gives us the victory through our Lord Jesus Christ. Therefore, my dear brothers, stand firm. Let nothing move you. Always give yourselves fully to the work of the Lord, because you know that your labor in the Lord is not in vain. 1 Corinthians 15:57-58 (NIV)

Be on your guard; stand firm in the faith; be men of courage; be strong. Do everything in love. 1 Corinthians 16:13-14 (NIV)

WORSHIP/OBEDIENCE

Am I desperate? I hope so!

Dear God, remind me to act desperate all the time—desperate for your help,
your guidance, and desperate for your advice today!
Remind me that the storms, trials, disappointments,
and limitations that I may face will force me to seek you!
I acknowledge that I have limitations without you but I want to
worship you with desperation every day of the week! Amen.

My great-grandmother always wanted to lean on my arm as she walked. Many times I would reach out and grab her arm or hand as we went down the steps, but she didn't like that at all. She did not want to be led along! She would grab my arm and hold on to me, but she made it clear that she wanted to do the leaning! I was her strength if she started to fall, got weary, or needed some extra power. My great-grandmother recognized the fact that she needed help, and was quick to grab for it. Do we recognize our need?

ADORATION/EXPLANATION

Our awe and adoration for what Jesus has done for us should result in a constant "leaning" on Him. We should not wait until we are falling, struggling, or drowning to reach out with flailing arms toward God. Although He loves us and is always there when we flail about, He wants us to understand that we need to make it a conscious habit to LEAN on Him in all circumstances.

"Ah, Sovereign Lord," I said, "I do not know how to speak; I am only a child." But the Lord said to me, "Do not say, 'I am only a child.' You must go to everyone I send you to and say whatever I command you. Do not be afraid of them, for I am with you and will rescue you," declares the Lord. Jeremiah 1:6-8 (NIV)

He who dwells in the shelter of the Most High will rest in the shadow of the Almighty. I will say of the Lord, "He is my refuge and my fortress, my God, in whom I trust." Psalm 91:1-2 (NIV)

When I said, "My foot is slipping," your love, O Lord, supported me. Psalm 94:18 (NIV)

Trust in the Lord with all your heart and lean not on your own understanding; Proverbs 3:5 (NIV)

WORSHIP/OBEDIENCE

Just as my great-grandmother wanted to lean on my arm, we need to always make it a habit to lean on God. Even if our way seems easy today and we feel sure-footed, we should lean on Him and NOT on our own understanding.

No more flailing arms of panic!

As spring is slowly approaching, I have noticed many deer in the fields, as well as those peeking from the wood lines along the road. They seem to be in search of the new tender shoots and plants. They are quietly observant and have a keen sense of what is going on around them.

ADORATION/EXPLANATION
It is amazing how many times the Bible compares us to deer. It talks about their desire for water, drive for food, and their strong hind feet that enable them to move swiftly. So why, you may be asking, are we compared to deer?

Yet I will rejoice in the Lord, I will be joyful in God my Savior. The Sovereign Lord is my strength; he makes my feet like the feet of a deer, he enables me to go on the heights. Habakkuk 3:18-19 (NIV)

With persuasive words she led him astray; she seduced him with her smooth talk. All at once he followed her like an ox going to the slaughter, like a deer stepping into a noose Proverbs 7:21-22 (NIV)

As the deer pants for streams of water, so my soul pants for you, O God. Psalm 42:1 (NIV)

Then will the lame leap like a deer, and the mute tongue shout for joy. Isaiah 35:6 (NIV)

WORSHIP/OBEDIENCE
The Bible gives the example of a deer panting and searching for water. Then it focuses on the deer's hind legs being able to carry it over high places. Deer are extremely quick and swift-footed animals, known to be able to leap high enclosures. How do I obey this advice today? Am I striving for God?

Dear God, give me the same desire for You that a deer has when driven for cool streams. Today, I want to run and leap with Your strength!

Today is going to be a "walk on water" kind of day! I am going to choose to rely so much on God that, if He asks me to step out of the boat and do something extraordinary for Him, I will. When Peter saw Jesus walking on water, he got out of the boat and started walking. In the days after the crucifixion and resurrection of Jesus, Peter was fishing and heard Jesus on the shore. He didn't calmly row back to the beach, but dove into the water head first and swam back in! It is going to be a "walk on water" kind of day!

ADORATION/EXPLANATION
We should want to stay in such awe of God and His power for our lives that we are not afraid to get out of the boat when the opportunity presents itself. If we continue to keep our gaze and focus on Christ, then nothing will dissuade us from stepping out into the water, even if it seems frightening!

Such confidence as this is ours through Christ before God. Not that we are competent in ourselves to claim anything for ourselves, but our competence comes from God. 2 Corinthians 3:4-5 (NIV)

But he said to me, "My grace is sufficient for you, for my power is made perfect in weakness." Therefore I will boast all the more gladly about my weaknesses, so that Christ's power may rest on me. 2 Corinthians 12:9 (NIV)

"Salvation is found in no one else, for there is no other name under heaven given to men by which we must be saved." When they saw the courage of Peter and John and realized that they were unschooled, ordinary men, they were astonished and they took note that these men had been with Jesus. Acts 4:12-13 (NIV)

WORSHIP/OBEDIENCE
Sitting in a boat is easy, and remaining in the boat when storms come up and the waves are rough is just common sense. But when Jesus is right there beside us, urging us to take a step, to get out of the boat, to actually dive into the water…*THAT* is when we need to really obey!

This may be a "walk on water" kind of day, and we don't want to miss it!

March 4

Do you have room for Jesus in your life? Oh, we're not talking about just on Sundays. Do you really have room for Jesus? Is there space in your schedule today to consult Him, pray and meditate on His Word, live by His example? Or is Jesus just kind of squeezed into the cracks, a filler, a last ditch solution in your daily grind?

ADORATION/EXPLANATION
We need to swing our heart's door wide open! There needs to be room. There needs to be a permanent spot with a continual, ongoing reservation that is only saved for Christ. Let Him enter your life daily. He will never push or force His way in or break down the door. You must give Him the key!

"Ask and it will be given to you; seek and you will find; knock and the door will be opened to you. For everyone who asks receives; he who seeks finds; and to him who knocks, the door will be opened." Matthew 7:7-8 (NIV)

Those whom I love I rebuke and discipline. So be earnest, and repent. Here I am! I stand at the door and knock. If anyone hears my voice and opens the door, I will come in and eat with him, and he with me. Revelation 3:19-20 (NIV)

While they were there, the time came for the baby to be born, and she gave birth to her firstborn, a son. She wrapped him in cloths and placed him in a manger, because there was no room for them in the inn. Luke 2:6-7 (NIV)

WORSHIP/OBEDIENCE
If people had really believed who Jesus was, there certainly would have been room for Him in the inn. We give preference to esteemed people. Movie stars, athletes, and important officials get the best tables, seats, and the most preferred room reservations in hotels. Who do you believe Jesus to be? He is standing there knocking. Is there any room available and what kind of room have you set aside for Him?

Give Him access to every situation that you encounter today!

We can conquer anger in our lives when we call on our authority from God. Am I saying that you will not have to get angry anymore? No, certainly not. I'm merely stating that when we believe we have authority from God to overpower bad habits in our lives, we can win the battle with anger.

ADORATION/EXPLANATION

We can only claim God's authority over issues in our lives when we really believe that we have it. The Bible tells us that we have great strength in God, yet not everyone is calling upon this. We go straight to anger instead of acting with a godly authority. We have authority from God to endure problems, yet still remain amazingly happy and joyful.

Be self-controlled and alert. Your enemy the devil prowls around like a roaring lion looking for someone to devour. Resist him, standing firm in the faith, because you know that your brothers throughout the world are undergoing the same kind of sufferings. And the God of all grace, who called you to his eternal glory in Christ, after you have suffered a little while, will himself restore you and make you strong, firm and steadfast. 1 Peter 5:8-10 (NIV)

I have given you authority to trample on snakes and scorpions and to overcome all the power of the enemy, nothing will harm you. Luke 10:19 (NIV)

In your anger do not sin. Do not let the sun go down while you are still angry, and do not give the devil a foothold. Ephesians 4:26-27 (NIV)

WORSHIP/OBEDIENCE

Letting anger control us instead of calling on God's authority over it in our lives is giving the devil a foothold. Pretty soon that becomes two or three footholds, and after a while, anger has a stronghold on us. We can choose today to go through our schedules being calm, stable, joyful, and peaceful all because of our authority in God!

Anger or authority—it's your choice!

Is obeying God's word better than sacrificing your time for God? Have you ever thought to yourself, "Hey, I go to church every week!" or "I go to a weekly Bible study and work in the church nursery!" Maybe you've thought this one: "I give money in the offering each week and I donate to charities! I make meals for the sick and elderly! I must definitely be pleasing God with all these sacrifices of my time and money for Him, RIGHT?"

ADORATION/EXPLANATION

Sacrificing our time and money is beautiful. It can be a wonderful thing to do and it sometimes is even pleasing to God. But the Bible is very clear in telling us that God is more interested in an *obedient heart*. The posture of a heart so obedient, that it will be demonstrated in all areas, not just in traditions, sacraments, or sacrifices. An attitude that results in following God's word…and then not even drawing attention to our sacrifices! Wow…I want that attitude!

Sacrifice and offering you did not desire, but my ears you have pierced, burnt offerings and sin offerings you did not require. Then I said, "Here I am, I have come—it is written about me in the scroll, I desire to do your will, O my God; your law is within my heart." Psalm 40:6-8 (NIV)

No man can redeem the life of another or give God a ransom for him—the ransom for a life is costly, no payment is ever enough... Psalm 49:7-8 (NIV)

O Lord, open my lips, and my mouth will declare your praise. You do not delight in sacrifice, or I would bring it; you do not take pleasure in burnt offerings. The sacrifices of God are a broken spirit; a broken and contrite heart, O God, you will not despise. Psalm 51:15-17 (NIV)

WORSHIP/OBEDIENCE

We need to read God's word and daily live it out in obedience to what it teaches. Easy? Not necessarily. But the more that we commit to obey God in every little area, in every little corner of our lives, it will result in the most prized sacrifice that God could ever desire from us. And do you want to know something neat? You won't even realize that you are sacrificing anything!

March 7

What is our function for God today? While both gifts and abilities are endowments from God, when mentioned in the Bible, gifts are talked about specifically to minister to other believers. God assigns each of us with a specific function and enables us by His grace to fulfill it.

ADORATION/EXPLANATION
In his discourse on spiritual functions in the book of Romans, the Apostle Paul uses the analogy of the human body. We all have different functions and, consequently, different gifts and talents that enable us to fulfill these functions in life.

For by the grace given me I say to every one of you; Do not think of yourself more highly than you ought, but rather think of yourself with sober judgment, in accordance with the measure of faith God has given you. Just as each of us has one body with many members, and those members do not all have the same function, so in Christ we who are many form one body, and each member belongs to all the others. We have different gifts, according to the grace given us. If a man's gift is prophesying, let him use it in proportion to his faith. If it is serving, let him serve; if it is teaching, let him teach; if it is encouraging, let him encourage; if it is contributing to the needs of others, let him give generously; if it is leadership, let him govern diligently; if it is showing mercy, let him do it cheerfully. Romans 12:3-8 (NIV)

Each one should use whatever gift he has received to serve others, faithfully administering God's grace in its various forms. 1 Peter 4:10 (NIV)

Now to each one the manifestation of the Spirit is given for the common good. 1 Corinthians 12:7 (NIV)

WORSHIP/OBEDIENCE
God assigns and has designed every person for an important function in the body of believers. Just as in the physical body, the body of believers needs us to function properly. Every Christian has a gift and every gift is important! What is your function? What is your job?

Are you performing to the best of your ability?

Only the trait of LOVE gives true value to our gifts. What? Not skill, talent, attitude, or purpose driven lives? Nope! Only LOVE gives true…lasting value.

ADORATION/EXPLANATION

Put a row of zeros on a piece of paper. Now put another row and another. What do they add up to? Absolutely nothing! But then put a number 1 in front of all these zeroes—now that's a lot! This is how love adds to our gifts, talents, and skill. They really aren't worth much of anything until we put love in front of them, but doing so makes them have immediate value. Genuine love can add exponentially greater value to our natural gifts!

Now you are the body of Christ, and each one of you is a part of it. 1 Corinthians 12:27 (NIV)

If I speak in the tongues of men and of angels, but have not love, I am only a resounding gong or a clanging cymbal. If I have the gift of prophecy and can fathom all mysteries and all knowledge, and if I have a faith that can move mountains, but have not love, I am nothing. If I give all I possess to the poor and surrender my body to the flames, but have not love, I gain nothing. Love is patient, love is kind. It does not envy, it does not boast, it is not proud. It is not rude, it is not self-seeking, it is not easily angered, it keeps no record of wrongs.

Love does not delight in evil but rejoices with the truth. It always protects, always trusts, always hopes, always perseveres. 1 Corinthians 13:1-7 (NIV)

WORSHIP/OBEDIENCE

Love must permeate every aspect of our lives. Love should not be exercised only in our various Christian duties, it is to be present in the home, at the office, in the classroom, on the tennis courts, in the convenience store, in the traffic jam, and in any place that we live and function. It is NOT a gift in itself, but rather the partner to any gift that God has bestowed upon us.

Everything is multiplied with love! Everything is better with love!

Today is going to be an extraordinary day! How do I know this? Because today, I am consciously going to choose to be thankful for all of the normal, average, "same old, same old" events that happen to me throughout my schedule. Yup…I said thankful!

ADORATION/EXPLANATION
God never asked us to look for an extraordinary existence and He never promised fantastic "wow moments" in our lives. It doesn't matter! Our praise to Him should be demonstrated in a heart that is thankful for even the mundane things that occur. It is only as we purpose to do this that God may allow us a glimpse of the extraordinary.

He has showed you, O man, what is good. And what does the Lord require of you? To act justly and to love mercy and to walk humbly with your God. Micah 6:8 (NIV)

So then, just as you received Christ Jesus as Lord, continue to live in him, rooted and built up in him, strengthened in the faith as you were taught, and overflowing with thankfulness. Colossians 2:6 (NIV)

And whatever you do, whether in word or deed, do it all in the name of the Lord Jesus, giving thanks to God the Father through him. Colossians 3:17 (NIV)

Make it your ambition to lead a quiet life, to mind your own business and to work with your hands, just as we told you, so that your daily life may win the respect of outsiders and so that you will not be dependent on anybody. 1 Thessalonians 4:11-12 (NIV)

WORSHIP/OBEDIENCE
I need to be thankful for my regular, calm, mundane, ordinary life. What is so bad about ordinary anyway? Absolutely nothing!

Dear Lord, prompt me to be thankful for the ordinary events today and to believe that in the midst of this, the extraordinary may show up! Amen.

It takes sadness to really know what happiness feels like. It takes noise to fully appreciate silence and peacefulness. When something is lost, we only then understand what it means to be found. It takes absence of someone in our lives to really love when they are near.

ADORATION/EXPLANATION
I wish that many hardships didn't have to happen to me in my life! But I am beginning to understand that the God that I love and praise knows better than I do. Only in these difficult circumstances of my every-day journey do I really learn to appreciate His faithfulness. Sad…to happy, noisy to complete peacefulness, absence to nearness, and lost…but now found! Wow!

Then Daniel praised the God of heaven and said: "Praise be to the name of God for ever and ever; wisdom and power are his. He changes times and seasons; he sets up Kings and deposes them. He gives wisdom to the wise and knowledge to the discerning. He reveals deep hidden things; he knows what lies in darkness, and light dwells with him. I thank and praise you, O God of my fathers: You have given me wisdom and power, you have made known to me what we asked of you, you have made known to us the dream of the king." Daniel 2:19b-23 (NIV)

The King asked Daniel, "Are you able to tell me what I saw in my dream and interpret it?" Daniel replied, "No wise man, enchanter, magician or diviner can explain to the king the mystery he has asked about, but there is a God in heaven who reveals mysteries." Daniel 2:26-28b (NIV)

WORSHIP/OBEDIENCE
So, is God telling us to worship Him, no matter what? It would seem so. He says in His word that wisdom and power are His! Daniel seemed to understand this. We want to understand it also, but most of the time we won't. We will not get it; we will not understand His ways; we will not get the whole plan. But when things happen such as sadness, sickness, noise, commotion, turmoil, absence, and loss, we must remember that there is a God in heaven who reveals mysteries.

He may explain or He may not, but He is always God! Trust!

March 11

Already, spring seems to be coming in with a flourish. Flower bulbs are peeking up through the lingering cold ground, which is, in some places, still dusted with snow! Even though I am sure that the season will change, the signs of the new season are not all the way evident yet.

ADORATION/EXPLANATION

How we act and behave when there are no clear signs of change coming is indicative of what we really believe. Do we believe that spring is right around the corner? Yes! What if our only sign is buried in the still-frozen ground? Yes! Because we know, beyond a shadow of a doubt that the season we long for, always comes. Likewise, our awe for God reminds us of His track record, and we know that spring is coming!

Now Daniel so distinguished himself among the administrators and satraps by his exceptional qualities that the king planned to set him over the whole kingdom. At this, the administrators and the satraps tried to find grounds for the charges against Daniel in his conduct of government affairs, but they were unable to do so. They could find no corruption in him, because he was trustworthy and neither corrupt or negligent. Finally these men said, "We will never find any basis for charges against this man Daniel unless it has something to do with the law of his God. Daniel 6:3-5 (NIV)

Now when Daniel learned that the decree had been published, he went home to his upstairs room where the windows opened toward Jerusalem. Three times a day he got down on his knees and prayed, giving thanks to his God, just as he had done before. Then these men went as a group and found Daniel praying and asking God for help. Daniel 6:10-11 (NIV)

WORSHIP/OBEDIENCE

When I was a child, I used to sing a song called "Dare to Be a Daniel" in Sunday school. Could I...would I...be someone with the courage of Daniel? As I reflect on that now, my obvious act of worship to God needs to be more then just singing a song. I need to act, behave, and live obediently, no matter what the possible outcome may be. As sure as I'm sitting here, I know that times change and spring is going to come. Daniel acted trustworthy in all affairs because he trusted God's track record in every season of his life. Try it! I dare you!

In yesterday's reading we realized that although the month of March seems to be roaring in like a lion; spring is on its way. Winter's winds and cold are still roaring about, but change is slowly seeping in. Even if the signs are not at all spring-like just yet, even if we do not feel it in the air, the season will change!

ADORATION/EXPLANATION

Once again we will read in the Old Testament book of Daniel how Daniel acted ethically and was trustworthy and consistent in his obedience to God in all his affairs— ALL of his affairs! At all times, during all seasons, in work, play and worship, Daniel was a righteous man. And what did he get for his troubles? A visit to the lion's den… that's what!

Then they said to the king, "Daniel, who is one of the exiles from Judah, pays no attention to you, O king, or to the decree you put in writing. He still prays three times a day." When the king heard this, he was greatly distressed; he was determined to rescue Daniel and made every effort until sundown to save him. Then the men went as a group to the king and said to him, "Remember, O king, that according to the law of the Medes and Persians no decree or edict that the king issues can be changed."

So the king gave the order, and they brought Daniel and threw him into the lions' den. The king said to Daniel, "May your God, whom you serve continually, rescue you!" A stone was brought and placed over the mouth of the den, and the king sealed it with his own signet ring and with the rings of his nobles, so that Daniel's situation might not be changed. Daniel 6:13-17 (NIV)

WORSHIP/OBEDIENCE

Daniel's situation went from a high position in government to being tossed down into a lion's den. His status, well-being, and safety changed drastically in a matter of days. He even lost control over his very life when a large boulder was rolled across his possible means of escape. Only one choice remained to him and that never wavered. He worshipped! He trusted! He prayed!

Continually, continuous, consistency…can any of these words describe your life of faith, your praying habits, or your personal walk with God? Think about it—when Daniel was young, his reputation was that he was honest, sincere, ethical, continually serving God, and trustworthy in all situations. He was elevated to a high government position for the king and he continued in this behavior so much so that others wanted to find fault with him. Jealousy at its best!

ADORATION/EXPLANATION

When given a decree that he must stop praying to God or risk losing his life, Daniel continued. When thrown into a lions' den, his behavior was still consistent. Do you think others noticed this? Yes! As a matter of fact, the last thing that the king yelled into the den was, "May your God, whom you serve continually, rescue you!"

At the first light of dawn, the king got up and hurried to the lions' den. When he came near the den, he called to Daniel in an anguished voice, "Daniel, servant of the living God, has your God, whom you serve continually, been able to rescue you from the lions?" Daniel answered, "O king, live forever! My God sent his angel, and he shut the mouths of the lions. They have not hurt me, because I was found innocent in his sight. Nor have I ever done any wrong before you, O king." The king was overjoyed and gave orders to lift Daniel out of the den. And when Daniel was lifted from the den, no wound was found on him, because he had trusted in his God. Daniel 6:19-23 (NIV)

"I issue a decree that in every part of my kingdom people must fear and reverence the God of Daniel." Daniel 6:26a (NIV)

WORSHIP/OBEDIENCE

Obviously we want our lives to be in consistent obedience to God, and Daniel's life was a great example of this beautiful trait! Will anyone notice our lives' consistency? Do we want to hear, "May your God, whom you serve <u>continually</u>, rescue you!"?

Are we serving continually in all areas of our lives? Ponder this!

While I'm writing this book, I happen to be living at the New Jersey shore. Not only do I love the ocean, but there is also a large lighthouse nearby that I enjoy visiting. The best time to see this lighthouse that looks out over Barnegat Bay is in the evening, because at that time, the light at the top is turned on.

ADORATION/EXPLANATION

When it begins to get dark and the light begins to come on in the lighthouse, there is no noise. No sirens, no warning bells, no announcements—just the light. I have been there when this happens and an awed hush comes over any visitors. Boats pass by loaded with tourists that look on and take pictures. We all adore a beautiful light that shines in the darkness!

This is the message we have heard from him and declare to you: God is light; in him there is no darkness at all. If we claim to have fellowship with him yet walk in the darkness, we lie and do not live by the truth. But if we walk in the light, as he is in the light, we have fellowship with one another. And the blood of Jesus, his Son, purifies us from all sin. 1 John 1:5-7 (NIV)

Anyone who claims to be in the light but hates his brother is still in the darkness. 1 John 2:9 (NIV)

"You are the light of the world. A city on a hill cannot be hidden.

In the same way, let your light shine before men, that they may see your good deeds and praise your Father in heaven." Matthew 5:14, 16 (NIV)

WORSHIP/OBEDIENCE

Does a lighthouse have to call attention to the fact that the light is turned on? Absolutely not! The beacon shining brightly out over the water is enough of an attraction to draw most gazes in that direction. Isn't it obvious how we, as believers in Christ, should be living our lives?

If our light is "turned on" and we're walking in the light,
we won't need sirens or announcements!

If I claim to be walking with God but do not love others, the Bible calls me a liar. What? But I go to a Bible study each week! Are you kidding me? I attend church, and help serve coffee every Sunday! I'm not a liar! My father is the pastor, my uncle is a deacon, my brother is an elder, my sister a nun, my cousin is a priest…what?

ADORATION/EXPLANATION

The question is, do you believe God and His Word or not? It doesn't matter who you are or who your relatives are or what you do weekly. It only matters who God is and what He says we must do—love everyone!

And if we don't, well, sorry to say, we are blind and we are liars!

———

We know that we have come to know him if we obey his commands. The man who says, "I know him," but does not do what he commands is a liar, and the truth is not in him. 1 John 2:3-4 (NIV)

But whoever hates his brother is in the darkness and walks around in the darkness; he does not know where he is going, because the darkness has blinded him. 1 John 2:11 (NIV)

If anyone says, "I love God," yet hates his brother, he is a liar. For anyone who does not love his brother, whom he has seen, cannot love God, whom he has not seen. And he has given us this command: Whoever loves God must also love his brother. 1 John 4:20-21 (NIV)

WORSHIP/OBEDIENCE

Woe to me, woe to you, woe to anyone who makes claims that they know Christ yet then try to rest on their own laurels instead of what He commands us to do in scripture. Let us not be known as liars!

God, please help me choose to follow your Word.
Travel along with me in my daily duties,
job, and schedule to look for those that I need to love.

———

March 16

Sometimes we as humans have a hard time accepting and believing everything in the Bible and about God. We have doubts. Is this normal? Yup! You may even carry some doubts for the rest of your life. If you were to pretend you never doubted anything, then you would be "only fooling yourself." Your doubts are not sin if they are honest questionings.

ADORATION/EXPLANATION

Treat your doubts as opportunities to grow. Bring them out into the open and ask Christian leaders the hard questions. Seek wise, godly counsel and confront God with your doubts. We have a God that is so awesome and loving that He wants us to seek Him when we feel doubts or trepidation. He already knows the tough paradoxes of Scripture and our universe. Why not ask Him?

But you, dear friends, build yourselves up in your most holy faith and pray in the Holy Spirit. Keep yourselves in God's love as you wait for the mercy of our Lord Jesus Christ to bring you to eternal life. Be merciful to those who doubt; Jude 1:20-22 (NIV)

Timothy, guard what has been entrusted to your care. Turn away from godless chatter and the opposing ideas of what is falsely called knowledge, which some have professed and in so doing have wandered from the faith. Grace be with you. 1Timothy 6:20-21 (NIV)

Blessed is the man who makes the Lord his trust, who does not look to the proud, to those who turn aside to false gods. Do not withhold your mercy from me, O Lord; may your love and your truth always protect me. Psalm 40:4, 11 (NIV)

WORSHIP/OBEDIENCE

Can we still obey or worship God when we have doubts? If so, how? Here's the panacea. Here is the remedy: relax! Follow Him despite your doubts and ask Him to lead your mind. He will! Many apostles and writers of Scripture had their own doubts and questions for God and sought His answers. They eventually understood God's truth, but they never stopped serving Him while they searched! Remember this—you can't expect to know it all. Only God himself does and this is where trust comes in!

Jesus refers to Satan quite a bit in the Bible. He calls him the prince of the powers of the air. But Christ's death on the cross defeated Satan, and we as believers share in Christ's victory. But be aware and never forget that once you become a part of God's family, you have taken on a new enemy. Satan is unhappy to have lost you, so he will continually throw a few things into your life to upset your balance and trust.

ADORATION/EXPLANATION

Doubt, discouragement, delays, distractions, and many other things are strategically thrown into our daily lives. On top of all this, Satan may cause us to feel depressed because we have these doubts and other feelings. But here is the good news—no, the GREAT news—be encouraged, for you have truth on your side! Jesus tells us to cheer up because the battle is already won!

Submit yourselves, then, to God. Resist the devil, and he will flee from you. James 4:7 (NIV)

So I find this law at work: When I want to do good, evil is right there with me. For in my inner being I delight in God's law; but I see another law at work in the members of my body, waging war against the law of my mind and making me a prisoner of the law of sin at work within my members. Romans 7:21 (NIV)

Be self-controlled and alert. Your enemy the devil prowls around like a roaring lion looking for someone to devour. 1 Peter 5:8 (NIV)

The Lord will rescue me from every evil attack and will bring me safely to his heavenly kingdom. To him be glory for ever and ever. Amen. 2 Timothy 4:18 (NIV)

WORSHIP/OBEDIENCE

We need to understand that all of Satan's attacks will be based on one thing: a lie. Jesus told us that the devil was a liar and a hater of truth. We need to constantly tell ourselves to be encouraged, for we have truth on our side. No matter how many doubts, depressed days, or discouragements we feel, Jesus has already handled it. We cannot get hung up on these attacks to our minds and spiritual health.

We are on the victor's side. Cheer up, because the battle has been won!

March 18

Do you believe that God has loved us for generations and generations? I do! He will also continue to love us for many generations to come. This is such a beautiful legacy of faith to pass on to our friends, family, children, and grandchildren. Even if doubts, fears, and discouragement come (which they will), we can still read about and watch God's promises down through the pages of Scripture.

ADORATION/EXPLANATION

Our awe of God's love and promises to believers should inspire us to live daily to honor Him. We should leave a legacy to all who know us, whether they are acquaintances, dear friends, or deeply loved family. The fifth book of the Old Testament, Deuteronomy, has some wonderful seeds of advice about remembering God's commands so that our lives will produce a legacy.

Know therefore that the Lord your God is God; he is the faithful God, keeping his covenant of love to a thousand generations of those who love him and keep his commands. Deuteronomy 7:9 (NIV)

Be careful to follow every command I am giving you today, so that you may live and increase and may enter and possess the land that the Lord promised on oath to your forefathers. Remember how the Lord your God led you all the way in the desert these forty years, to humble you and to test you in order to know what was in your heart, whether or not you would keep his commands. He humbled you, causing you to hunger and then feeding you with manna, which neither you nor your fathers had known, to teach you that man does not live on bread alone but on every word that comes from the mouth of the Lord.

Observe the commands of the Lord your God, walking in his ways and revering him. Deuteronomy 8:1-4, 6 (NIV)

WORSHIP/OBEDIENCE

Even in the days of old, there was one prevalent guideline for believers: follow God's commands! Be careful to follow, remember to follow, do not neglect to follow…can it get any simpler? Our obvious way to worship is obedience to God in all situations, and not only in good times but also in times of testing, doubts, and hardships. Are you following?

You are responsible to leave a legacy!

March 19

We leave lasting effects upon the people that we meet. Whether they are co-workers, neighbors, friends, or family, we make some kind of impression. Yesterday we talked about leaving a legacy to generations to follow but today let's think about the smaller picture—TODAY! We need to remember what we've learned in the Bible and what God is teaching us daily, and take every opportunity to give God the credit. We may not have tomorrow to affect the life of someone that we meet in passing.

ADORATION/EXPLANATION

God once again reminds the people in Deuteronomy that their own eyes saw and witnessed God's might and power. They need to remember this and give God the glory. They need to talk about it to their children and to everyone that they meet! Talk about it!

Love the Lord your God and keep his requirements, his decrees, his laws and his commands always. Remember today that your children were not the ones who saw and experienced the discipline of the Lord your God; his majesty, his mighty hand, his outstretched arm;

But it was your own eyes that saw all these great things the Lord has done. Deuteronomy 11:1-3a, 7 (NIV)

Fix these words of mine in your hearts and minds; tie them as symbols on your hands and bind them on your foreheads. Teach them to your children, talking about them when you sit at home and when you walk along the road, when you lie down and when you get up. Write them on the doorframes of your houses and on your gates. Deuteronomy 11:18-20 (NIV)

WORSHIP/OBEDIENCE

Are you talking about God? Not just throwing out random Bible verses to people, but are you really talking about what God has done and is doing for you daily? Are you making a point to remember to fix God's words and provisions for you in your heart and mind so that you can tell others, or are you forgetting and going on with your day? What effect for God are you having upon the lives of people today? Will they remember that you were even there?

March 20

For any of us to leave a legacy, have an effect on people, or just live individually for God from day to day with a purpose, there is one component of our bodies that has to change—our heart! According to the Bible, our hearts, minds, and soul all work together. But what is going on in our heart will most likely dictate how we act and speak.

ADORATION/EXPLANATION
In biblical times, circumcision was a sign of a covenant between God and Israel. It was a deliberate act of cutting and discarding of the male body's foreskin to demonstrate cleanliness and rightness before God. This outward sign of obedience by the Jewish people later became something flaunted as a legalistic, human effort to please God. It became just an outward physical act and God desired a deliberate, inward change. God speaks in the Old and New Testament concerning a circumcision of the HEART. Circumcise your heart? What is this?

Circumcision has value if you observe the law, but if you break the law, you have become as though you had not been circumcised. If those who are not circumcised keep the law's requirements, will they not be regarded as though they were circumcised? A man is not a Jew if he is only one outwardly, nor is circumcision merely outward and physical. No, a man is a Jew if he is one inwardly; and circumcision is circumcision of the heart, by the Spirit, not by the written code. Such a man's praise is not from men, but from God. Romans 2:25-26, 28-29 (NIV)

Circumcise your hearts, therefore, and do not be stiff-necked any longer. For the Lord your God is God of gods and Lord of lords, the great God mighty and awesome, who shows no partiality and accepts no bribes. Deuteronomy 10:16 (NIV)

WORSHIP/OBEDIENCE
Just as physical circumcision is a deliberate act of cutting away, so must be the circumcision of our hearts. We should not choose to be stiff-necked and stubborn or try to hold onto what needs to be carved out of our souls. God is a careful surgeon… but He is deliberate! God is looking for the inward change that only the Spirit can make. Can He see it? Is there a change?

March 21

Spring is busting out all over! The weather is just turning balmy and pleasant, and I feel a renewed hope as the winter season seems to be receding. There is something about the buds, flowers, trees, and grass popping up that reminds me that everything was alive all along. By this I mean that even in the cold of winter when I didn't see any sign of buds or flowers, I still knew they existed. They would come back!

ADORATION/EXPLANATION

My flowers may have been dormant all winter, but what was happening underground will insure beautiful blooms this spring. God reminds us of these same principles in living the Christian life each day. Even if we have been in a dormant state, we don't have to worry or fret for too long. Whatever is truly going on in our hearts will insure beautiful, fragrant blossoms to come.

"Make a tree good and its fruit will be good, or make a tree bad and its fruit will be bad, for a tree is recognized by its fruit. You brood of vipers, how can you who are evil say anything good? For out of the overflow of the heart the mouth speaks. The good man brings good things out of the good stored up in him, and the evil man brings evil things out of the evil stored up in him. Matthew 12:33-35 (NIV)

Above all else, guard your heart, for it is the wellspring of life. Proverbs 4:23 (NIV)

Then hear from heaven, your dwelling place. Forgive and act; deal with each man according to all he does, since you know his heart (for you alone know the hearts of all men)…

But your hearts must be fully committed to the Lord our God, to live by his decrees and obey his commands, as at this time. 1 Kings 8:39a, 61 (NIV)

WORSHIP/OBEDIENCE

"In my heart there rings a melody!" Spring is here!

God, let the words of my mouth and the emotions of my heart
burst force with a pleasing flourish for you.
Help me display the benefits of a healthy heart.

Do I have to go to church this week? Should I go to church every week? What about Bible study? What if I spend some volunteer time down at my local homeless shelter? Don't these other activities count towards going to church? What does God want? According to the Bible, God clearly expects us to worship. It is our purpose!

ADORATION/EXPLANATION

In the Old Testament times, the people in the wilderness pitched a tent or a tabernacle and this is where God's presence lived among them. They went to the tabernacle to worship and learn of God's glory. God does desire worship from us, but He desires believers to build each other up, encourage, and spur one another on. How can this be done if we do not meet together regularly?

Let us hold unswervingly to the hope we profess, for he who promised is faithful. And let us consider how we may spur one another on toward love and good deeds. Let us not give up meeting together, as some are in the habit of doing, but let us encourage one another—and all the more as you see the Day approaching. Hebrews 10:23-25 (NIV)

I rejoiced with those who said to me, "Let us go to the house of the Lord." Psalm 122:1 (NIV)

Therefore, since we are receiving a kingdom that cannot be shaken, let us be thankful, and so worship God acceptably with reverence and awe, Hebrews 12:28 (NIV)

WORSHIP/OBEDIENCE

Once again the question may arise, "Do I have to go to church?" Here are a few questions to ponder: Can you regularly worship with other believers without a local congregation? Are you being taught and growing steadily in words, deeds, faith, and in Bible knowledge? Are you able to meet regularly and encourage, sing praises, and spur on other believers? I decided long ago to trade in a stale spiritual obligation and enjoy the privilege of attending a worship service weekly to focus and respond to God. If you were offered a free breakfast each week from a local restaurant, would you go?

You are offered a free spiritual breakfast each week! Do you want it?

God's Word really doesn't matter to your life unless you respond to what it teaches. Your personal response to what it says is everything! We will only make time to worship a God when we truly learn to comprehend how much He loves us, what His attributes are, how much He desires our conversation and prayer, how much He wants to bless us, help us through sorrow, and join with us in praise and joy.

ADORATION/EXPLANATION

Part of my personal worship to God is reading, studying, and meditating on what the Bible tells me. There are wonderful experiences with God that only come in times of private worship and study. Make time to read and think…

But seek first his kingdom and his righteousness, and all these things will be given to you as well. Matthew 6:33 (NIV)

Your attitude should be the same as that of Christ Jesus: Philippians 2:5 (NIV)

For everything that was written in the past was written to teach us, so that through endurance and the encouragement of the Scriptures we might have hope. May the God who gives endurance and encouragement give you a spirit of unity among yourselves as you follow Christ Jesus, so that with one heart and mouth you may glorify the God and Father of our Lord Jesus Christ. Romans 15:4-6 (NIV)

WORSHIP/OBEDIENCE

To seek first God's kingdom and His way of life is a continuous action. We need to strive for, desire strongly, pursue, and study God's word. Then we need to respond to and practice it in our daily life. Simple? Hardly ever! Excuses seem to pop up easily to take away our concentration from seeking. Sometimes the excuses are valid in and of themselves; but DO NOT let the excuses take first place.

First place belongs to God!
What is first place in your life?

March 24

Turn off the television, shut down the computer, power off your electronic gadgets and mute your phone. Unplug? Many people today cannot exist without constantly being attached, hooked up, or turned on to their social media devices. Oh yes, they will make all the typical excuses about important e-mails, shows, news, messages, and phone calls, even insisting that they could not, should not, or dare not unplug for even a day.

ADORATION/EXPLANATION

What if we had this same attitude about our relationship with God? Sorry friends, there is just NO WAY that I can put God on mute. Wow! Imagine telling others around us, "Sorry! I can't turn God off, it might be important! I refuse to power down, unplug, or even mute God during this meeting, lunch, dinner date, conversation, vacation, or relaxing time." Could you? Would you?

Now that would be something to behold!

May the God of hope fill you with all joy and peace as you trust in him, so that you may overflow with hope by the power of the Holy Spirit. I myself am convinced, my brothers, that you yourselves are full of goodness, complete in knowledge and competent to instruct one another. Romans 15:13-14 (NIV)

"What good will it be for a man if he gains the whole world, yet forfeits his soul? Or what can a man give in exchange for his soul?" Matthew 16:26 (NIV)

"Woe to the world because of the things that cause people to sin! Such things must come, but woe to the man through whom they come! Matthew 18:7 (NIV)

WORSHIP/OBEDIENCE

Many devices are wonderfully made and God has given them to us for our pleasure and work. Our lives are easier because of modern electronics. Things we may consider indispensable cannot compare with the greater value of a daily connection to Jesus Christ. Let your act of obedience and worship today include a concerted effort to unplug from the world and plug in to God!

"Today is the first day of the rest of your life." "Let's make a new start." "Let's start fresh" and so on! How many times have we heard these sayings? But to start over, to start fresh, to begin again, or to start anything, you have to recognize exactly where you are now! Whether you are traveling, in a mall, in school, desiring a new job, or plotting any kind of new course for your life, you must acknowledge where you're standing right now. Rarely does anybody "accidentally" end up on the right road.

ADORATION/EXPLANATION
The process of redirecting our course in life can be slow, painful, confusing, and sometimes likely to make us want to give up. Do NOT! Run, walk, trudge, or crawl straight toward God with your plans. Hard times do not mean that you should quit. They are producing perseverance! We have a mighty God!

The word of the Lord came to Jonah son of Amittai: "Go to the great city of Nineveh and preach against it, because its wickedness has come up before me." But Jonah ran away from the Lord and headed for Tarshish. He went down to Joppa, where he found a ship bound for that port. After paying the fare, he went aboard and sailed for Tarshish to flee from the Lord. Then the Lord sent a great wind on the sea, and such a violent storm arose that the ship threatened to break up. Jonah 1:1-4 (NIV)

This terrified them and they asked, "What have you done?" (they knew he was running away from the Lord, because he had already told them so.) The sea was getting rougher and rougher. So they asked him, "What should we do to you to make the sea calm down for us?" "Pick me up and throw me into the sea," he replied, "and it will become calm. I know that it is my fault that this great storm has come upon you." Then they took Jonah and threw him overboard, and the raging sea grew calm. Jonah 1:10-12, 15 (NIV)

WORSHIP/OBEDIENCE
Can you imagine the difficult process of redirecting your path? God does not always pursue those of us that run from His path; but in this case, He did have a particular mission in mind for Jonah. Sometimes God just lets us run because He knows that our running away will result in us eventually turning to Him for guidance.

Do you need redirecting? Start today!

Whether by pursuing us or by letting us run, God's goal for us seems to be the same. He wants to work in our daily lives, firmly and lovingly, to redirect us towards His best plan. Somewhere along the line, the prophet Jonah got his directions crossed. Through a drastic chain of events, Jonah began to get his head together in the belly of a gigantic fish. Rolling around in seaweed, bile, and seawater might help redirect most of us. Yikes!

ADORATION/EXPLANATION

Jonah cries out to God, shouts for mercy, and recites Scripture. He makes promises, makes more vows, and prays. What else can he do? He <u>has</u> to cry "Uncle"! This resulted because Jonah knew exactly where he was and admitted to what got him in his present situation. All stubbornness had to leave before this admission could be made!

But the Lord provided a great fish to swallow Jonah, and Jonah was inside the fish three days and three nights. Jonah 1:17 (NIV)

From inside the fish Jonah prayed to the Lord his God. He said: "In my distress I called to the Lord, and he answered me. From the depths of the grave I called for help, and you listened to my cry. You hurled me into the deep, into the very heart of the seas, and the currents swirled about me; all your waves and breakers swept over me. I said, 'I have been banished from your sight; yet I will look again toward your holy temple.' The engulfing waters threatened me, the deep surrounded me; seaweed was wrapped around my head." Jonah 2:1-5 (NIV)

Worship/Obedience

Swallowed by a whale? That would certainly get my attention! Or would it?

God got Jonah's attention in a very dramatic way and it changed his attitude, but God does not always use the dramatic. He most likely will not use a whale in our case, but take a moment today to look around. Pull that seaweed off your head and listen to God's voice! He may be directing…

We sometimes have a restricted view of God and His presence in our daily lives. We limit Him to church, Bible studies, or religious concerts and such. That is exactly why Jonah thought that he could flee from God. If he was not in the temple, then surely God couldn't find him! Do I act this way sometimes? Do I believe that God cannot find me and certainly will not pursue me when I try to ignore him?

ADORATION/EXPLANATION
My awe and adoration of God and His mighty ways keep me from trying to run and hide. I realize who He is! God wants to make His perfect will known to people everywhere. Anyone who chooses to seek will find. It may not always be crystal clear in the beginning, but as I follow and obey in faith, I just may start to see the path that God wants me on.

To the roots of the mountains I sank down; the earth beneath barred me in forever. But you brought my life up from the pit, O Lord my God. "When my life was ebbing away, I remembered you, Lord, and my prayer rose to you, to your holy temple. Those who cling to worthless idols forfeit the grace that could be theirs. But I, with a song of thanksgiving, will sacrifice to you. What I have vowed I will make good. Salvation comes from the Lord." And the Lord commanded the fish, and it vomited Jonah onto dry land. Jonah 2:6-10 (NIV)

The Lord is close to the brokenhearted and saves those who are crushed in spirit. Psalm 34:18 (NIV)

WORSHIP/OBEDIENCE
Jonah found God in the stomach of a large sea creature. He started out making his own plans and encountered a storm. He was tossed overboard and engulfed by waves, while wearing a seaweed turban. Next on God's schedule, was his encounter with a whale.

Lord, I do NOT need a large fish to get my attention.
Today I desire to trust you, even in times of distress. If my heart is broken,
still I will trust. If my spirit is crushed, still I will trust!
If you can turn a disobedient prophet around,
then I believe that you can make something beautiful out of my life.

Have you ever noticed that when we seem to have it all together in our own lives, we are the most impatient with others who do not? We wonder why they are so thick-headed or rebellious. Why can't they get their lives on track? Why don't they change? What exactly is the matter with them?

ADORATION/EXPLANATION

I love reading the Bible for the very fact that it teaches me great personal lessons. In the Scripture, we once again see the great pendulum swing of Jonah's personality. Didn't he learn patience with others after his own episode with the whale? It didn't appear as if he did. I would! (Wouldn't I?)

Then the word of the Lord came to Jonah a second time: "Go to the great city of Nineveh and proclaim to it the message I give you." Jonah obeyed the word of the Lord and went to Nineveh.

When God saw what they did and how they turned from their evil ways, he had compassion and did not bring upon them the destruction he had threatened. Jonah 3:1-3a, 10 (NIV)

But Jonah was greatly displeased and became angry. He prayed to the Lord, "O Lord, is this not what I said when I was still at home? That is why I was so quick to flee to Tarshish. I knew that you are a gracious and compassionate God, slow to anger and abounding in love, a God who relents from sending calamity.

But the Lord replied, "Have you any right to be angry?" Jonah 4:1-2, 4 (NIV)

We who are strong ought to bear with the failings of the weak and not to please ourselves. Romans 15:1 (NIV)

WORSHIP/OBEDIENCE

Today, let us choose to view others through the lens of God's grace. This is the same grace that has been extended to us during our many attempts and failings. Who are we to get angry? Have we any right to be angry at other people's issues? NO!

We should choose to strive for graciousness and compassion.

March 29

Isn't living with grace and extending it freely to others risky? When we believe that we are declared righteous by Christ and His death on the cross, we are basically set free by God's grace. It doesn't mean that we are perfect or that we stop sinning, but there has been a judicial pronouncement made on us through Christ's substitution for our sin. If you can wrap your mind around this concept, it will radically change your daily life!

ADORATION/EXPLANATION

We are not perfect, but God views us through what Jesus has done. We are not sinless, but God has declared us righteous in His eyes because of the crucifixion of His Son. If we really understand this, really believe this, really "get" it, then we will want to live a transformed life! We can live up to how we are viewed by God. How amazing!

Who has saved us and called us to a holy life—not because of anything we have done but because of his own purpose and grace. This grace was given us in Christ Jesus before the beginning of time, but it has now been revealed through the appearing of our Savior, Christ Jesus who has destroyed death and has brought life and immortality to light through the gospel. 2 Timothy 1:9-10 (NIV)

Here is a trustworthy saying that deserves full acceptance: Christ Jesus came into the world to save sinners—of whom I am the worst. But for that very reason I was shown mercy so that in me, the worst of sinners, Christ Jesus might display his unlimited patience as an example for those who would believe on him and receive eternal life. 1Timothy 1:15-16 (NIV)

WORSHIP/OBEDIENCE

Living a holy life does not necessarily mean living in sinless perfection. We cannot do this on our own no matter how much we try, hence the reason that we need God's amazing grace shed on us! Living holy means to first and foremost dedicate our daily lives to the Lord. Living each and every day, striving and motivated to faithfully honor and serve God in even our most mundane schedules.

God displays His unlimited patience on us. What a calming notion that is when we completely believe! Unlimited patience…

March 30

I do not know when your birthday is, but I can tell you that today is mine! As I look outside to the tulips, daffodils, hyacinths, and other springtime flowers, I reflect on my years here on this earth. Spring was always a great time to have my birthday. New life is just poking out its head through the soil, in the trees, and in the air. Smell the breeze! Breathe it in!

ADORATION/EXPLANATION

I am in awe of the fact that my earthly parents gave me life, two beautiful people that God chose just for me, to be my parents! I am fortunate because they also taught me the fact that I needed a spiritual birth. March 30 was always a wonderful day with parties, presents and a celebration of my physical age. But much more important is the fact that I also had a spiritual birthday. I cannot recall the exact day, but around the age of six, I chose to make Jesus Christ my personal Savior. This is my spiritual birthday! Have you had yours?

Praise be to the God and Father of our Lord Jesus Christ! In his great mercy he has given us new birth into a living hope through the resurrection of Jesus Christ from the dead, and into an inheritance that can never perish, spoil or fade—kept in heaven for you, 1 Peter 1:3-4 (NIV)

Jesus answered, "I tell you the truth, no one can see the kingdom of God unless he is born of water and the Spirit. Flesh gives birth to flesh, but the Spirit gives birth to spirit. You should not be surprised at my saying, 'You must be born again.'" John 3:5-7 (NIV)

Therefore, if anyone is in Christ, he is a new creation; the old has gone, and the new has come! 2 Corinthians 5:17 (NIV)

WORSHIP/OBEDIENCE

Today is my birthday and, because of the fact that I also have a spiritual birthday, I can celebrate each coming year in anticipation of what God is going to do in my life! Smell the breeze! Breathe it in! I love birthdays!

Someone is building a new house right next door to my home. Beginning at 7:00 a.m., there are hammers, nail guns, and loud noises coming from the lot. I try to drown the construction sounds out, but nothing seems to work. Even trying to read can pose a problem if my windows are open. Soon though, the job will be complete and the noise will subside. In the meantime, I must put up with the commotion or find some way to block it out.

ADORATION/EXPLANATION

There's a lot of noise in our society. Even when the world outside is quiet, there may still be a lot of racket going on inside our hearts and heads. We need to learn to somehow push the noise back enough to hear the voice of God. Listen…be still…meditate. Do you hear Him?

"At this my heart pounds and leaps from its place. Listen! Listen to the roar of his voice, to the rumbling that comes from his mouth. He unleashes his lightning beneath the whole heaven and sends it to the ends of the earth. After that comes the sound of his roar; he thunders with his majestic voice. When his voice resounds, he holds nothing back. God's voice thunders in marvelous ways; he does great things beyond our understanding. Job 37:1-5 (NIV)

The Lord came and stood there, calling as at the other times, "Samuel! Samuel!" Then Samuel said, "Speak, for your servant is listening." 1 Samuel 3:10 (NIV)

He who has ears, let him hear. Matthew 11:15 (NIV)

WORSHIP/OBEDIENCE

To push or block out the noise sometimes takes a lot more effort than it does at other times. The key appears to be in learning to filter out the din of everyday living long enough to hear the gentle voice of our God, encouraging, lifting, soothing, challenging, teaching, and loving.

Be still and listen. There's no other sound quite like it.

April 1

Today is often referred to as April Fools, and it's a day when jokes and pranks are played on people. April Fools Day (aka "All Fools Day") is of unknown origin, but may have begun around 1582 in France when the Gregorian calendar was introduced and New Year's Day changed from April 1st to January 1st. Whether you even think of jokes or not on this day, the thing that everyone wants to avoid is being made to look a fool!

ADORATION/EXPLANATION

The Bible talks a lot about NOT being a fool. This sage advice does not have anything to do with jokes but more often with NOT following or listening to God.

The fool says in his heart, "There is no God." Psalm 14:1a (NIV)

For the foolishness of God is wiser than man's wisdom, and the weakness of God is stronger than man's strength. 1 Corinthians 1:25 (NIV)

Whoever loves discipline loves knowledge, but he who hates correction is stupid.

The way of a fool seems right to him, but a wise man listens to advice.

A fool shows his annoyance at once, but a prudent man overlooks an insult. Proverbs 12:1, 15-16 (NIV)

A wise man fears the Lord and shuns evil, but a fool is hotheaded and reckless. Proverbs 14:16 (NIV)

It is to a man's honor to avoid strife, but every fool is quick to quarrel. Proverbs 20:3 (NIV)

WORSHIP/OBEDIENCE

Whether it is the first day of April or any other day, we should desire to listen to God's advice and avoid living like a fool. We need not be worried about the world's version of foolishness if we keep our eyes, ears, hearts, minds, and souls focused on things above. Now that is NO joke!

I do not like lukewarm coffee, tea, hot chocolate, or soup. I also do not relish taking a tepid bath. If I am supposed to have a hot drink, I personally like it to be hot! And a nice, hot bath needs to be just that—nice and hot! It also goes the other way. If I desire a cold drink such as soda, water, milk, or iced tea, then it had better be freezing cold!

ADORATION/EXPLANATION

According to the Bible, God has some real thoughts about His people being luke-warm followers. He desires our whole-hearted commitment in living out our daily lives for Him. Would you want a lackluster, dull, drab, pallid kind of relationship with anyone? I wouldn't! God certainly does not want, desire, nor even seem to tolerate this kind of relationship with His children.

If they have escaped the corruption of the world by knowing our Lord and Savior Jesus Christ and are again entangled in it and overcome, they are worse off at the end than they were at the beginning. It would have been better for them not to have known the way of righteousness, than to have known it and then to turn their backs on the sacred command that was passed to them. 2 Peter 2:20-21 (NIV)

The Lord is not slow in keeping his promise, as some understand slowness. He is patient with you, not wanting anyone to perish, but everyone to come to repen-tance. 2 Peter 3:9 (NIV)

I know your deeds, that you are neither cold nor hot. I wish you were either one or the other! So, because you are lukewarm—neither hot nor cold—I am about to spit you out of my mouth.

Those whom I love I rebuke and discipline. So be earnest, and repent. Revelation 3:15-16, 19 (NIV)

WORSHIP/OBEDIENCE

People who are lukewarm in their faith have just enough pretense of Christianity to convince themselves that they are okay. They may be convinced that they are put-ting in the required time, attendance, or whatever is the case to just "get by" with God. But in truth, they may risk missing a wonderful, fulfilling relationship with God altogether.

Dear Lord, make me hot, hot, hot!

April 3

To remain a "hot" follower of Christ and avoid becoming lukewarm, we must continue to make an effort to look for ways to praise God. When praise is in our hearts, minds, and on our lips, there will not be much room left for sinful words and sentiments to pop out!

When we truly remember that God is worthy of praise, it will start to happen naturally and spontaneously in our everyday lives.

ADORATION/EXPLANATION

When I watch a professional ball game, listen to a great concert, or view a show-stopping performance by a great actor, I normally express my appreciation through applause, cheers, shouts, and compliments. Shouldn't our response to God flow out just as easily and joyously? Not necessarily loudly…but freely?

"You are worthy, our Lord and God, to receive glory and honor and power, for you created all things, and by your will they were created and have their being." Revelation 4:11 (NIV)

I will sing of the Lord's great love forever; with my mouth I will make your faithfulness known through all generations. Psalm 89:1 (NIV)

I will sing of your love and justice; to you, O Lord, I will sing praise. Psalm 101:1 (NIV)

Praise the Lord. Praise God in his sanctuary; praise him in his mighty heavens. Praise him for his acts of power; praise him for his surpassing greatness.

Let everything that has breath praise the Lord. Psalm 150:1-2, 6 (NIV)

WORSHIP/OBEDIENCE

How should we praise and give thanks to God? With all that we are and everything that we have! God is worthy of the best that we can do in our worship.

Take a look around you, and choose this day to give praise to the One who deserves it most! Easily…joyously…and freely!

Do you pass the test of faithfulness? Are you considered trusted, reliable, consistent, and steadfast? What about over a long period of time, through thick and thin, in good times and in bad? Do you pass the test or do you fail?

ADORATION/EXPLANATION

We have the privilege to faithfully represent God in our daily grind. Each new morning is a chance to remain faithful in our actions, words, attitudes, and love toward God. The marvelous fact is that even if we fail today, we can re-take the test tomorrow! Unlike a college exam, God always offers a re-test. He wants us to pass! So don't let a failing grade today get you bogged down in depression. God's mercies are new every morning, and tomorrow is another chance at the re-take.

❧❧❧

For we do not have a high priest who is unable to sympathize with our weaknesses, but we have one who has been tempted in every way, just as we are—yet was without sin. Let us then approach the throne of grace with confidence, so that we may receive mercy and find grace to help us in our time of need. Hebrews 4:15-16 (NIV)

What you heard from me, keep as the pattern of sound teaching, with faith and love in Christ Jesus. Guard the good deposit that was entrusted to you—guard it with the help of the Holy Spirit who lives in us. 2 Timothy 1:13-14 (NIV)

Remind the people to be subject to rulers and authorities, to be obedient, to be ready to do whatever is good, to slander no one, to be peaceable and considerate, and to show true humility toward all men. Titus 3:1-2 (NIV)

WORSHIP/OBEDIENCE

Faithful people are willing to stay under God's guidance with a correct attitude. They are willing to stay faithful right where they are at, even if it is NOT fun, and in many cases it isn't. Faithful followers of Christ do not worry about what everyone else is doing. They choose to act faithfully over and over and over again!

Here is the question once more…
do you pass the test of faithfulness?

❧❧❧

I love the word "flee." It is much more descriptive then run, hustle, skip, scoot, or even scurry. It reminds me of leaving or getting out of someplace very quickly, so quickly that you barely even have time to look back. Flee!

ADORATION/EXPLANATION
When God warns us in His Word to flee something, we should not take that advice lightly. We need to heed the message and move swiftly away from whatever God is speaking of, because He is God, and He knows better.

Flee from sexual immorality. All other sins a man commits are outside his body, but he who sins sexually sins against his own body. 1 Corinthians 6:18 (NIV)

Therefore, my dear friends, flee from idolatry. 1 Corinthians 10:14 (NIV)

Flee the evil desires of youth, and pursue righteousness, faith, love and peace, along with those who call on the Lord out of a pure heart. 2 Timothy 2:22 (NIV)

Submit yourselves, then, to God. Resist the devil, and he will flee from you. James 4:7 (NIV)

Where can I go from your Spirit? Where can I flee from your presence? Psalm 139:7 (NIV)

WORSHIP/OBEDIENCE
When God says, "flee" we need to flee! Don't walk, don't dawdle, and don't drag your feet. Turn and run, and do not stop to take a second glance back! God provides all the strength that we need for today's battles. But here's the best news yet: we can never flee His presence. He is always there to guide and strengthen us, if we just call on His name! Awesome!

April 6

Some days I just wake up tired! I seemed to have a wonderful night of sleep, but I still struggled to get myself going. I'm yawning, dragging, and moving slowly. Why? I'm not exactly sure, but I have been thinking and dwelling on many things lately. Sometimes mental stress, anxiety, or just every day issues of life can drain you of your energy. I need more than coffee to get me inspired today. I need help!

ADORATION/EXPLANATION

Today I will commit to read, re-read, then meditate and dwell on God's Word. "Shouldn't I commit to doing this every day?" you are probably asking. The answer is a resounding "Yes!" But on days when we struggle just a little bit more than usual, we can commit to focus all the more intently on truth. We should refuse to focus on how we may feel physically and mentally but on the truth in Scripture.

But the Lord is faithful, and he will strengthen and protect you from the evil one. 2 Thessalonians 3:3 (NIV)

The Lord is my light and my salvation—whom shall I fear? The Lord is the stronghold of my life—of whom shall I be afraid? Psalm 27:1 (NIV)

I lift my eyes to the hills—where does my help come from? My help comes from the Lord, the maker of heaven and earth. Psalm 121:1-2 (NIV)

Finally, be strong in the Lord and in the strength of His might. Ephesians 6:10 (NASB)

In the same way, the Spirit helps us in our weakness. We do not know what we ought to pray for, but the Spirit himself intercedes for us with groans that words cannot express. Romans 8:26 (NIV)

WORSHIP/OBEDIENCE

Can't get moving? Don't know what's wrong? Tired? Worn out? Stressed?

Call out to God in prayer and meditate all day long on verses of help! And don't worry about the words that you use. Just talk to God and let Him know all about your battles. He knows that you are tired. He already cares!

April 7

In order to correctly celebrate a risen savior on Easter morning, we must first remember His death on the cross. It is a somber occasion but should NOT be a sad one. Why? Isn't it horrible the kind of death that Jesus was put through? Yes, it surely was, but the wonderful fact is that He willingly gave his life up for us so that we could be washed free from sin! Solemn, yes! Sad? Never!

ADORATION/EXPLANATION

"Grace, grace… God's grace! Grace and sacrifice and mercy and justification and cleansing that are greater than all of our sin." A free gift from God! Wow…are we blessed or what?

"You are a king, then!" said Pilate. Jesus answered, "You are right in saying I am a king. In fact, for this reason I was born, and for this I came into the world, to testify to the truth. Everyone on the side of truth listens to me." "What is the truth?" Pilate asked. With this he went out again to the Jews and said, "I find no basis for a charge against him. But it is your custom for me to release to you one prisoner at the time of Passover. Do you want me to release 'the king of the Jews'?" They shouted back, "No, not him! Give us Barabbas!" John 18:37-40a (NIV)

Then Pilate took Jesus and had him flogged. The soldiers twisted together a crown of thorns and put it on his head. They clothed him in a purple robe and went up to him again and again, saying, "Hail, king of the Jews!" And they struck him in the face.

But they shouted, "Take him away! Take him away! Crucify him! "Shall I crucify your king?" Pilate asked. "We have no king but Caesar," the chief priests answered. Finally Pilate handed him over to them to be crucified. John 19:1-3, 15-16 (NIV)

WORSHIP/OBEDIENCE

Dear God, never let me forget the cross.
Never let me forget the awesome sacrifice of your own perfect,
sinless Son for me, an imperfect sinner.
"Grace, grace…God's grace!" Thank you.

The most important fact about Jesus' death on the cross and His subsequent burial was the fact that He didn't stay dead and He didn't remain in the tomb. He was resurrected from the grave just as He said would happen. Up from the tomb He arose, rolling the stone away and walking right past the sleeping guards.

ADORATION/EXPLANATION
We serve a risen Savior who lives and is seated at the right hand of God. "He lives, He lives! Christ Jesus lives today!"

Early on the first day of the week, while it was still dark, Mary Magdalene went to the tomb and saw that the stone had been removed from the entrance. So she came running to Simon Peter and the other disciple, the one Jesus loved, and said, "They have taken the Lord out of the tomb, and we don't know where they have put him!" So Peter and the other disciple started for the tomb. Then Simon Peter, who was behind him, arrived and went into the tomb. He saw the strips of linen lying there, as well as the burial cloth that had been around Jesus' head. The cloth was folded up by itself, separate from the linen. John 20:1-3, 6-7 (NIV)

Then the disciples went back to their homes, but Mary stood outside the tomb crying. As she wept, she bent over to look into the tomb and saw two angels in white, seated where Jesus' body had been, one at the head and the other at the foot. They asked her, "Woman, why are you crying?" "They have taken my Lord away," she said, "and I don't know where they have put him." At this, she turned around and saw Jesus standing there, but she did not realize that it was Jesus.

Jesus said to her, "Mary." She turned toward him and cried out in Aramaic, "Rabboni!" (which means Teacher.) Mary Magdalene went to the disciples with the news: "I have seen the Lord!" John 20:10-14, 16, 18a (NIV)

WORSHIP/OBEDIENCE
Wouldn't you have loved to be Mary on that early Easter morning, the first to see the risen Savior? Wouldn't it have been wonderful to be the one to cry out, "He lives! He lives! I have seen the Lord!" Today, we have a daily opportunity to demonstrate this to those in our lives. Do you see the Lord? Act on it!

THIS…is living the obvious!

April 9

Whether you are a teenager, young single woman, or a married lady, you can profit from reading the Old Testament book of Proverbs, chapter 31. Some readers have questioned if the passage known as "The Wife of Noble Character" is a realistic model for today's women. Well, why not? This is not a list of all-encompassing expectations, but it should inspire godly women to find fullness and contentment in their home, family, community, and/or career. Go for it!

ADORATION/EXPLANATION
God said it, I believe it! God allowed it in the Bible, so I'll read it!

A wife of noble character who can find? She is worth far more than rubies. Her husband has full confidence in her and lacks nothing of value. She brings him good, not harm, all the days of her life. She selects wool and flax and works with eager hands. She is like the merchant ships, bringing her food from afar. She gets up while it is still dark; she provides food for her family and portions for her servant girls. She considers a field and buys it; out of the earnings she plants a vineyard. She sets about her work vigorously; her arms are strong for her tasks. She sees that her trading is profitable, and her lamp does not go out at night. In her hand she holds the distaff and grasps the spindle with her fingers. She opens her arms to the poor and extends her hands to the needy. When it snows, she has no fear for her household; for all of them are clothed in scarlet. She makes coverings for her bed; she is clothed in fine linen and purple. Her husband is respected at the city gate, where he takes his seat among the elders of the land. She makes linen garments and sells them, and supplies the merchants with sashes. She is clothed with strength and dignity; she can laugh at the days to come. She speaks with wisdom, and faithful instruction is on her tongue. She watches over the affairs of her household and does not eat the bread of idleness. Her children arise and call her blessed; her husband also, and he praises her; "Many women do noble things, but you surpass them all."

Charm is deceptive, and beauty is fleeting; but a woman who fears the Lord is to be praised. Give her the reward she has earned, and let her works bring her praise at the city gate. Proverbs 31:10-31

WORSHIP/OBEDIENCE
Dear God, help me to be a woman of noble character!

April 10

Have you ever made a vow to someone? A vow (as in a marriage vow) is a promise or commitment. When I got married, I vowed to stay yoked together with my husband whether we were richer or poorer, in sickness and in health, for better or worse, until death parted us. I personally take these vows very seriously.

ADORATION/EXPLANATION
In the Old Testament, worshippers often vowed to do something if God answered their prayer request. Vows were not required by God but, once made, it was crucial that the vow be fulfilled. Careless or frivolous vows should not be made.

Guard your steps when you go to the house of God. Go near to listen rather than to offer sacrifice of fools, who do not know that they do wrong.

Do not be quick with your mouth, do not be hasty in your heart to utter anything before God. God is in heaven and you are on earth, so let your words be few.

As a dream comes when there are many cares, so the speech of a fool when there are many words.

When you make a vow to God, do not delay in fulfilling it. He has no pleasure in fools; fulfill your vow. It is better not to vow than to make a vow and not fulfill it. Much dreaming and many words are meaningless. Therefore stand in awe of God. Ecclesiastes 5:1-5, 7 (NIV)

It is a trap for a man to dedicate something rashly and only later to consider his vows. Proverbs 20:25 (NIV)

WORSHIP/OBEDIENCE
God never goes back on His promises. What He has promised in the Bible to His faithful children, He will most certainly fulfill. We have an imperishable home and inheritance in heaven when we leave this earth, and we have strength and power for each new day while we are living here. Commit to being thankful today and to worship God with honor, reverence, and awe.

Lord, we stand in awe of you!

Does the character trait of meekness represent weakness to you? It always seemed so to me, until I really grasped what God's concept of the virtue really meant. Meekness and gentleness of your inner spirit is the key. It can be described as a kind of resolve and power that your inner spirit possesses and chooses to remain in control of. This does not come easily or naturally to most folks. It takes self-control, inner discipline and practice.

ADORATION/EXPLANATION

When God speaks to us in His word and tells us that we are blessed if we are meek, and that we will inherit the earth if we are meek, then who wouldn't strive to obtain this characteristic? True meekness of spirit is recognized as strength under control! It is difficult to be meek in heart but if the God that we love and adore recommends that we practice meekness, we must. Practice makes permanent!

But the meek will inherit the land and enjoy great peace. Psalm 37:11 (NIV)

Blessed are the meek, for they will inherit the earth. Blessed are the peacemakers, for they will be called the sons of God. Matthew 5:5, 9 (NIV)

By the meekness and gentleness of Christ, I appeal to you—I Paul, who am "timid" when face to face with you, but "bold" when away! For though we live in the world, we do not wage war as the world does. 2 Corinthians 10:1, 3 (NIV)

WORSHIP/OBEDIENCE

Meekness does not mean that we are stepped on, looked over, or sappy. It is anything BUT weakness, but it is a difficult fruit to bear in our daily lives. Meekness means keeping quiet when we would rather say something. It is curbing our tempers when we would like to slap someone upside the head! It is being right but choosing to give up our rights and letting God handle the situation.

Meekness is an inner quality, an inner virtue that produces beautiful outward fruit!

April 12

Have you every played the opposite game as a child? You say black, I say white! I say go, you say stop! Wet, dry…high, low…loud, quiet…hard, soft! Whatever one person says, the other must think of the opposite. This was entertaining to me as a child, but as an adult, I prefer things to be clear and concise. Yet God has a way of changing conventional thinking in order to make us ponder His words.

ADORATION/EXPLANATION

In the book of Matthew, Jesus teaches reversed values. Why? Isn't this confusing to the readers? Jesus taught that what the world thought of as being blessed by God was not always the correct picture. If your current situation does not seem to be blessed, it is only temporary in God's view of reality. Wealth, influence, and happiness are not the only sign of blessings. When you read this passage, called the Beatitudes, think to yourself as you read: Let THIS be my attitude in my current situation today!

And he began to teach them, saying:

"Blessed are the poor in spirit, for theirs is the kingdom of heaven. Blessed are those who mourn, for they will be comforted. Blessed are the meek, for they will inherit the earth. Blessed are those who hunger and thirst for righteousness, for they will be filled. Blessed are the merciful, for they will be shown mercy. Blessed are the pure in heart, for they will see God. Blessed are the peacemakers, for they will be called sons of God. Blessed are those who are persecuted because of righteousness, for theirs is the kingdom of heaven. Blessed are you when people insult you, persecute you and falsely say all kinds of evil against you because of me. Rejoice and be glad, Matthew 5:2-12a

WORSHIP/OBEDIENCE

In today's busy schedule, how do we obviously live this out in obedience?

Let THIS…be your ATTITUDE!

Yesterday we discussed learning to have the correct attitude and observing blessings in all situations. Yet I have been stunned with the realization that rejoicing and being glad are one thing, while actually doing something and getting up to follow Christ is another. Sometimes we understand God's Word, but we sit paralyzed and do not react.

ADORATION/EXPLANATION

In the Gospel of Matthew, we read how Jesus called the first disciples to follow Him. At first read, it seems as if they were acting on impulse. But the more that we observe and grasp the awesome power of Jesus and His very spirit-filled life, we can conclude that their immediate response to Him is an example for our very own lives. Get up and follow!

As Jesus was walking beside the Sea of Galilee, he saw two brothers, Simon called Peter and his brother Andrew. They were casting a net into the lake, for they were fishermen. "Come, follow me," Jesus said, "and I will make you fishers of men." At once they left their nets and followed him. Going on from there, he saw two other brothers, James son of Zebedee, preparing their nets. Jesus called them, and immediately they left the boat and their father and followed him. Matthew 4:18-22 (NIV)

As Jesus went on from there, he saw a man named Matthew sitting at the tax collector's booth. "Follow me," he told him, and Matthew got up and followed him. Matthew 9:9 (NIV)

WORSHIP/OBEDIENCE

Don't you just love this? No hesitation, no hemming and hawing, no "what ifs!" There was just an immediate reaction to Jesus' words. The disciples didn't ask tons of questions and try to figure out the plan (although they may have been thinking it). They got up and moved. They trusted that Jesus had it covered.

Dear Lord, let me react to your words today!

April 14

A harvest can mean a season or time of gathering in crops, or the action of gathering in the fields or crops. We have all probably heard of harvest time around the fall holiday of Thanksgiving, but as followers of Christ, the harvest that Jesus talks about in the Bible is not limited to one season. After Jesus brought the opportunity of salvation to the world through His death on the cross, the harvest is always ready to begin. The real question is…where are the workers?

ADORATION/EXPLANATION
The season for God to change lives is always here and the time to gather is continually in front of us. God's message of love, salvation, and the free gift of His son are available and free to all who ask. Let God do the planting in your friend's and family's lives through the Holy Spirit's prompting. He will get their attention! Our job is to stand in awe and be ready to gather.

He who gathers crops in summer is a wise son, but he who sleeps during harvest is a disgraceful son. Proverbs 10:5 (NIV)

"Do you not say, 'Four months more and then the harvest'? I tell you, open your eyes and look at the fields! They are ripe for harvest." John 4:35 (NIV)

Then he said to his disciples, "The harvest is plentiful but the workers are few. Ask the Lord of the harvest, therefore, to send out workers into his harvest field." Matthew 9:37 (NIV)

"He who is not with me is against me, and he who does not gather with me scatters." Matthew 12:30 (NIV)

WORSHIP/OBEDIENCE
Let us open our eyes and look at the fields and be able to spot the harvest of people who are ready to seek God.

Lord, help me to live my daily life in such a way as to draw others toward Your free offer of salvation. I am willing to work!

April 15

God calls His disciples and He tells them that the harvest is ready and the workers are needed. This is taught in various places in Scripture, but sometimes we do not feel like following or being the worker. We have enough worries keeping our own lives on track, let alone being concerned for others. There are plenty of other believers who can set the example, aren't there? Why me? God will certainly understand.

ADORATION/EXPLANATION
God loves us no matter what, but if we really grasp the amazing grace and love that He has for us, we will not be able to help ourselves from living for Him. We should choose to sit in His classroom of life, with our hands raised up high, shouting, "Pick me, pick me!"

"You are the light of the world. A city on a hill cannot be hidden. In the same way, let your light shine before men, that they may see your good deeds and praise your Father in heaven. Matthew 5:14, 16 (NIV)

Preach the Word; be prepared in season and out of season; correct, rebuke and encourage—with great patience and careful instruction. 2 Timothy 4:2 (NIV)

He said to them, "Go into all the world and preach the good news to all creation. Mark 16:15 (NIV)

Then I heard the voice of the Lord saying, "Whom shall I send? And who will go for us?" And I said, "Here am I. Send me!" Isaiah 6:8 (NIV)

WORSHIP/OBEDIENCE
We are called to be a light in the world. Where exactly in this world are we to be this light? Obviously it will be a different location for each of us. For some it will be a mission on a foreign continent, and for others it will be in their hometowns, going about daily life and schedules. At work, home, school, play, or in far-away places, a light turned off is of no use. So turn your light on!

April 16

We don't have to be a pastor, priest, nun, evangelist, or even a teacher to be used by God. The beautiful trait of our heavenly Father is that He loves us, sees the best in us, and can use our personal talents and personality exactly where we are. Only one thing is required on our part: a willingness to let our talents and personality be of service to others.

ADORATION/EXPLANATION

In the book of Acts, a woman disciple named Dorcas (or Tabitha) used her talent as a seamstress to help others. Nothing seemed extraordinary, fantastic, or super-spiritual about her, but Dorcas made enough of an impact on people's lives that when she died, the Apostle Peter made a special trip to raise her from the dead.

In Joppa there was a disciple named Tabitha (which, when translated, is Dorcas), who was always doing good and helping the poor. About that time she became sick and died, and her body was washed and placed in an upstairs rom. Lydda was near Joppa; so when the disciples heard that Peter was in Lydda, they sent two men to him and urged him, "Please come at once!"

Peter went with them, and when he arrived he was taken upstairs to the room. All the widows stood around him, crying and showing him the robes and other clothing that Dorcas had made while she was still with them. Peter sent them all out of the room; then he got down on his knees and prayed. Turning toward the dead woman, he said, "Tabitha, get up." She opened her eyes, and seeing Peter she sat up. He took her by the hand and helped her to her feet. Then he called the believers and the widows and presented her to them alive.

This became known all over Joppa, and many people believed in the Lord. Acts 9:36-42 (NIV)

WORSHIP/OBEDIENCE

Did you notice that the first way the Bible describes Dorcas is by calling her a disciple of Christ? She was also probably a very humble woman and that is why so many mourned her death. Dorcas was a Christian not because she sewed robes and did other charitable services. Rather, she sewed and did charitable services BECAUSE she was a Christian.

Father, let me be a disciple like Dorcas today!

Faith and obedience to God will move mountains and remove mountains! But if you desire to have a mountain-moving kind of life, then faith and obedience must go hand in hand. As a child, I used to hear the verse about moving mountains and think to myself, "Wouldn't it be cool to tell a mountain to move and it actually happen?" But that was a childish thought and not necessarily the kind of mountain that God was speaking about for our lives. Oh man…

ADORATION/EXPLANATION

God tells us that if we have faith the size of a mustard seed, we can move mountains. Wow! I used to have a necklace as a young girl with a small glass ball on it. Encased in the drop of glass was a mustard seed. So tiny and insignificant really, but it served to remind me that I only needed that much faith in order to move mountains in my life. We could start with the smallest of seeds, but we need to nourish it with obedience to God if it is ever going to move mountains. Do we have that much faith?

He told them another parable: "The kingdom of heaven is like a mustard seed, which a man took and planted in his filed. Though it is the smallest of all your seeds, yet when it grows, it is the largest of the garden plants and becomes a tree, so that the birds of the air come and perch in its branches." Matthew 13:31-32 (NIV)

He replied, "Because you have so little faith, I tell you the truth, if you have faith as small as a mustard seed, you can say to this mountain, 'Move from here to there' and it will move. Nothing will be impossible for you." Matthew 17:20 (NIV)

WORSHIP/OBEDIENCE

A small amount of faith, coupled with obedience, will grow and grow. Mountains can be removed! Mountains of difficulty and depression, mountains of sin and evil, mountains of anger, frustration and bitterness, mountains of jealousy and pride, mountains of sadness and being afraid—what mountain do you want to remove? Find a small seed of faith and get cracking!

Faith should grow as we live out our lives trusting in God. Trials, temptations, and tribulations only prove that our faith can get stronger as we pray and trust in God's power. Yikes…but isn't that tough? Yup! But we must remember that He is omnipotent! He is all-powerful! We aren't.

ADORATION/EXPLANATION

When we practice praying in faith, we will willingly leave room for God's perfect will to overrule any request that we make. It doesn't mean that we don't ask, implore, or petition God with our heart's desires and hurts. As a matter of fact, we should willingly bring everything before the feet of Jesus and watch for God's plan. Start with that little mustard seed. Bring it all! Throw it down!

"Have faith in God," Jesus answered. "I tell you the truth, if anyone says to this mountain, 'Go, throw yourself into the sea,' and does not doubt in his heart but believes that what he says will happen, it will be done for him. Therefore I tell you, whatever you ask for in prayer, believe that you have received it, and it will be yours. And when you stand praying, if you hold anything against anyone, forgive him, so that your Father in heaven may forgive you your sins." Mark 11:22-25 (NIV)

Now faith is being sure of what we hope for and certain of what we do not see. Hebrews 11:1 (NIV)

So do not throw away your confidence; it will be richly rewarded. You need to persevere so that when you have done the will of God, you will receive what he has promised.

But we are not of those who shrink back and are destroyed, but of those who believe and are saved. Hebrews 10:35-36, 39 (NIV)

WORSHIP/OBEDIENCE

As the writer of the book of Hebrews says, "Do not throw away your confidence"! Persevere, pray, and press on! Follow God's will and realize that your faith WILL be tested and tried, but that is okay! The testing brings about growth and maturity and passing the test is a privilege.

Today let us worship God by NOT shrinking back!

At this particular juncture in time and history, as I am writing this book, I do not happen to personally like or agree with the president of our country. I disagree morally, financially, and politically. I didn't vote for him, but he did win and was elected as the leader of our nation. Doing so, at least to me, means that he deserves my respect.

ADORATION/EXPLANATION
Does God want us to honor the office and pray for our leaders even when we do not agree? The Bible gives us a resounding "Yes!" on that one! I still may not like, agree, or even believe the man deserves my prayers, but God tells us to pray anyway! I will not go on a personal vendetta to destroy him or post constant defamatory comments, stories, etc. Hard to do? Yes! Do I have to like and agree with him? No! But my personal behavior is all in the pursuit of godliness and holiness. Have I forgotten that God is in charge?

I urge, then, first of all, that request, prayers, intercession and thanksgiving be made for everyone—for kings and all those in authority, that we may live peaceful and quiet lives in all godliness and holiness. This is good, and pleases God our Savior, who wants all men to be saved and to come to a knowledge of the truth. 1Timothy 2:1-4 (NIV)

Everyone must submit himself to the governing authorities, for there is no authority except that which God has established. The authorities that exist have been established by God. Consequently, he who rebels against authority is rebelling against what God has instituted, and those who do so will bring judgment on themselves. For rulers hold no terror for those who do right, but for those who do wrong. Do you want to be free from fear of the one in authority? Then do what is right and he will commend you.

This is also why you pay taxes, for the authorities are God's servants, who give their full time to governing. Give everyone what you owe him: If you owe taxes, pay taxes; if revenue, then revenue; if respect, then respect; if honor, then honor. Romans 13:1-4, 6-7 (NIV)

WORSHIP/OBEDIENCE
So I have to pray, pay, and give thanks for our leaders? Yes! In the book of Romans, the Apostle Paul prayed for Nero even though he was not a servant or follower of God. He understood that praying for and obeying the leaders of the time would enable the ultimate outcome of spreading the gospel to happen. Pray, pay, and give thanks!

Who or what is your confidence placed in? Where is your security? Is it your family name, your job, your spouse, your looks, your money, or your talents? All of these things can and will fade and disappoint you over a period of time. Your confidence needs to be placed in Jesus Christ alone. He needs to be our cornerstone and our rock!

ADORATION/EXPLANATION

Many times we forgetfully place our confidence and well being in external sources. We think that if we can just get more money, a better house, marry that person, look a certain way, or get a certain job, then everything will all be secure. These things are all mirages! Like a thirsty man in a desert, we plod along thinking and dreaming that we see water. We become fooled!

God is NOT a mirage. He is the real deal.

For it is we who are the circumcision, we who worship by the Spirit of God, who glory in Christ Jesus, and who put no confidence in the flesh—

But whatever was to my profit I now consider loss for the sake of Christ. What is more, I consider everything a loss compared to the surpassing greatness of knowing Christ Jesus my Lord, for whose sake I have lost all things. I consider them rubbish, that I may gain Christ and be found in him, not having a righteousness of my own that comes from the law, but that which is through faith in Christ—the righteousness that comes from God and is by faith. Philippians 3:3, 7-9 (NIV)

However, as it is written: "No eye has seen, no ear has heard, no mind has conceived what God has prepared for those who love him…" 1 Corinthians 2:9 (NIV)

WORSHIP/OBEDIENCE

No mirages…no false pictures, promises, or dreams to place our hope and confidence in. Only the wonderful love of our Savior, Jesus Christ! His righteousness and confidence can cover every area of our lives. He is the provider of wealth, friends, family, time, health, and talents. We should be thankful for all that we have and are, but we should put no confidence in any of these areas—only in Christ alone. He is the real deal!

Cornerstone or capstone…what is it? A cornerstone or capstone is a firm foundation or stronghold upon which all others could rest, a corner of strength upon which our faith can be built. In other words, a solid rock!

ADORATION/EXPLANATION

The capstone may have been the most important part of the early ancient construction. A keystone was used to hold up the many arches in the building and a cornerstone was placed at the base of the bisecting walls. They were definitely very important to the strength and integrity of the structure! Jesus is described as the cornerstone of our lives and the foundation for our faith!

I will give you thanks, for you answered me; you have become my salvation. The stone the builders rejected has become the capstone; Psalm 118:21-22 (NIV)

As you come to him, the living Stone—rejected by men but chosen by God and precious to him—you also, like living stones, are being built into a spiritual house to be a holy priesthood, offering spiritual sacrifices acceptable to God through Jesus Christ. For in Scripture it says: "See, I lay a stone in Zion, a chosen and precious cornerstone, and the one who trusts in him will never be put to shame." 1 Peter 2:4-6 (NIV)

Consequently, you are no longer foreigners and aliens, but fellow citizens with God's people and members of God's household, built on the foundation of the apostles and prophets, with Christ Jesus himself as the chief cornerstone. Ephesians 2:19-20 (NIV)

WORSHIP/OBEDIENCE

You and I are spiritual construction projects. God has taken up residence in our lives (if we have accepted His free gift of salvation) and the ongoing work and construction process has begun. The best news for our architectural blueprints is that our foundation is already in place, strong, perfect, and complete. We need to make sure that we are placing the strength of our dwellings on that solid rock.

Our buildings cannot help but be awesome with the perfect cornerstone!

April 22

Sometimes I feel old, and some days I am definitely more tired and weary than others. I glance in the mirror only to see another gray hair, another wrinkle, another pound of weight. Time is marching on and taking all of us with it! (At least it's taking me…)

ADORATION/EXPLANATION

God already has our days and years numbered. The only thing that we can do is use our time here on earth to the best of our ability. We can choose to look and dress our best, exercise, and eat right, but we can NOT slow down time. We are aging as we speak. My parents are moving quickly towards eighty and my children towards thirty years of age. This should not cause us to be afraid! What this should do is inspire us to cherish every moment given to us and stand in awe of our creator!

Gray hair is a crown of splendor; it is attained by a righteous life. Proverbs 16:31 (NIV)

The righteous will flourish like a palm tree, they will grow like a cedar of Lebanon…

They will still bear fruit in old age, they will stay fresh and green. Psalm 92:12, 14 (NIV)

What man can live and not see death, or save himself from the power of the grave? Psalm 89:48 (NIV)

Teach us to number our days aright, that we may gain a heart of wisdom. Psalm 90:12 (NIV)

Who of you by worrying can add a single hour to his life? Matthew 6:27 (NIV)

WORSHIP/OBEDIENCE

Whenever you notice a gray hair, wrinkles, or any other signs of aging, commit to giving thanks to God for your time here on earth. When you feel like lamenting about growing older, instead declare your worship for God by being thankful for the years that you have already enjoyed.

Look expectantly to the future for ways to serve Him.

How can we expect God to gently speak to our souls when we are making so much noise with our own rapid thoughts, ideas, and reflections? Our minds seem to run on high octane all of the time. We have a long to-do list of places to go, people to see, and many problems to be solved. Another sticky note is on the counter!

ADORATION/EXPLANATION

God keeps the planets spinning, the sun shining, the seasons changing, and each new day dawning. His to-do list is a lot more important than mine and He never drops the ball! So if I truly realized how omnipotent and powerful God is, then I would not fret at His timing in guiding my own life.

"Be still before the Lord, all mankind, because he has roused himself from his holy dwelling." Zechariah 2:13 (NIV)

"The Lord your God is with you, he is mighty to save. He will take great delight in you, he will quiet you with his love, he will rejoice over you with singing." Zephaniah 3:17 (NIV)

This is what the Sovereign Lord, the Holy One of Israel, says:

"In repentance and rest is your salvation, in quietness and trust is your strength, but you would have none of it." Isaiah 30:15 (NIV)

The work of righteousness will be peace, and the service of righteousness, quietness and confidence forever. Isaiah 32:17 (NASB)

WORSHIP/OBEDIENCE

Simply holding still is not a sign of weakness. Actually, as a follower of Christ, it is just the opposite. Standing still means trusting God even when we do not seem to be hearing His voice or understanding His plan. Stop thinking so hard! Stop trying to figure it all out! Sometimes the most obvious act of obedience to God is to simply hold still.

God is on His own schedule, not yours!

If you thumb through any magazine on the supermarket rack, you will find more beauty tips, aids, creams and secrets than ever before. We are inundated with styles, diets, and make-up products. Look better, feel better, and live better is the typical headline, but eventually we all come to the conclusion that reality is not going to be as smooth and perfect as the pictures in a magazine.

ADORATION/EXPLANATION

There is absolutely nothing wrong or sinful with wanting to look your best, or at least in wanting to make your outside package prettier. New clothes, a fresh haircut, or even just a shower all improve the body that God created for you to enjoy. Yet the greatest beauty secret has nothing to do with fashion or make-up. The greatest beauty secret is learning to live daily as a woman who delights in God.

Charm is deceptive, and beauty is fleeting; but a woman who fears the Lord is to be praised. Proverbs 31:30 (NIV)

The king again asked, "Queen Esther, what is your petition? It will be given you. What is your request? Even up to half the kingdom, it will be granted." Then Queen Esther answered, "If I have found favor with you, O king, and if it pleases your majesty, grant me my life—this is my petition. And spare my people—this is my request." Esther 7:2b-3 (NIV)

Your beauty should not come from outward adornment, such as braided hair and the wearing of gold jewelry and fine clothes. Instead, it should be that of your inner self, the unfading beauty of a gentle and quiet spirit, which is of great worth in God's sight. 1 Peter 3:3-4 (NIV)

WORSHIP/OBEDIENCE

A heart that seeks after God is the most beautiful thing in the world! Queen Esther had a beautiful body AND heart. She used her inner and outer beauty to help her people and save their lives! Go ahead, put on a new outfit, get a stylish haircut, or try a new brand of make-up, but never forget that true style and beauty are a reflection of your relationship with God!

Strive for substance—a discerning mind, controlled lips, and a loving demeanor.

Faithfulness is very important to our earthly well-being because humans were made to operate on the very principle of faith. We live on a planet without a visible means of support, that spins on its own in a vast space. We can't perpetuate the spinning, and we can't even try to fix it if it begins to go wrong. To get up each morning requires large amounts of faith. We breathe air that we cannot see, eat food that we have not examined under a microscope, drive through green traffic signals that we trust will prevent an accident, and ride on planes regularly because we have faith that they will stay up in the air until we arrive at our destination.

ADORATION/EXPLANATION

When we consider the root of faithfulness, our starting point must be God Himself. He created us to operate and thrive in an environment of faith and dependence on Him.

So, if you think you are standing firm, be careful that you don't fall! No temptation has seized you except what is common to man. And God is faithful; he will not let you be tempted beyond what you can bear. But when you are tempted, he will also provide a way out so that you can stand up under it. 1 Corinthians 10:12-13 (NIV)

Love the Lord, all his saints! The Lord preserves the faithful, Psalm 31:23a (NIV)

First, I thank my God through Jesus Christ for all of you, because your faith is being reported all over the world. I long to see you so that I may impart to you some spiritual gift to make you strong—that is, that you and I may be mutually encouraged by each other's faith. Romans 1:8, 11-12 (NIV)

WORSHIP/OBEDIENCE

God's faithfulness to us is trustworthy because He always means what He says and says what He means. The ultimate hope of our salvation experience is laid up in heaven for us, guaranteed by our faithful God. Today, may those who watch and come behind us find us faithful, not by an absence of mistakes but through our faithfulness to stand firm and depend on God! We can do this by "living the obvious" each day and then giving Him ALL the glory.

Have you ever seen a yield sign? I'm sure that you have. The word "yield" means "to give up possession of, demand of, to surrender or relinquish a right, or to give place and precedence to someone else." As a road sign, it dictates that I need to slow down, pause, and give way to someone that is already driving on the road. If I fail to yield to on-coming traffic, I could cause dire problems for myself and others.

ADORATION/EXPLANATION

As we yield to God in our relationships with others, our words will reflect it. Conversation patterns such as gossip, slander, criticisms, false witness, and words that stir up strife in others will give way to words and conversations that protect reputations, show genuine concern for others, encourage peace and love, and offer opportunities to compliment and promote pure, kind thoughts.

———

Be wise in the way you act toward outsiders; make the most of every opportunity. Let your conversation be always full of grace, seasoned with salt, so that you may know how to answer everyone. Colossians 4:5-6 (NIV)

Do nothing out of selfish ambition or vain conceit, but in humility consider others better than yourselves. Each of you should look not only to your own interest, but also to the interests of others. Philippians 2:3-4 (NIV)

Avoid godless chatter, because those who indulge in it will become more and more ungodly. Don't have anything to do with foolish and stupid arguments, because you know they produce quarrels. 2 Timothy 2:16, 23 (NIV)

WORSHIP/OBEDIENCE

Just like failing to yield to a road sign, if we fail to yield to others in our conversations and relationships, we could cause dire problems for ourselves and others.

Dear God, give me the strength today to remember to follow the YIELD signs.

———

We hear a lot about the self-made man or woman and how important it is to be self-sufficient, self-determined, and able to pull yourself up by your own bootstraps. But God also knows that pure self-sufficiency can breed a sinful pride in us.

ADORATION/EXPLANATION

Success sometimes goes straight to a person's head. We begin to think that we are "all that!" When we forget that what we are and have is because of God, we become spoiled with pride. That is about the time that the Bible needs to remind us that we adore a God who is the ultimate source of everything. God often reminded the Israelites of this in the Old Testament.

Be careful to follow every command I am giving you today, so that you may live and increase and may enter and possess the land that the Lord promised on oath to your forefathers. Remember how the Lord your God led you all the way in the desert these forty years, to humble you and to test you in order to know what was in your heart, whether or not you would keep his commands.

He gave you manna to eat in the desert, something your fathers had never known, to humble and to test you so that in the end it might go well with you. You may say to yourself, "My power and the strength of my hands have produced this wealth for me." But remember the Lord your God, for it is he who gives you the ability to produce wealth, and so confirms his covenant, which he swore to your forefathers, as it is today. Deuteronomy 8:1-2, 16-18 (NIV)

WORSHIP/OBEDIENCE

Sometimes God permits suffering instead of success and true humility demands that we submit to God's provision in bad times as well as good. Our obvious act of obedience and worship should be to practice going from a self-sufficient mindset that breeds pride to a God-sufficient attitude that breeds a grateful, worshipping heart.

April 28

Music appeared early in the history of mankind and has been an important part of every known culture of every age. I love music and God has provided us with talents to create so many varieties and genres for our pleasure. Music can pump you up for a workout or it can soothe your soul after a hard day. Music appeared early in the history of mankind and has been an important part of every known culture of every age.

ADORATION/EXPLANATION
The major scriptural function of music is for the praise and worship of God. The Bible is full of many examples of music being use to glorify and magnify the might of God, especially in the Old Testament. We need to leave our worries of perfect tone or pitch behind and just sing!

Then Moses and the Israelites sang this song to the Lord:

"I will sing to the Lord, for he is highly exalted. The horse and its rider he has hurled into the sea. The Lord is my strength and my song; he has become my salvation. Exodus 15:1-2 (NIV)

Sing to him, sing praises to him: tell of all his wonderful acts.

Sing to the Lord, all the earth; proclaim his salvation day after day.

Then the trees of the forest will sing, they will sing for joy before the Lord, for he comes to judge the earth. 1 Chronicles 16:9, 23, 33 (NIV)

Speak to one another with psalms, hymns and spiritual songs. Sing and make music in your heart to the Lord, Ephesians 5:19 (NIV)

WORSHIP/OBEDIENCE
God made man with a responsiveness to music and has enabled us to write various words and notes to new songs each day. Even creation is described as singing out in praise to God! So once again, throw out your worries of a perfect sound or pitch and just sing. Sing a song and sing it long!

April 29

Are you aware that music is part of heaven? In many places in the Bible, music and musical instruments are mentioned when speaking of angels and heaven. Just the thought of singing and instruments sounding makes me feel like a preschooler in their first band. Remember those tambourines, sticks, cymbals, bells, and a metal triangle, all joyfully unrestrained and clanging away? Doesn't it make you smile?

ADORATION/EXPLANATION
When the Lord returns to this earth, the signal is represented as a musical one. Are you listening for the music?

Listen, I tell you a mystery: We will not all sleep, but we will all be changed—in a flash, in the twinkling of an eye, at the last trumpet. For the trumpet will sound, the dead will be raised imperishable, and we will be changed. 1 Corinthians 15:51-52 (NIV)

"The Lord your God is with you, he is mighty to save. He will take great delight in you, he will quiet you with his love, he will rejoice over you with singing." Zephaniah 3:17 (NIV)

He came and took the scroll from the right hand of him who sat on the throne. And they sang a new song: "You are worthy to take the scroll and to open its seals, because you were slain, and with your blood you purchased men for God, from every tribe and language and people and nation.

Then I looked and heard the voice of many angels, numbering thousands upon thousands, and ten thousand times ten thousand. In a loud voice they sang:

"Worthy is the Lamb, who was slain, to receive power and wealth and wisdom and strength and honor and glory and praise!" Revelation 5:7, 9, 11a-12 (NIV)

Is anyone happy? Let him sing songs of praise. James 5:13b (NIV)

WORSHIP/OBEDIENCE
Can you imagine the sound of tens of thousands of angels singing? Today, let's choose to not only listen to the music but to sing with the angels and give thanksgiving for every blessing that we have. Worthy is the Lamb!

God places a very high value on our physical bodies. He created Adam in the beginning and He is responsible for the creation of our body also. God also considered the various parts of the human body of sufficient importance that He often refers to them specifically in the Bible.

ADORATION/EXPLANATION

God uses the connecting relationships of the parts of the human body as an example of the oneness of the body of believers in Christ. The most exciting thing about this information is the necessity of all the parts in both bodies! God created you and me to be necessary!

For you created my inmost being; you knit me together in my mother's womb. I praise you because I am fearfully and wonderfully made; your works are wonderful, I know that full well. My frame was not hidden from you when I was made in the secret place. When I was woven together in the depths of the earth, your eyes saw my unformed body. All the days ordained for me were written in your book before one of them came to be. Psalm 139:13-16 (NIV)

Just as each of us has one body with many members, and these members do not all have the same function, so in Christ we who are many form one body, and each member belongs to all the others. Romans 12:4-5 (NIV)

Instead, speaking the truth in love, we will in all things grow up into him who is the Head, that is, Christ. From him the whole body, joined and held together by every supporting ligament, grows and builds itself up in love, as each part does its work. Ephesians 4:15-16 (NIV)

WORSHIP/OBEDIENCE

Jesus Christ is the head of the body of believers (the church). In the church we all have jobs and should function together under the leadership of Christ. Our act of obedience and worship should also let Christ be the head and guide our physical bodies as well. He created us and knows us intimately.

How fearfully and wonderfully we are made!

The fact that our human body is so wonderfully made should also remind us that God cares about its needs. Food, clothing, shelter, rest, exercise, and love are needs that our God wants to provide for us. We were created in His image and He already knows our every requirement. Why should we worry? Oh…but we do!

ADORATION/EXPLANATION
God prepared a human body for the vehicle of His Son to come to earth and live among us. How unique and fantastic our forms must be to Him! Each and every part was intimately created to function together. I am still in awe of the individuality of each new child's birth!

The body is a unit, though it is made up of many parts; and though all its parts are many, they form one body. So it is with Christ.

If the foot should say, "Because I am not a hand, I do not belong to the body," it would not for that reason cease to be part of the body. And if the ear should say, "Because I am not an eye, I do not belong to the body," it would not for that reason cease to be part of the body.

But in fact God has arranged the parts in the body, every one of them, just as he wanted them to be. If they were all one part, where would the body be? As it is, there are many parts, but one body. The eye cannot say to the hand, "I don't need you!" And the head cannot say to the feet, "I don't need you!"

But God has combined the members of the body and has given greater honor to the parts that lacked it, so that there should be no division in the body, but that its parts should have equal concern for each other. If one part suffers, every part suffers with it; if one part is honored, every part rejoices with it. 1 Corinthians 12:12, 15-16, 18-21, 24b-27 (NIV)

So God created man in his own image, in the image of God he created him; Genesis 1:27 (NIV)

WORSHIP/OBEDIENCE
Dear God, please help me not to take my body for granted. It was composed especially for me, by YOU, and I need to honor that fact. I promise to take care of this beautiful gift and all its parts to the best of my ability. I am thankful for every part. I will place my trust in You to remember all my other needs today. Thank you!

May 2

Almost every one of us has something that we prize very highly. It may be jewelry, clothes, dishes, furniture, a letter, a poem, a painting, a house, or even a certain person! Whatever it is, we probably hold it in high value and would be upset if it were gone.

ADORATION/EXPLANATION

Whatever our treasures may be, God is clear in His word that we should not hold on to them too tightly. The real valuables in our treasure chest of life should be minerals and gemstones such as the gold of keeping the commands of the Lord; the silver of a continual strong love for God; the diamonds of keeping our lips from lies, gossip, and slander; and the rubies of keeping our feet from running to evil.

Praise the Lord. Blessed is the man who fears the Lord, who finds great delight in his commands. Psalm 112:1 (NIV)

Jesus replied: "'Love the Lord your God with all your heart and with all your soul and with all your mind.' This is the first and greatest commandment." Matthew 22:37-38 (NIV)

Do not lie to each other, since you have taken off your old self with its practices and have put on the new self, which is being renewed in knowledge in the image of its Creator. Colossians 3:9-10 (NIV)

Do not set foot on the path of the wicked or walk in the way of evil men. Avoid it, do not travel on it; turn from it and go on your way. Psalm 4:14-15 (NIV)

WORSHIP/OBEDIENCE

Is God telling us to not consider anything that we have valuable or worthy? Do you mean my grandma's dishes, my son's painting, or a beautifully penned letter from my husband cannot be held in high esteem to me? No, God is not saying that. Rather He is asking us to keep our earthly treasures in perspective. Enjoy precious things, but do not hold them so tightly that you forget about what God has deemed as treasure.

Hold Him in the place of MOST importance.

As I peer out of my window, I can see my lawn turning a beautiful shade of green. Although I do not love all the April showers, I do love how it encourages the grass to spring forth. What was brown and sparse all winter long is now filling in, growing up, and soon will need to be mowed. What a change from the cold season that just passed!

ADORATION/EXPLANATION

God wants us to enjoy this good, green earth, but no doubt about it, our beautiful green lawns will eventually whither away. We can enjoy it while we can by watering it, laying in it, playing on it, and loving its scent when freshly cut. But our awe for God needs to be placed on the real things of substance that NEVER wither or fade.

As for man, his days are like grass, he flourishes like a flower of the field; Psalm 103:15 (NIV)

For "All men are like grass, and all their glory is like the flowers of the field; the grass withers and the flowers fall, but the word of the Lord stands forever." 1 Peter 1:24-25 (NIV)

The Lord is my shepherd, I shall not be in want. He makes me lie down in green pastures, he leads me beside quiet waters, Psalm 23:1-2 (NIV)

So neither he who plants nor he who waters is anything, but only God, who makes things grow. For we are God's fellow workers; you are God's field, God's building. 1 Corinthians 3:7, 9 (NIV)

WORSHIP/OBEDIENCE

Go green! Well, maybe not the environmentalist mindset (unless that's your thing, of course!), but by loving your grass, your park, your flowers, your fields, your gardens, or whatever bit of nature that God has placed near you. Enjoy and give thanks, and choose to remind yourself that you are God's field. Take care of yourself…you are worth it!

Are you fading? Withering? If so, start watering and go green!

Have you ever been convicted? If you ask most people this question, they believe that you are asking them if they have ever been found guilty of a crime. One of the definitions of being convicted is to find or prove someone guilty of an error or crime, but another meaning for conviction is a strong persuasion, feeling, compulsion, or belief in something. Have you ever been convicted?

ADORATION/EXPLANATION
I have been convicted! As a matter of fact, I have had many, many convictions!

My convictions all come from God and His presence in my life. The beauty of this fact is that my life is so much more fulfilling and free because of them. My faith in God and His word direct me to seek forgiveness when I am guilty of a transgression and to live my life following His commands and directives. My faith also convicts me to look expectantly for His blessings and promises. Without any convictions (urgings) from the Holy Spirit, what would ever motivate us to live as faithful followers?

<hr>

But if we hope for what we do not yet have, we wait for it patiently. In the same way, the Spirit helps us in our weakness. We do not know what we ought to pray for, but the Spirit himself intercedes for us with groans that words cannot express. And he who searches our hearts knows the mind of the Spirit, because the Spirit intercedes for the saints in accordance with God's will. Romans 8:25-27 (NIV)

But I tell you the truth: It is for your good that I am going away. Unless I go away, the Counselor will not come to you; but if I go, I will send him to you. When he comes, he will convict the world of guilt in regards to sin and righteousness and judgment: in regard to sin, because men do not believe in me; in regard to righteousness, because I am going to the Father, where you can see me no longer…

But when he, the Spirit of truth, comes, he will guide you into all truth. He will not speak on his own; he will speak only what he hears, and he will tell you what is yet to come. John 16:7-10, 13 (NIV)

WORSHIP/OBEDIENCE
Our trust in Jesus Christ has given us the Holy Spirit as our inner guide. We need never make guesses about what to be convicted or not convicted about! Wow!

<hr>

May 5

Do you know what *kintsugi* or *kintsukuroi* is? No, it's not something edible or a martial arts term or even the name of a weapon. Kintsukuroi is the Japanese art of fixing broken pottery with gold or silver resin. When kintsukoroi is performed, the cracks in the vessel become part of the art and history of the piece, a part of its story rather than something to hide! The cracks and breaks, scars and chips now filled with a gleaming substance; all contribute to making the pottery more beautiful than before it was broken!

ADORATION/EXPLANATION
God is in the process of performing this exact same technique with our lives. If we allow Him he takes our foibles and failures, struggles and strife, hurts, humiliations, disasters, and devastations and fills them with His love, care, and hope. Then we become vessels repaired by the Master to be better than we were before the breaks occurred. Better after the repairs? Yes!

You turn things upside down, as if the potter were thought to be like the clay! Shall what is formed say to him who formed it, "He did not make me"? Can the pot say of the potter, "He knows nothing"? Isaiah 29:16 (NIV)

Yet, O Lord, you are our Father. We are the clay, you are our potter; we are all the work of your hand. Isaiah 64:8 (NIV)

For God, who said, "Let light shine out of darkness," made his light shine in our hearts to give us the light of the knowledge of the glory of God in the face of Christ. But we have this treasure in jars of clay to show that this all-surpassing power is from God and not from us. 2 Corinthians 4:6-7 (NIV)

WORSHIP/OBEDIENCE
Just as in the Japanese art of kintsukoroi, we can become more beautiful after having been broken. We just need to stop fretting about our cracks and breaks and allow God to fill them with His gold and silver words of hope…actually a very priceless resin. We must let the potter do his best work in our lives because he will not work without our permission.

Being a "cracked pot" can help us show God's light!

May 6

In the Apostle Peter's day, when clay pots were fired or baked for strength, very often some would crack and be rendered useless. If the pot made it safely through the firing, it would be stamped with a maker's mark of quality. This mark was the same word used for "genuine" that Peter uses in his first chapter. Are you able to be marked as genuine?

ADORATION/EXPLANATION

Just as in the ancient art of kintsugi, our earthly vessels can still be marked "genuine" even if we have cracks. We are never rendered useless if we give God permission to fix and repair us. We actually become more valuable to God than before. How we handle these struggles is what puts a stamp of God's power on us. We are genuine!

❦

"O house of Israel, can I not do with you as this potter does?" declares the Lord. "Like clay in the hand of the potter, so are you in my hand, O house of Israel. Jeremiah 18:6 (NIV)

Does not the potter have the right to make out of the same lump of clay some pottery for noble purposes and some for common use? Romans 9:21 (NIV)

In this way you greatly rejoice, though now for a little while you may have had to suffer grief in all kinds of trials. These have come so that your faith—of greater worth than gold, which perishes even though refined by fire—may be proved genuine and may result in praise, glory and honor when Jesus Christ is revealed. 1 Peter 1:6-7 (NIV)

WORSHIP/OBEDIENCE

Our earthly bodies are just vessels to carry around our faith in Jesus Christ. They may get cracked, pitted, chipped, and worn down, but that is the sign of a well-used piece of stoneware. Our concern need not lie in our chips or faults but in the amazing work that these chips and faults will enable God to do. There is no need to hide our flaws!

Our only desire should be to live in such a way that when the cracks do show to the outside world, the word "genuine" is stamped right next to them.

❦

The secret to a happy life is to enjoy the passage of time! Life can be a lovely ride if we just learn to relax in the arms of God. Troubles, hardships, disappointments, illness, and death are all inevitable, but many people are looking and waiting with so much bated breath that they never ever really enjoy the life that the Lord created for them!

ADORATION/EXPLANATION

You mean to tell me that we are supposed to love and enjoy our life here on earth? Yes! But what about…? I don't get…? I never really understood…?

How can that work…? Why does God…?

Relax, breathe, trust! It's been said that even Einstein never really understood it all. And, sorry to say, most of us aren't Einstein. A newborn baby's face, the planets spinning in space, flowers peeking up through the soil, or the sensation of the overwhelming love of a good friend! Whew!

There was a man alone; he had neither son nor brother. There was no end to his toil, yet his eyes were not content with his wealth. "For whom am I toiling," he asked, "and why am I depriving myself of enjoyment?" This too is meaningless—a miserable business! Two are better than one, because they have a good return for their work; if one falls down, his friend can help him up. Ecclesiastes 4:8-10a (NIV)

Command those who are rich in this present world not to be arrogant nor to put their hope in wealth, which is so uncertain, but to put their hope in God, who richly provides us with everything for our enjoyment. 1Timothy 6:17 (NIV)

The earth is the Lord's and everything in it, the world, and all who live in it; Psalm 24:1a (NIV)

Mercy, peace and love be yours in abundance. Jude 1:2 (NIV)

WORSHIP/OBEDIENCE

The secret of life is to enjoy the passage of time. Whether you are on the way up the hill, at the top, or sliding down the other side, live a life full of thanksgiving for our God.

Open up your heart and enjoy the ride!

In the world of boxing, when people talk about worthy opponents, they call them "contenders." He is a possible contender. The word "contend" basically implies that there is something worth fighting for or to strive in a contest.

ADORATION/EXPLANATION

To "contend" and be "contentious" are slightly different. A contentious person has a constant or even weary tendency to fight, quarrel, and dispute everything. These kinds of folks can be belligerent and don't stop to think if something is worth fighting for. They just quarrel. God's children should contend for their faith but never be labeled contentious. Hmm…good thought!

Dear friends, although I was very eager to write to you about the salvation we share, I felt I had to write and urge you to contend for the faith that was once for all entrusted to the saints.

These men are grumblers and faultfinders; they follow their own evil desires; they boast about themselves and flatter others for their own advantage. But, dear friends, remember what the apostles of our Lord Jesus Christ foretold. They said to you, "In the last times there will be scoffers who will follow their own ungodly desires." These are the men who divide you, who follow mere natural instincts and do not have the Spirit. But you, dear friends, build yourselves up in your most holy faith and pray in the Holy Spirit. Jude 1:3, 16-20 (NIV)

Whatever happens, conduct yourselves in a manner worthy of the gospel of Christ. Then, whether I come and see you or only hear about you in my absence, I will know that you stand firm in one spirit, contending as one man for the faith of the gospel without being frightened in any way by those who oppose you. Philippians 1:27-28a (NIV)

Timothy, guard what has been entrusted to your care. Turn away from godless chatter and the opposing ideas of what is falsely called knowledge, 1 Timothy 6:20 (NIV)

WORSHIP/OBEDIENCE

We should contend for our faith if it is challenged, but in doing so, not become contentious people.

Dear Lord, teach and lead me today in ways to stand firm, yet also help me conduct myself in a way that represents You and your grace in my life.

Have you ever been so distracted that you could not focus on the day ahead of you? I have! My mind can get so occupied with things and issues and problems that I might not be able to focus on the day. This is not a good place to dwell! I am not usually nice, or at my best when I am distracted.

ADORATION/EXPLANATION
God has to remind me so many times to focus; stay looking up; keep on plodding forward. When we get distracted from His plan or His purpose, we need to read the Bible and meditate on the thoughts and advice that God has given us. In the Old Testament, Joshua felt this way and God sent down some awesome advice: be strong and courageous!

"No one will be able to stand up against you all the days of your life. As I was with Moses, so I will be with you; I will never leave you or forsake you. Be strong and courageous, because you will lead these people to inherit the land I swore to their forefathers to give them. Be strong and very courageous. Be careful to obey all the law my servant Moses gave you; do not turn from it to the right or to the left, that you may be successful wherever you go. Do not let this Book of the Law depart from your mouth; meditate on it day and night, so that you may be careful to do everything written in it. Then you will be prosperous and successful. Have I not commanded you? Be strong and courageous. Do not be terrified; do not be discouraged, for the Lord your God will be with you wherever you go." Joshua 1:5-9 (NIV)

"But you are to hold fast to the Lord your God, as you have until now." Joshua 23:8 (NIV)

WORSHIP/OBEDIENCE
Focus your mind on God today, on His plans, His purposes, and His perfectly timed schedule. Allow Him to help you focus on what you need to accomplish at work, at home, or wherever you go, without getting frustrated and distracted.

Lord, teach me to focus straight ahead and not look to the right or the left. Help me be strong and very courageous! Thank you ahead of time for Your help.

We've all had our rainy days. For instance, right now it's pouring outside and I'm not talking about a sprinkling or drizzling of rain. No, it's actually pouring down torrential buckets of water and thunder is rumbling in the distance. It's a gray, dreary, downcast kind of day to be sure.

ADORATION/EXPLANATION

Then again, why does it have to be downcast? Why consider it dreary?

God gave us days like these for a reason. We can set aside time to read, listen to music, meditate, or even just enjoy the rain from indoors. Try to remember that God is providing nourishment and sustenance for our world that could not be accomplished on a hot, sunny day. What a gift rain can be!

"Wherever I bring clouds over the earth and the rainbow appears in the clouds, I will remember my covenant between me and you and all living creatures of every kind. Never again will the waters become a flood to destroy all life. Whenever the rainbow appears in the clouds, I will see it and remember the everlasting covenant between God and all living creatures of every kind on the earth." Genesis 9:14-16 (NIV)

But I tell you: Love your enemies and pray for those who persecute you, that you may be sons of your Father in heaven. He causes his sun to rise on the evil and the good, and sends rain on the righteous and unrighteous. Matthew 5:44-45 (NIV)

"Bring the whole tithe into the storehouse, that there may be food in my house. Test me in this," says the Lord Almighty, "and see if I will not throw open the floodgates of heaven and pour out so much blessing that you will not have room enough for it." Malachi 3:10 (NIV)

WORSHIP/OBEDIENCE

What if, instead of rain, the downpour I'm looking at was a downpour of blessings? How cool would that be? Maybe, just maybe it is? Suppose I choose to look at it as torrential buckets of blessings? The day doesn't seem so dreary after all!

May 11

When I was a small child, I attended a series of church gatherings held in a big outdoor tent called "revival meetings." Usually a guest speaker or traveling evangelical pastor would teach a week of inspiring lessons on how to get a revival going in the church and in our own lives. The meetings were never dull! They were meant to revive!

ADORATION/EXPLANATION

In order to restore something to consciousness again, renew, or to return something to a state of flourishing, we have to first acknowledge that it has wilted or become inactive. Is our life as a faithful follower inactive? Useless? Are we making a difference? We as believers in Christ need to have a constant revival going on in our lives. We must not wait for unconsciousness to set in!

***

Will you not yourself revive us again, that your people may rejoice in you? Show us your lovingkindness, O Lord, and grant us your salvation. Psalm 85:6-7 (NASB)

Restore us, O Lord God Almighty; make your face to shine upon us, that we may be saved. Psalm 80:19 (NIV)

To him who is able to keep you from falling and to present you before his glorious presence without fault and with great joy—to the only God our Savior be glory, majesty, power and authority, through Jesus Christ our Lord, before all ages, now and forevermore! Amen. Jude 1:24-25 (NIV)

WORSHIP/OBEDIENCE

Let's choose to make a conscious effort to allow God's Spirit to revitalize our daily lives. Don't wait for someone else to spur you on towards personal revival. Renew your mind, recall God's words, and live like you have a Savior who will present you faultless and without blemish before God! Revive!

Hallelujah, God, You are the glory!

***

If you really desire a revival or a revitalization of your daily life, then you will quickly learn that you need to stop trying to compete or impress everyone else. Recognize who you are in Christ and where you are in your walk of faith. No competition necessary!

ADORATION/EXPLANATION
The truth of God's Word is not relative to the age we live in, how we feel, or what is going on today. Truth is truth! Everything that we are and may become is because of God's might and power in our daily journey. Is He walking with you?

"Come now, let us reason together," says the Lord. "Though your sins are like scarlet, they shall be white as snow; though they are red as crimson, they shall be like wool. If you are willing and obedient, you will eat the best from the land;" Isaiah 1:18-19 (NIV)

But for you who revere my name, the sun of righteousness will rise with healing in its wings. And you will go out and leap like calves released from the stall. Malachi 4:2 (NIV)

Peter turned and saw that the disciple whom Jesus loved was following them. When Peter saw him, he asked, "Lord, what about him?" Jesus answered, "If I want him to remain alive until I return, what is that to you? You must follow me." John 21:20-22 (NIV)

WORSHIP/OBEDIENCE
It sounds like Jesus was basically telling Peter to mind his own business! What is that to you? Keep your eyes, heart, and mind focused on God's plan for you. Do not be distracted by other people, do not look to the right or the left, and do not compare your life to another. Just continue to walk daily in the obvious ways that God demonstrates through His word. There still remains a question to be asked: can this walking with God thing become difficult? Yes, absolutely! But you do have the Lord's might, power, and Spirit walking right beside you.

Keep Him there, grab His hand, and just start walking.

It takes faith to live daily in this crazy world, but on some days our faith does not seem to be enough to get us through the difficult circumstances. Sometimes we're just not sure that we're strong enough. We reach the point that we're not even convinced that our faith is growing stronger! We start to feel doubtful. We begin to feel weak…

ADORATION/EXPLANATION

Are you feeding your faith? Remember, faith is the only thing that pleases God because it is our faith that causes us to study, seek, serve, worship, and trust.

How then do we feed our faith? How do we grow it? Start by reading the Bible, seeking opportunities to learn, study, and hear the instructions of the faithful God that we claim we are following. God wants us to feed our faith in the same way that we feed our face…daily!

That if you confess with your mouth, "Jesus is Lord," and believe in your heart that God raised him from the dead, you will be saved.

Consequently, faith comes from hearing the message, and the message is heard through the word of Christ. Romans 10:9, 17 (NIV)

And without faith it is impossible to please God, because anyone who comes to him must believe that he exists and that he rewards those who earnestly seek him. Hebrews 11:6 (NIV)

So do not throw away your confidence; it will be richly rewarded. You need to persevere so that when you have done the will of God, you will receive what he has promised. Hebrews 10:35-36 (NIV)

WORSHIP/OBEDIENCE

Stop your worrying and doubting! That is Satan's prime way of bringing you down and discouraging your daily walk. Do not throw away your confidence! When we feed our body healthy food, we believe that it is nourishing us and helping us grow. We also need to feed ourselves with the truth of Scripture.

Continue daily to feed your soul healthy food.

Faith growth happens from the inside out!

Have you ever heard the phrase, "We don't see eye-to-eye?" It basically means that you do not agree on something with another person. Although it is not a big issue to differ with the people in our lives, it is a big deal NOT to see eye-to-eye with God.

ADORATION/EXPLANATION

If we really, truly understand how incredible God's power and grace is, and that it is available to those that trust and obey, then we will not only desire to see eye-to-eye, but will not be satisfied until we are face-to-face with Him!

Open my eyes, that I may behold wonderful things from your law. Psalm 119:18 (NASB)

Look to the Lord and his strength; seek his face always. 1 Chronicles 16:11 (NIV)

My heart says of you, "Seek his face!" Your face, Lord, I will seek. Psalm 27:8 (NIV)

But my eyes are fixed on you, O Sovereign Lord; in you I take refuge– Psalm 141:8 (NIV)

Now the Lord is the Spirit, and where the Spirit of the Lord is, there is freedom. And we, who with unveiled faces all reflect the Lord's glory, are being transformed into his likeness with ever-increasing glory, 2 Corinthians 3:17-18a (NIV)

WORSHIP/OBEDIENCE

We do not have the option to disagree with God's standard of living. We have to see eye-to-eye" with Him because He is God and we are not! As a faithful follower of Christ, each of us must choose to learn, study, and apply biblical principles to every area of our daily lives.

Dear Lord, help me continually keep my eyes, my face, and my life focused on you. I want to see eye-to-eye with you so that my face reflects Your glory to someone today!

May 15

Many people nowadays seem to have the audacity to think that the Bible is not relevant anymore. It's out of date, out of style, and underrated. It seems that a lot of folks want to pick and choose what parts to obey and what sections they want to ignore. This arrogance has pervaded the media and our culture. It is on just about every television channel and in almost every magazine. A seemingly disrespect for God's truth?

ADORATION/EXPLANATION
Here's a news flash: God is the authority, we are not! God has the might and power, not us! According to His word, He is not interested in assumption, audacity, or arrogance. As a matter of fact, it is exactly the opposite. He loves a humble, obedient heart! When we are weak, He is strong.

If my people, who are called by my name, will humble themselves and pray and seek my face and turn from their wicked ways, then will I hear from heaven and will forgive their sin and will heal their land. 2 Chronicles 7:14 (NIV)

"The Lord bless you and keep you; the Lord make his face shine upon you and be gracious to you; the Lord turn his face toward you and give you peace." Numbers 6:24-26 (NIV)

Therefore I will boast all the more gladly about my weaknesses, so that Christ's power may rest on me. 2 Corinthians 12:9b (NIV)

I will instruct you and teach you in the way you should go; I will counsel you and watch over you. Many are the woes of the wicked, but the Lord's unfailing love surrounds the man who trusts in him. Psalm 32:8, 10 (NIV)

WORSHIP/OBEDIENCE
What should our obvious act of worship look like in light of these verses? Well to start, it should show humility, an honest heart, a turn from our sinful habits, prayer, and the desire to seek God's face! The Bible is our final authority. It is the living, breathing, inspired Word of God. God can only work through us when we accept our weaknesses and depend on Him.

He does his best work in humble hearts. God said it, so I believe it!

Is it healthy for us to think about ourselves as sinful? I may be a louse, but I don't want my self-esteem totally destroyed by thinking of myself as that bad. Where will it get me by telling myself that I'm a crummy person all the time? There are plenty of folks worse off than I am? Real sinners! Does God desire this attitude from us?

ADORATION/EXPLANATION

Self-honesty is the best road to spiritual health. We are selfish creatures by nature and to ignore this is like ignoring cancer. Looking within, you will also see the incredibly high potential you have. Your goodness or badness is irrelevant—we're all sinners, after all! But you have a new life in Christ, so you live in His goodness in front of God the Father. He does not see a crummy person!

***

"Do not let your hearts be troubled. Trust in God; trust also in me." John 14:1 (NIV)

Jesus replied, "If anyone loves me, he will obey my teaching. My Father will love him, and we will come to him and make our home with him. He who does not love me will not obey my teaching. These words you hear are not my own; they belong to the Father who sent me." John 14:23-24 (NIV)

"O our God, will you not judge them? For we have no power to face this vast army that is attacking us. We do not know what to do, but our eyes are upon you."

"This is what the Lord says to you: 'Do not be afraid or discouraged because of this vast army. For the battle is not yours, but God's.' 2 Chronicles 20:12, 15b (NIV)

WORSHIP/OBEDIENCE

War will always rage inside us. Your old self will clash against the new, so expect some conflict between your sinful human nature and God's plan. We don't need to feel crummy, just conviction. So buckle up, pray, and prepare to watch God give you the victory over these conflicts. Remember, the battle is not yours to fight in your own strength!

God's plan in this world is to draw out a community of people who will love Him forever and, because you've personally trusted in Him, you're one of them!

***

May 17

Life is full of expectations, but many things in this world do not pan out as we hope they will. Perhaps jobs, families, health, and even relationships are some of the things that are not like you imagined they'd be. Sometimes this can be very disappointing and discouraging. What happened?

ADORATION/EXPLANATION

God never disappoints, though not necessarily because things always turn out the way we want and expect. Rather, it's because He is a mighty God. He already sees the future and knows that some of our expectations are not in our best interest. We must trust in His sovereignty, His knowledge, and His perfect will for our lives.

Give ear to my words, O Lord, consider my sighing. Listen to my cry for help, my King and my God, for to you I pray. In the morning, O Lord, you hear my voice; in the morning I lay my requests before you and wait in expectation. Psalm 5:1-3 (NIV)

For we are God's workmanship, created in Christ Jesus to do good works, which God prepared in advance for us to do. Ephesians 2:10 (NIV)

What then shall we say? Is God unjust? Not at all! For he says to Moses,

"I will have mercy on whom I have mercy, and I will have compassion on whom I have compassion." It does not, therefore, depend on man's desire or effort, but on God's mercy. Romans 9:14-16 (NIV)

WORSHIP/OBEDIENCE

Living obviously, in obedience to God, means laying our prayers, praises, and expectations at His feet. What if He doesn't answer our requests the way we want Him to? What if we are disappointed? Here's the simple solution: realize and accept that we should wait with expectancy for God to work, but do not wait with expectancy for Him to work in OUR way or on OUR time schedule.

When we realize that God wants and already knows the best answer for our prayer requests, we will wait with expectation to see how He is going to work.

May 18

Giving seems very easy for some people. Giving of time, labor, service, and money seems to be a natural character trait for many Christians. Is it because they have a lot of these resources? Is it from an overflow of money? Is it because they have a more joyful heart than others? Are they less selfish? Or could it be in direct obedience to God, no matter what their circumstance or financial position? No matter how joyful they feel?

ADORATION/EXPLANATION

In the following scripture from the Old Testament book of 1 Kings, we see that the Prophet Elijah's resources for food and water ran out. He then approaches a poor, starving widow for help. What…poor? Yes! Not only poor, but depressed, desperate, and destitute, and God still asks her to give in those circumstances!

Then the word of the Lord came to him: "Go at once to Zarephath of Sidon and stay there. I have commanded a widow in that place to supply you with food." So he went to Zarephath. When he came to the town gate, a widow was there gathering sticks. He called to her and asked, "Would you bring me a little water in a jar so that I may have a drink?" As she was going to get it, he called, "And bring me, please, a piece of bread." "As surely as the Lord your God lives," she replied, "I don't have any bread—only a handful of flour in a jar and a little oil in a jug. I am gathering a few sticks to take home and make a meal for myself and my son, that we may eat it and die." Elijah said to her, "Don't be afraid. Go home and do as you have said. But first make a small cake of bread for me from what you have and bring it to me, and then make something for yourself and your son. For this is what the Lord, the God of Israel, says; 'The jar of flour will not be used up and the jug of oil will not run dry until the day the Lord gives rain on the land.'" She went away and did as Elijah had told her. 1 Kings 17:8-15 (NIV)

WORSHIP/OBEDIENCE

How did this woman do it? She barely had enough for her family, she was desperate, and she was ready to call it quits and die. But amazingly enough, the story goes on to tell us that she obeyed and her food miraculously never ran out. Talk about a big "wow" moment! We need to learn from this story to give in a way that may seem hard or maybe even impossible, but to trust that God can take care of the rest.

A change may be right around the corner!

May 19

Change, change…I want to make a change! Many people have uttered these thoughts at some point in their lives, yet never actually got around to making the changes. I wonder why? What is stopping the change?

ADORATION/EXPLANATION

There is a fine line between <u>wanting</u> to make a change and really accepting and allowing God to <u>bring</u> a change into your daily life. Seeing a need to change is the first step, but obeying God, even when it seems so difficult or unrealistic, is the key to a permanent life-changing walk. He is the author of our stories!

Then the word of the Lord came to Elijah: "Leave here, turn eastward and hide in the Kerith Ravine, east of the Jordan. You will drink from the brook, and I have ordered ravens to feed you there." So he did what the Lord had told him. He went to the Kerith Ravine, east of the Jordan, and stayed there. The ravens brought him bread and meat in the morning and bread and meat in the evening, and he drank from the brook. Some time later the brook dried up because there had been no rain in the land. Then the word of the Lord came to him: "Go at once to Zarephath of Sidon and stay there. I have commanded a widow in that place to supply you with food." So he went to Zarephath. 1 Kings 17:2-10a (NIV)

After a long time, in the third year, the word of the Lord came to Elijah: "Go and present yourself to Ahab, and I will send rain of the land." So Elijah went to present himself to Ahab. 1 Kings 18:1-2a (NIV)

WORSHIP/OBEDIENCE

Do you see the obvious principle at work here in yesterday's story of the widow? It is one of sheer obedience. Elijah did exactly what the Lord told him to do and went exactly where he was told to go. When the brook dried up and when the ravens stopped bringing food, when the widow stopped supplying…Elijah allowed God to make a change. He understood that God was the author of his destiny and was NOT afraid of what may have seemed like nonsensical proposals.

Will you obey the author of your story?

May 20

In many books of the Bible, we hear about the Word of the Lord coming to people and then they obey. Have you ever heard the Word of the Lord coming to you? No, I don't mean in an audible voice, but through His Word, through people, or through circumstances? Are you actually listening or are you too busy doing all the speaking?

ADORATION/EXPLANATION

Sometimes even strong believers face a personal crisis of faith. We doubt our identity, vision, and purpose for God. We feel exhausted. We have human weaknesses and worries. These factors may be blaring so loudly in your mind and soul that you cannot hear the voice of God, even if you tried. Learn to quiet your mind and listen. Really listen! Do you hear Him?

"I have had enough, Lord," he said. "Take my life; I am no better than my ancestors." Then he lay down under the tree and fell asleep. The angel of the Lord came back a second time and touched him and said, "Get up and eat, for the journey is too much for you." So he got up and ate and drank. Strengthened by that food, he traveled forty days and forty nights until he reached Horeb, the mountain of God. There he went into a cave and spent the night.

The Lord said, "Go out and stand on the mountain in the presence of the Lord, for the Lord is about to pass by." Then a great and powerful wind tore the mountains apart and shattered the rocks before the Lord, but the Lord was not in the wind. After the wind there was an earthquake, but the Lord was not in the earthquake. After the earthquake came a fire, but the Lord was not in the fire. And after the fire came a gentle whisper. When Elijah heard it, he pulled his cloak over his face and went out and stood at the mouth of the cave. 1 Kings 19:4b-5, 7-9, 11-13a (NIV)

WORSHIP/OBEDIENCE

Exhaustion, hunger, worries, and stress can clutter our minds so that we cannot actually hear God's leading. The prophet Elijah had to sleep, eat, and then go into a cave to clear his head and heart. Then he had to be able to persevere past the strong winds, crashing rocks, earthquake, and fire! His forty days of traveling and all these other events most likely covered a big stretch of time. But the beautiful and wonderful payoff for Elijah's tenacity was the arrival of the gentle whisper from God.

Wait for the whisper!

Do you realize that God is in the business of working through you to accomplish His tasks? Do you really, I mean really, think about this? Tasks in our lives may seem impossible, but God has shaped us with personality traits, experiences, and training that prepares us for purposes way beyond our scope of comprehension. Wow!

ADORATION/EXPLANATION

Nehemiah was a character from the Old Testament and, just like most of us, he was an ordinary person. However, he was placed in a unique spot to accomplish a special goal for God. But Nehemiah did something that many of us forget—he always prayed before he acted! He first talked with God then he walked with confidence!

When I heard these things, I sat down and wept. For some days I mourned and fasted and prayed before the God of heaven.

The king said to me, "What is it that you want?" Then I prayed to the God of heaven, and I answered the king, "If it pleases the king and if your servant has found favor in his sight, let him send me to the city in Judah where my fathers are buried so that I can rebuild it." And because the gracious hand of my God was upon me, the king granted my requests. Then I said to them, "You see the trouble we are in; Jerusalem lies in ruins, and its gates have been burned with fire. Come, let us rebuild the wall of Jerusalem, and we will no longer be in disgrace." I also told them about the gracious hand of my God upon me and what the king had said to me. They replied, "Let us start rebuilding." So they began this good work. I answered them by saying, "The God of heaven will give us success." Nehemiah 1:4; 2:4-5, 8b, 17-18, 20a (NIV)

WORSHIP/OBEDIENCE

Have you ever felt inadequate to meet a challenge? I have! Read the whole story of Nehemiah in the Old Testament. He struggled with criticism, weariness, and motivation. But from the beginning to the end of his account, he never hesitated to ask God for favor and help. He trusted God before he went into any kind of situation and proved himself faithful and of good leadership quality. Even Nehemiah's enemies grudgingly admitted that God was with him in his impossible task of rebuilding the Jerusalem wall.

Do you talk and walk with God? Start a conversation with Him today.

Even if you are praying regularly and trusting God with projects, accomplishments, and tasks in your daily life, you still may get criticism from others. As a matter of fact, you will mostly likely receive criticism and doubt if you are doing anything that seems impossible. Faith to do the seemingly impossible things in life will always draw comments, distractions, and criticisms. Don't listen!

ADORATION/EXPLANATION

As Nehemiah and the people of Jerusalem were in the process of rebuilding their city wall, many naysayers came around to discourage them. Mean comments can be hurtful when you are trying to accomplish something, but God can overrule any words, comments, or fears of failure if we just keep our mind focused on Him and NOT on others. Pray continually during any task. Trust God!

When Sanballat heard that we were rebuilding the wall, he became angry and was greatly incensed. He ridiculed the Jews, and in the presence of his associates and the army of Samaria, he said, "What are these feeble Jews doing? Will they restore their wall? Will they offer sacrifices? Will they finish in a day? Can they bring the stones back to life from those heaps of rubble—burned as they are?

Tobiah the Ammonite, who was at his side, said, "What they are building—if even a fox climbed up on it, he would break down their wall of stones!" Nehemiah 4:1-3 (NIV)

For we are taking pains to do what is right, not only in the eyes of the Lord but also in the eyes of men. 2 Corinthians 8:21 (NIV)

WORSHIP/OBEDIENCE

You may not have the strength or ability to continue on under strong criticism. God does! Your job today is to press on and work on in obedience to God's word in actions and attitude. There are two obvious ways to travel through your schedule today: First, continue to be a person who talks to God, not once, not twice, but continually. Welcome Him into your thoughts and plans. Second, walk with God today. Do not let critical words, taunts, or doubts get you down. Behave in the right way in front of all who cheer or jeer.

God may have an amazing mission waiting just for you!

Satan will very often try to discourage our plans by creeping stealthily into our minds. We start to listen more closely to what others think instead of what God says! We need to stand up and fight these discouraging thoughts daily if we are to accomplish anything for God.

ADORATION/EXPLANATION
While rebuilding the wall of Jerusalem, Nehemiah and the people realized that they were also fighting a battle. They posted guards, they stood watch, and they carried their swords. They had a plan, and they carried it out even amidst the jeers and physical threats. Yet Nehemiah's main focus was not on the enemy. Instead, his main focus was always on God and His purposes. Throughout the rebuilding of the wall, Nehemiah sought God's guidance and strength first. He proclaimed with confidence, "Our God will fight for us!"

So we rebuilt the wall till all of it reached half its height, for the people worked with all their heart.

They all plotted together to come and fight against Jerusalem and stir up trouble against it. But we prayed to our God and posted a guard day and night to meet this threat. After I looked things over, I stood up and said to the nobles, the officials and the rest of the people, "Don't be afraid of them. Remember the Lord, who is great and awesome, and fight for your brothers, your sons and your daughters, your wives and your homes." The officers posted themselves behind all the people of Judah who were building the wall. Those who carried materials did their work with one hand and held a weapon in the other, and each of the builders wore his sword at his side as he worked.

"Wherever you hear the sound of the trumpet, join us there, Our God will fight for us!" Nehemiah 4:4, 8-9, 14, 16b-18a, 20 (NIV)

WORSHIP/OBEDIENCE
Do you hear the sound of the trumpet? God will do the battle for you today. Do your work diligently but, like the Jewish people, carry your sword in one hand at all times? Come on…a sword? Really? I need a sword for today's schedule? YES!! God's word (the Bible) is your sword of the Spirit. What you have studied, learned, meditated on, and memorized should be your main weapon of choice. Pray, trust God, and do your work, but keep your sword in one hand because your enemy roars all around you.

The battle is yours because God will fight for you!

There are times of battle, sorrow, grieving, and mourning in the lives of believers. Even with our faith in God, we as humans fail, fight, and get discouraged. These are normal emotions and it is fine to go through them, but the key is not to reside there.

ADORATION/EXPLANATION

God wants us to cheer up! He desires joy and laughter. There is a time for mourning but there is also a time for feasting, cheering, and joy. Are you residing in a place of sadness and depression? As Nehemiah instructed the Hebrew people in the Scripture, the joy of the Lord can lift you up! The time of crying is over. Chose this day to stand up and praise!

Then Nehemiah the governor, Ezra the priest and scribe, and the Levites who were instructing the people said to them all, "This day is sacred to the Lord your God. Do not mourn or weep." For all the people had been weeping as they listened to the words of the Law. Nehemiah said, "Go and enjoy choice food and sweet drinks, and send some to those who have nothing prepared. This day is sacred to our Lord. Do not grieve, for the joy of the Lord is your strength." Nehemiah 8:9-10 (NIV)

And the Levites—Jeshua, Kadmiel, Bani, Hashabneiah—said: "Stand up and praise the Lord your God, who is from everlasting to everlasting." "Blessed be your glorious name, and may it be exalted above all blessing and praise." Nehemiah 9:5 (NIV)

So with you: Now is your time of grief, but I will see you again and you will rejoice, and no one will take away your joy. John 16:22 (NIV)

WORSHIP/OBEDIENCE

Isn't it amazing that God wants us to be filled with joy? We are allowed a time of sadness but then it is time to stand up and praise. Our worship and obedience to God's word is obviously seen in the way we behave. We must not wait or delay any longer. Don't rely on your own mood or emotions. Remember, the joy of the Lord is your strength! Chose today to get up, get out of bed, and go enjoy a great meal. Grieving time is over!

Thank God for the things He has done for you and by all means…
stand up and praise Him!

May 25

Have you ever noticed that people say some of the most negative things? Even the most positive of folks cannot help but mutter some silly expressions without thinking. Sadly, we very often say these negative phrases to ourselves and then we start to believe them. I'll never get that job…I'm never going to lose the weight…I'll never pass this test…he'll never change his ways…she'll never invite me…it's never going to pan out!

ADORATION/EXPLANATION

The God that we love does not put these negative, silly thoughts in our head! Satan's goal is to get our minds to focus on the negative and the "nevers" in each day. The Apostle Paul warns us in the Bible to stay away from wasted conversations and thoughts. Thank you, Lord, for your optimistic lessons!

Do not let any unwholesome talk come out of your mouths, but only what is helpful for building others up according to their needs, that it may benefit those who listen. Nor should there be obscenity, foolish talk or coarse joking, which are out of place, but rather thanksgiving. Be careful, then, how you live—not as unwise but as wise, making the most of every opportunity, because the days are evil. Ephesians 4:29; 5:4, 15-16 (NIV)

Finally, brothers, whatever is true, whatever is noble, whatever is right, whatever is pure, whatever is lovely, whatever is admirable—if anything is excellent or praiseworthy—think about such things. Philippians 4:8 (NIV)

WORSHIP/OBEDIENCE

Sometimes our negative comments and thoughts are what Paul calls foolish, idle talk. A waste of time! If we are to make the most of every opportunity, value each day, and cherish each moment, then we cannot allow ourselves to think or speak negative thoughts. Satan will try to squeak them into our minds, but we can override them with God's truth. Our obvious act of obedience today will be to follow what the Bible tells us to focus on: thoughts that are truthful, noble, right, pure, and lovely.

Look for the positives. Start practicing!

Sometimes we fight battles that we do not need to fight. Why is this? We seem to think that it is our duty to fix things, make something right or just speak up. We get involved where we do not need to get involved, make comments that we do not need to make and try to solve problems that may not be ours to solve. We then set about wondering why we have so many trials, scuffles, and confrontations with others. Isn't it our right to get involved?

ADORATION/EXPLANATION
Whether we have a right to argue, confront or dispute with others or not, God tells us that the battle is His. If there truly is a war to wage, then God is the one who will do the fighting. Our job is to step back, control ourselves, and not try to handle everything in our own strength. If He needs our help…He will make it very clear to us. This takes discipline!

"If calamity comes upon us, whether the sword of judgment, or plague or famine, we will stand in your presence before this temple that bears your Name and will cry out to you in our distress, and you will hear us and save us." "O our God, will you not judge them? For we have no power to face this vast army that is attacking us. We do not know what to do, but our eyes are upon you."

He said: "Listen, King Jehoshaphat and all who live in Judah and Jerusalem! This is what the Lord says to you: 'Do not be afraid or discouraged because of this vast army. For the battle is not yours, but God's.'" 2 Chronicles 20:9, 12, 15 (NIV)

For though we live in the world, we do not wage war as the world does. The weapons we fight with are not the weapons of the world. On the contrary, they have divine power to demolish strongholds. We demolish arguments and every pretension that sets itself up against the knowledge of God, and we take captive every thought to make it obedient to Christ. 2 Corinthians 10:3-5 (NIV)

WORSHIP/OBEDIENCE
Imagine if we took every thought, word, and argument captive and obedient to Christ! We would have so many less daily battles.

Lord, please help me to remember that if there is a battle to be fought…it is not mine, but yours!

Have you ever felt beaten up? Maybe not physically, but emotionally and spiritually beaten and battered? The Bible records that the Apostle Paul had been stoned (almost to death), beaten with rods three times, and beaten with the cat-of-nine-tails five times. Thirty-nine lashes was the usual beating with the whip. If we multiply the nine tails with the thirty-nine lashes, then multiply again by five for each separate beating, Paul most likely had over 1,750 marks on his body! This does not even count the stoning or the three beatings recorded with rods. Talk about feeling beaten up!

ADORATION/EXPLANATION

In the New Testament book of Acts, we read of Paul and Silas sitting in prison when an earthquake strikes. Can you just picture them sitting on a cold stone floor, feet in chains, and backs bleeding from their latest beating? The amazing thing about this story is that they were not just sitting and sulking. No, they were singing and praising God!

After they had been severely flogged, they were thrown into prison, and the jailer was commanded to guard them carefully. Upon receiving such orders, he put them in the inner cell and fastened their feet in the stocks. About midnight Paul and Silas were praying and singing hymns to God, and the other prisoners were listening to them. Suddenly there was such a violent earthquake that the foundations of the prison were shaken. At once all the prison doors flew open, and everybody's chains came loose. The jailer woke up, and when he saw the prison doors open, he drew his sword and was about to kill himself because he thought the prisoners had escaped. But Paul shouted, "Don't harm yourself! We are all here!" The jailer called for lights, rushed in and fell trembling before Paul and Silas. He then brought them out and asked, "Sirs, what must I do to be saved?" Acts 16:23-30 (NIV)

WORSHIP/OBEDIENCE

What a testimony to their faith and trust in God! The other prisoners and the jailer could not help but see and hear these strange men who were singing and praising God in the midst of their problems. Sometimes God allows problems in our lives in order to minister to others who are observing us. Do you tend to sulk or sing when you feel beaten up? Someone may be learning from you today.

Do you have the habit of pouting or praising?

May 28

Sometimes God allows earthquake-sized problems that shake the very founda-tions of our lives. Financial earthquakes, occupational earthquakes, relational earth-quakes, physical or psychological earthquakes, and spiritual earthquakes can affect your relationship with God and others if you let them. Has the foundation of your life been shaken recently?

ADORATION/EXPLANATION
In the account of Paul and Silas in prison, the earthquake shook open doors and released the chains that bound them. We still have chains that bind us today. We are wrapped in chains such as guilt, doubt, depression, loneliness, emptiness, distrust, dishonesty, dissatisfaction, and fear. Later in scripture, Paul reminds us that we can be thankful for problems, trials, and even earthquakes for we know that they are good for us and can help open doors and release our chains!

For day and night your hand was heavy upon me; my strength was sapped as in the heat of summer. Then I acknowledged my sin to you and did not cover up my iniq-uity. I said, "I will confess my transgressions to the Lord"—and you forgave the guilt of my sin. Therefore let everyone who is godly pray to you while you may be found; surely when the mighty waters rise, they will not reach him. You are my hiding place you will protect me from trouble and surround me with songs of deliverance. Psalm 32:4-7 (NIV)

Remember Jesus Christ, raised from the dead, descended from David. This is my gospel, for which I am suffering even to the point of being chained like a criminal. But God's word is not chained. 2 Timothy 2:8-9 (NIV)

WORSHIP/OBEDIENCE
What are the chains in your life that are keeping you locked up? What is the sin, the habit, the problem, the issue, or the relationship that is keeping you in bondage? Be honest with yourself! As the Psalmist says, "I will confess my transgressions to the Lord." Will you confess? God may be allowing earthquakes to shake open some doors and to loosen some chains.

Look for the benefit of these storms and then SING!

Even though I am a believer and I know that I have eternal life through my faith in Jesus Christ's death on the cross for my sin, I do not really like the idea of death. I am not afraid of it, exactly, but I sincerely enjoy my life here on earth. Yet if I am to live my existence making any difference at all, then I need to realize that death is imminent for all of us and my time here needs to be purposeful.

ADORATION/EXPLANATION

The Apostle Paul and many others had the courage to die for their beliefs. Why would it take courage to die? Paul, Silas, and countless others realized that through their faith in Christ, death had lost its power to warp and distort life with constant fear. It is because of this that the Christian must dare to live openly, conscious of death, yet never balking at its threat. There is no threat! Our salvation is secure! Faith forces us to a constant awareness of final things and the real purpose of daily life. Paul got it!

Since no man knows the future, who can tell him what is to come? No man has power over the wind to contain it; so no one has power over the day of his death. Ecclesiastes 8:7-8a (NIV)

"Death has been swallowed up in victory. Where, O death, is your victory? Where, O death, is your sting? The sting of death is sin, and the power of sin is the law. But thanks be to God! He gives us the victory through our Lord Jesus Christ. Therefore, my dear brothers, stand firm. Let nothing move you. Always give yourselves fully to the work of the Lord, because you know that your labor in the Lord is not in vain. 1 Corinthians 15:54b-58 (NIV)

WORSHIP/OBEDIENCE

As Christians, we <u>need</u> to be aware…we must live being aware of an eternal dimension to our lives. We also realize that eternal dimension is in a sharp contrast and juxtaposition with our everyday life. Today and tomorrow are only separated by a line called death. This does not have to be a fearful thought. It is a fact! We must choose to face our fear of death and rest on the arm of our Savior.

If life and death are only separated by a thin line, how will we live today for God?

Have you every made a commitment to live courageously? Not just exist, but really live life with courage? Have you committed yourself to learn more about God and His purposes for life? People that live without commitments that bind life to meaning greater than themselves may be unable to cope with life. Suicide ranks as a very high cause of death for people between the ages of fifteen and forty. Increasing addictions and other escape routes show that without commitments to live, we are entirely vulnerable to the devouring vultures of life.

ADORATION/EXPLANATION

God can empower us with a strength born of a commitment to live a life pleasing to Him, and He can give us the courage to put that commitment ahead of any personal fulfillment. What… ahead of any personal plans or gain? You are kidding, right? The Apostle Paul could sing in prison because he understood that true personal fulfillment came from his commitment to live courageously.

Someone asked him, "Lord, are only a few people going to be saved?" He said to them, "Make every effort to enter through the narrow door, because many, I tell you, will try to enter and will not be able to. Once the owner of the house gets up and closes the door, you will stand outside knocking and pleading, 'Sir, open the door for us.' "But he will answer, 'I don't know you or where you come from.' Luke 13:23-25 (NIV)

I eagerly expect and hope that I will in no way be ashamed, but will have sufficient courage so that now and always Christ will be exalted in my body, whether by life or by death. For to me, to live is Christ and to die is gain. If I am to go on living in the body, this will mean fruitful labor for me. Yet what shall I choose? I do not know! Philippians 1:20-22 (NIV)

WORSHIP/OBEDIENCE

Paul's cost to remain alive seemed immense. He wanted to live fruitfully, but that may have meant more preaching, teaching, traveling, and beatings! Yikes! Is it any small wonder that he contemplated death? But he chose to live courageously with his commitment to the gospel of Christ. With this example in front of us, we can live daily with a commitment to our Savior. We can rely on God's strength for today's schedule wherever it may take us.

In obedience, I can wake up each day and recommit to living courageously!

I can have all the latest cookware, cook books, and equipment in my kitchen, I can have plenty of food in my pantry, and I can still fail to put a meal on the table. I can have a treadmill with all the tilts, speeds, and terrains and still not exercise. I can have an electric toothbrush and special whitening toothpaste and still not brush my teeth. I can have a library full of religious books, self-help guides, and reams of notes from church sermons and still be out of tune with God.

ADORATION/EXPLANATION

The outward things are easy to attain. Kitchen equipment, cookbooks, notes, and Bibles are all examples of tools to help us accomplish tasks. But tools and equipment are just that until we faithfully use them and put them into practice.

So the question really is…how is your inner life? Are you using your tools? Are you practicing? Or…are you disillusioned with the Christian life?

For Ezra had devoted himself to the study and observance of the Law of the Lord, and to teaching its decrees and laws in Israel. Ezra 7:10 (NIV)

Therefore we do not lose heart. Though outwardly we are wasting away, yet inwardly we are being renewed day by day. 2 Corinthians 4:16 (NIV)

In the same way, let your light shine before men, that they may see your good deeds and praise your Father in heaven. Matthew 5:16 (NIV)

And find out what pleases the Lord. Ephesians 5:10 (NIV)

WORSHIP/OBEDIENCE

The point is, the Lord looks at you right now through the lens of Jesus Christ and sees you as His child and loves you. He loves your efforts to live for Him, even though they may just seem like feeble attempts. Obviously, we are to "find out what pleases the Lord." This can only be done by using the biggest and best tool at our disposal—the Bible!

We must commit to study and stay informed to live for God in our everyday life.
Use your tool!

Ninety percent of American households probably own at least one Bible, and though they own the main component for inner growth they live grey, struggling lives. Many so-called Christians (Christ followers) are living the same way. They say they believe and have faith in God, but they truly do not comprehend the vastness of the power living within them. They own the tool—the Bible—and might have two or three of them, but they are not reading and studying it to find the answers. The secrets for growth…

ADORATION/EXPLANATION

God desires to show His great power in our daily lives and we think we need to jump in and help. We must have to DO something, right? Wrong! Accept His enormous power and strength for your life, believe in it, and be ready for God to work miracles. The only "doing" that God wants from us is obedience to His Word. Use the Bible as a day planner for your everyday schedules at work, play, and home.

He then brought them out and asked, "Sirs, what must I do to be saved?" They replied, "Believe in the Lord Jesus, and you will be saved—you and your household." Acts 16:30-31 (NIV)

Therefore, my dear friends, as you have always obeyed—not only in my presence, but now much more in my absence— Philippians 2:12a (NIV)

Don't let anyone look down on you because you are young, but set an example for the believers in speech, in life, in love, in faith and purity. Be diligent in these matters; give yourself wholly to them, so that everyone may see your progress. Watch your life and doctrine closely. Persevere in them, 1Timothy 4:12, 15-16a (NIV)

WORSHIP/OBEDIENCE

Be diligent in these matters of speech, life, love, faith, and purity. Have a problem? Open God's Word. Come across a glitch in a relationship? Open God's Word. His power is sufficient for any obstacle that you're struggling with. Our greatest act of worship to the Christ who we profess to follow and love is obedience! Open the Book!

I love the ocean. I enjoy salt water, salt air, and anything to do with the sea. I love to watch the waves rolling in and the mysterious underwater powers at work. The ancient Israelites were not friendly with the sea, and they even labeled their maps so that the Mediterranean was always behind them. Palestine had no natural harbors. Seagoing people from this region were the exception to the rule. The mysterious power and unfathomable might of a roaring ocean seemed fearsome to them.

ADORATION/EXPLANATION
In Psalm 93, we observe a short hymn-like passage that exalts God's power over the raging sea. The Israelite's only hope was that God was stronger than the sea, higher than the waves, and more constant than the tides. They needed to believe and sing about the fact that God was greater than their biggest fear.

The Lord reigns, he is robed in majesty; the Lord is robed in majesty and is armed with strength. The world is firmly established; it cannot be moved. Your throne was established long ago; you are from all eternity.

The seas have lifted up, O Lord, the seas have lifted up their voice; the seas have lifted up their pounding waves. Mightier than the thunder of the great waters, mightier than the breakers of the sea—the Lord on high is mighty. Your statutes stand firm; holiness adorns your house for endless days, O Lord. Psalm 93 (NIV)

WORSHIP/OBEDIENCE
After speaking about God's power over the mightiest thing in creation, the sea, the psalmist concludes by asserting the truthfulness and steadfastness of God's word and His holiness. The climax to this hymn can also be looked at as the conclusion to any argument. God is stronger than anything He makes, so will He not be truthful? God is greater than the mightiest sea. Will He not also be holy?

What represents the sea in your life? What is something that makes you fearful, worried, and scared?

The last couple of lines of this psalm are a strong affirmation of God's unlimited power and strength over your issues and fears. Read them again…then head out to sea!

What does a woman of strength look like? What constitutes a great woman in God's eyes? Are they super-strong, extra intelligent, of extraordinary genetics, exceptionally beautiful, or of a domineering nature? The Bible shows that all of God's people, both men and women, are strong when they call on His strength and weak when they try to do everything in their own human strength. So ordinary women like you and me, with the ability to realize that real strength does not ignore weakness, can have a quiet strength that comes from knowing who you are in God. This knowledge is a gentle power that grows inside with character, wisdom, and purpose.

ADORATION/EXPLANATION

If you take time to peruse through Scripture, you will find many examples of strong women. There is Deborah, Priscilla, Esther, Rahab, Dorcas, Phoebe, Naomi, Ruth, Sarah, and Mary, just to name a few. None of these ladies were doormats or dominators, but they all had an inner strength that came from their relationship and faithfulness to God.

The mouth of the righteous man utters wisdom, and his tongue speaks what is just. The law of his God is in his heart; his feet do not slip. Psalm 37:30-31 (NIV)

And Mary said: "My soul glorifies the Lord and my spirit rejoices in God my Savior, Luke 1:46-47 (NIV)

The wise in heart accept commands, but a chattering fool comes to ruin. Proverbs 10:8 (NIV)

She sets about her work vigorously; her arms are strong for her tasks. She speaks with wisdom, and faithful instruction is on her tongue. Proverbs 31:17, 26 (NIV)

WORSHIP/OBEDIENCE

What does a woman of strength do daily? What does she look like?

She honors her physical being by taking care of it, she honors her relationship to God by using her abilities to serve, and she honors her own heart by standing steadfast in her convictions and beliefs. A woman of strength remains a faithful follower even when times get tough!

Like a little black dress…a woman of strength never goes out of style!

The Bible tells us that Enoch walked with God. Noah was also reported to have daily and faithfully walked with God. Can you say that about yourself? Do you daily and faithfully make an appointment to meet with God? Do you even acknowledge that He is walking right beside you all day long? Do you chat, converse, or share any thoughts or conversations with Him during your long list of errands?

ADORATION/EXPLANATION
Imagine your eulogy and epitaph. This is the speech that someone would give at your funeral or the final thought that could be printed on your gravestone. What would it say? Are you living with such awe of God and His wonderful grace and mercy that people would say that you walked with God? Start walking today!

And after he became the father of Methuselah, Enoch walked with God 300 years and had other sons and daughters. Enoch walked with God; then he was no more, because God took him away. Genesis 5:22, 24 (NIV)

But Noah found favor in the eyes of the Lord. This is the account of Noah. Noah was a righteous man, blameless among the people of his time, and he walked with God. Genesis 6:8-9 (NIV)

By faith Enoch was taken from this life, so that he did not experience death; he could not be found, because God had taken him away. For before he was taken, he was commended as one who pleased God. And without faith it is impossible to please God, because anyone who comes to him must believe that he exists and that he rewards those who earnestly seek him. Hebrews 11:5-6 (NIV)

WORSHIP/OBEDIENCE
How cool! Can you imagine walking with God? You may think you can't experience this until you get to heaven, but actually, we still have that opportunity today. God is still with us and we can and should be walking with Him. We may not be able to see Him but that is where our faith comes in. Spend time reading His word, praying, sharing your thoughts, and just plain acknowledging His presence throughout your day. Feel the sun on your face, look at the flowers, notice the sky…He is there!

What are you waiting for? Start walking!

Ultra-distance runners take their bodies to the limit and beyond. They run farther and faster than most people ever will. Ultra-runners do not have to be the most talented, necessarily, but they train harder, study endurance harder, and put their brain, heart and gut into their running. These runners push themselves with incredible determination and endurance of body, mind, and spirit.

ADORATION/EXPLANATION

God has given us the ability to run the Christian life with endurance. The key is to call on God's strength to run the race and not on our own. Part of our goal in continuing to train is to pass on our experience and knowledge and to motivate and inspire others with our life of faith. Will you go the distance?

Do you not know that in a race all the runners run, but only one gets the prize? Run in such a way as to get the prize. Everyone who competes in the games goes into strict training. They do it to get a crown that will not last; but we do it to get a crown that will last forever. Therefore I do not run like a man running aimlessly; I do not fight like a man beating the air. 1 Corinthians 9:24-26 (NIV)

Such confidence as this is ours through Christ before God. Not that we are competent in ourselves to claim anything for ourselves, but our competence comes from God. 2 Corinthians 3:4-5 (NIV)

I have fought the good fight, I have finished the race, I have kept the faith. 2 Timothy 4:7 (NIV)

WORSHIP/OBEDIENCE

The Apostle Paul spoke these words from the book of Timothy as he was sitting in prison. Wow, talk about going the distance! How are you running?

Lord, help me dedicate time, stretch my mind,
train smart, prepare and focus on Your will and Your word daily.
I do not want to run my race aimlessly but rather with
Your grace and Your purpose as my finish line. Amen.

Loving parents want to give their children what they ask for, as long as it is good for them. They do not substitute dangerous or harmful gifts for good ones. Neither does God. He wants us to have the awesome things that we pray for so we need to let Him know what we need. The process of continually asking for our own needs is called "petition."

ADORATION/EXPLANATION

Praise, thanksgiving, and confession are aspects of prayer that center around our response to God, but asking for ourselves, or petitioning, is learning how He responds to you. As you go to God with your petitions, He supplies what you need. Jesus himself taught that asking for things in prayer is very important to our spiritual life.

"Ask and it will be given to you; seek and you will find; knock and the door will be opened to you. For everyone who asks receives; he who seeks finds; and to him who knocks, the door will be opened. Matthew 7:7-8 (NIV)

"If you believe, you will receive whatever you ask for in prayer." Matthew 21:22 (NIV)

"This, then, is how you should pray: 'Our Father in heaven, hallowed be your name, your kingdom come, your will be done on earth as it is in heaven.'" Matthew 6:9-10 (NIV)

Do not be anxious about anything, but in everything, by prayer and petition, with thanksgiving, present your requests to God. Philippians 4:6 (NIV)

WORSHIP/OBEDIENCE

When we ask God to supply our needs, there are certain attitudes and conditions that He expects of us. Our obvious act of worship and obedience needs to be complete trust without anxiety, a thankful heart for the things that God has already provided, and a presentation of our requests daily. We must fully realize that God has everything to offer, and even if the answer does not come in the form that we would like, He has our best interests before him.

Trust without anxiety? Can you accept that?

June 7

Why do we even waste time reading Bible passages that deal with stress, crying out to God, and troubling situations? Shouldn't we be spending our time on joyous and encouraging reading? Well hard times, distress, and trouble of some sort will eventually come to everyone. Don't you want to be ready when it does? We can learn what the writers of old were going through then, and what God wants us to learn, now.

ADORATION/EXPLANATION

The psalmist begins his writing in Psalm 77 with much complaining and thinking of himself and his hard situation. His lament is very negative, but near the end of the psalm, he seems to have a change of heart. Can we still remain in awe of a God who seems distant or uncaring? Yes! The writer seems to ask many questions of God but never seems to offer any sorrow or guilt about his own part in this picture. Failing to admit guilt is a far greater spiritual problem than suffering from too many guilty feelings. Guilty feelings and admission of sin helps us realize our need for a savior.

I cried out to God for help; I cried out to God to hear me. When I was in distress, I sought the Lord; at night I stretched out untiring hands and my soul refused to be comforted. You kept my eyes from closing; I was too troubled to speak. "Will the Lord reject forever? Will he never show his favor again? Has his unfailing love vanished forever? Has his promise failed for all time? Has God forgotten to be merciful? Has he in anger withheld his compassion?" Psalm 77:1-2, 4, 7-9 (NIV)

"I the Lord search the heart and examine the mind, to reward a man according to his conduct, according to what his deeds deserve." Jeremiah 17:10 (NIV)

WORSHIP/OBEDIENCE

We have a beautiful opportunity to cry out to God as many times as we want, but we must also be quick to look for opportunities to ask for forgiveness. We may be guilty of bringing some of the stress upon ourselves.

Lord, if stressful situations occur in my schedule today,
help me call out to you and then trust you completely in the circumstances.
Search my heart!

161

What's the big appeal with the occult and Satanism? From witches to rock groups, some people just aren't afraid to advertise their connection with Satan. Of course some people will say that it is just a marketing ploy, but is it? And even if it is, why play around with something so dangerous? The word "occult" basically means hidden or secret, and it is this secretive world that draws thousands of people in. People are usually curious about witchcraft, magic, predicting the future, their fortunes, or the spirit world, and just dipping a toe in seems harmless enough. Be warned: this wellspring is full of nothing but evil, torment, and lies.

ADORATION/EXPLANATION

If you haven't participated in these activities, thank God for His mercy and make a firm commitment to not even dabble in them. If you have been involved in any occult practices, turn around now and ask God for strength to change. The God that we should stand in awe of warns and reminds us to be aware of Satan's desire to assault our minds, thoughts, and desires. Be aware!

"Do not turn to mediums or seek out spiritists, for you will be defiled by them. I am the Lord your God." Leviticus 19:31 (NIV)

"'I will set my face against the person who turns to mediums and spiritists to prostitute himself by following them, and I will cut him off from his people. Consecrate yourselves and be holy, because I am the Lord your God. Keep my decrees and follow them. I am the Lord, who makes you holy.'" Leviticus 20:6-7 (NIV)

The acts of the sinful nature are obvious: sexual immorality, impurity and debauchery; idolatry and witchcraft; hatred, discord, jealousy, fits of rage, selfish ambition, dissensions, factions and envy; Galatians 5:19-20 (NIV)

WORSHIP/OBEDIENCE

How do we put this Biblical advice into every day use? The Bible tells us to resist the devil and he will flee. Be aware! Watch the material that you read, movies you see, and the videos or games that you and others play. Guard your mind.

What we think about or focus on shapes the person that we become.

June 9

The Bible tells us to pursue a godly life. How can we know if we have a godly character? Most of us wear many hats: son, daughter, mom, dad, student, teacher, grandparent, business partner, and so on. It's easy to develop different personalities for each of these roles, but a person's true character can be measured by a couple of traits: consistency and integrity.

ADORATION/EXPLANATION

Jesus lived a life as consistently as they come. What He said He would do, He did! What He taught that God would say and do, He did! He could be counted on. Do you know any two-faced people? That's a laugh, isn't it? We all know, or have been ourselves, people who act differently to please people and fit in. Consistency and integrity/honesty shows a strong, godly character. Christ never changed His values, His beliefs, the way He talked, or what He said about people in order to win approval. Pursue this example!

Righteousness will be his belt and faithfulness the sash around his waist. Isaiah 11:5 (NIV)

I saw heaven standing open and there before me was a white horse, whose rider is called Faithful and True. With justice he judges and makes war. Revelation 19:11 (NIV)

"Whoever has my commands and obeys them, he is the one who loves me. He who loves me will be loved by my Father, and I too will love him and show myself to him." John 14:21 (NIV)

WORSHIP/OBEDIENCE

A great life isn't a destination but a journey. We will find that it is a process of trying and failing and learning from mistakes. But we all should have only one face, and we need to follow Christ's example daily to let it shine through to others. Never change your values, beliefs, honesty, or conversation to win approval from others. Choose today, this minute, to stand strong in all situations with a God-like character. One face…one true character!

Your character is who you are and who you choose to be…even when no one is looking!

The message of the cross is two-fold for our lives: there is a vertical relationship with God through His son's death on the cross, and a horizontal relationship with relatives, friends and others. Sometimes though, we neglect one or the other of those relationships that are analogous to the simple wooden structure of the cross. We have a wonderful vertical relationship with God, yet we forget others around us. Or we have great relationships with people but forget to nurture our relationship with God. How can this be? We need both pieces of the cross to make it complete! Vertical and horizontal!

ADORATION/EXPLANATION

In order for the cross of Calvary to be something more than just a symbol, we must strive to live it out fully. If we look to God, follow His Word, and allow Jesus Christ to be an example for our lives, then we will have the vertical piece of the cross in place. If this relationship is honestly and truly strengthened, then the horizontal relationship to others should follow.

"And anyone who does not take his cross and follow me is not worthy of me. Whoever finds his life will lose it, and whoever loses his life for my sake will find it." Matthew 10:38-39 (NIV)

Then he said to them all "If anyone would come after me, he must deny himself and take up his cross daily and follow me. What good is it for a man to gain the whole world, and yet lose or forfeit his very self?" Luke 9:23, 25 (NIV)

I have been crucified with Christ and I no longer live, but Christ lives in me. The life I live in the body, I live by faith in the Son of God, who loved me and gave himself for me. Galatians 2:20 (NIV)

WORSHIP/OBEDIENCE

Don't you just love this last verse from the Apostle Paul? If we really believe that we (our old nature and habits) have been crucified with Christ and what He did for us on the cross, then we have no choice but to live a life that reflects this in our daily agendas. To make a cross we obviously need two pieces of wood to intersect each other for the symbol to be recognized.

Are you one straight wooden beam, or do people recognize the cross in you?

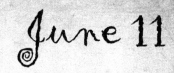
There is a diet pill on the market that advertises that it can significantly reduce body fat. The company spokesman announces that users of this product are not asked to change their daily life, perform exercise, or make changes to the way they eat. What? No changes?

ADORATION/EXPLANATION
If there really were a pill to change our lives to be more like Christ, many people would rush to take it. But in the daily walk with God, just as in a correct diet, there ARE changes that need to be made. True growth as a believer, just as in healthy eating, DOES require changes. It is in this sometimes slow, trudging pursuit that we see ourselves becoming more like the Christ that we follow. No magic pills needed!

If you really change your ways and your actions and deal with each other justly, then I will let you live in this place, in the land I gave your forefathers for ever and ever. But look, you are trusting in deceptive words that are worthless. Jeremiah 7:5, 7-8 (NIV)

He called a little child and had him stand among them. And he said: "I tell you the truth, unless you change and become like little children, you will never enter the kingdom of heaven. Therefore, whoever humbles himself like this child is the greatest in the kingdom of heaven." Matthew 18:2-4 (NIV)

WORSHIP/OBEDIENCE
Jesus gives us the perfect example of a little child. They do not know enough to be proud, conceited, or think that they need no changing. But like little children, we sometimes fight the change or discipline that the Lord places upon us in order to make us better. Humility makes us realize that our slow process, sometimes accompanied by no change at all, is the very obedience that God desires!

*Study God's Word diligently because users of <u>this</u> product
will see the need for changes to their daily life!*

June 12

A couple of days ago we talked about learning to represent the cross in our life. The well-known symbol of the cross is a horizontal wooden beam that intersects a vertical beam. The horizontal beam represents the relationships with people and this world, and the vertical beam represents our relationship with Christ. But think for a moment about which beam is the foundation? It is the deeply rooted beam. The piece that insures that the cross stands up. The vertical!

ADORATION/EXPLANATION

If the upright beam of wood is not put firmly into the ground, then the cross will fall and just become a pile of useless wood. Think for a moment: they nailed Jesus to the cross, pierced his hands and feet, lifted the cross precariously up, and then dropped it into a deep hole. Thud! With the weight *of* the cross and the weight *on* the cross, the vertical beam had to be deeply rooted to keep the cross upright.

"Salt is good, but if it loses its saltiness, how can you make it salty again? Have salt in yourselves, and be at peace with each other." Mark 9:50 (NIV)

Whoever speaks, is to do so as one who is speaking the utterances of God; whoever serves is to do so as one who is serving by the strength which God supplies; so that in all things God may be glorified through Jesus Christ, to whom belongs the glory and dominion forever and ever. Amen. 1 Peter 4: 11 (NASB)

If we claim to have fellowship with him yet walk in darkness, we lie and do not live by the truth. But if we walk in the light, as he is in the light, we have fellowship with one another, and the blood of Jesus, his Son, purifies us from all sin. 1 John 1:6-7 (NIV)

WORSHIP/OBEDIENCE

The vertical beam of the cross was sunk deep into the ground to hold up the body of Christ. In order for us to represent the cross of Christ to people in our everyday lives, we have to have our vertical relationship with God firmly, deeply planted. Living this out obviously means that we need to walk in the light of God's truths as mapped out in the Bible. When we commit to study, pray, and obey God's Word, we are sinking the foundation of the cross deeper and deeper into our lives.

How is your cross standing?

Good friends are united. They stand together and hold on tight when trouble comes. To find a companion, friend, or spouse like this is to find a treasure worth more than gold. God has created us for companions and friends and ordains many wonderful relationships during our lives. Make new friends but never forget to cherish the old!

ADORATION/EXPLANATION

God watches over our friendships and protects them. He gives us the courage to stand by them when they need us, and the wisdom to do and act in the right way. Love one another!

"May there be peace within your walls and security within your citadels."

For the sake of my brothers and friends, I will say, "Peace be within you." For the sake of the house of the Lord our God, I will seek your prosperity. Psalm 122:7-9 (NIV)

An unfriendly man pursues selfish ends; he defies all sound judgment. Proverbs 18:1 (NIV)

As iron sharpens iron, so one man sharpens another. Proverbs 27:17 (NIV)

Greater love has no one than this, that he lay down his life for his friends. You are my friends if you do what I command. John 15:13-14 (NIV)

The Lord would speak to Moses face to face, as a man speaks with his friend. Exodus 33:11a (NIV)

WORSHIP/OBEDIENCE

Wow…can you imagine talking face-to-face with God as if He were a friend? But He is! In fact, He is not only a friend, but our heavenly Father and our personal Savior too! He is the most devoted friend that we can ever have and as the New Testament book of John states, He laid his life down for us.

Greater love does not exist! What a beautiful example of friendship!

June 14

Roses, roses, and more beautiful roses! I have a large climbing rose bush that started out as a small shrub over twenty years ago. Every year around this time, it is covered in a profusion of hundreds of small, pink blossoms. I have had elementary graduation parties, high school graduations, anniversary parties, and even a wedding in my yard at this time of year. The rose bush is a constant, consistent natural decoration at every event, and I am delighted every time I look at it!

ADORATION/EXPLANATION
Just as I take great delight in seeing my roses bloom year after year, God wants us to take great delight in Him. Sometimes we become too casual or complacent about His ways, His creation, His promises, His commands, and with His Word. To delight means to find great joy, bliss, ecstasy, and happiness. If my rose bush brings me delight year after year, shouldn't God and all His glory bring me just as much? No… much *more*! Just look for the blooms!

Then my soul will rejoice in the Lord and delight in his salvation. Psalm 35:9 (NIV)

Delight yourself in the Lord and he will give you the desires of your heart. Psalm 37:4 (NIV)

Who is a God like you, who pardons sin and forgives the transgression of the remnant of his inheritance? You do not stay angry forever but delight to show mercy. Micah 7:18 (NIV)

I delight greatly in the Lord; my soul rejoices in my God. For he has clothed me with garments of salvation and arrayed me in a robe of righteousness, Isaiah 61:10a (NIV)

WORSHIP/OBEDIENCE
Living out the principle of being delighted in God is not as hard as it may seem. We need to choose today to open our eyes—really open them—to see even the simple things that God has blessed us with. Look for obvious ways to be joyful. Just as in the fact that I KNOW…and wait with expectation that my rose bush is going to bloom every June and I am still delighted when it does. We can look anew and with delight at our salvation, God's love for us, and His simple blessings.

Keep looking with expectation for the blooms!

Yesterday I talked about being delighted in my beautiful rose bush. It blooms every year, but I never lose the excitement of viewing it again. In this same way, God never loses the excitement of being delighted in us. What? God delights in watching us? Aren't we supposed to take delight in Him?

ADORATION/EXPLANATION
We are supposed to take delight in Him, but one of the most comforting reasons that we can delight in God is because He wants to and does delight in those that follow and pursue Him. When was the last time that someone was delighted in you? How awesome is it that the God of the universe does delight in us.

If the Lord delights in a man's way, he makes his steps firm; Psalm 37:23 (NIV)

The Lord detests lying lips, but he delights in men who are truthful. Proverbs 12:22 (NIV)

"The Lord your God is with you, he is mighty to save. He will take great delight in you, he will quiet you with his love, he will rejoice over you with singing." Zephaniah 3:17 (NIV)

This is what the Lord says: "Let not the wise man boast of his wisdom or the strong man boast of his strength or the rich man boast of his riches, but let him who boasts boast about this: that he understands and knows me, that I am the Lord, who exercises kindness, justice and righteousness on earth, for in these I delight," declares the Lord. Jeremiah 9:23-24 (NIV)

WORSHIP/OBEDIENCE
God desires for us to know Him and understand His ways. He delights when His children study and model the character qualities that are taught in His Word. Truthfulness, honesty, love, kindness, joy, peacefulness, and patience need to be the order of our days.

If we desire God's delight, then we will choose today to live
in obvious ways that will make Him delighted!

June 16

Many people, including Christians, are insensitive to the big problems of destructive speech. We tend to excuse ourselves with rationalizations such as, "If they didn't want folks to talk, they never should have done it." Or maybe, "Well, it's the truth, isn't it? And we are supposed to speak the truth, right?" Perhaps the subtlest one amongst Christians is, "Let me share this juicy detail with you so that we can pray about it."

Right. Pray about it?

ADORATION/EXPLANATION

If a frog is placed in a pan of cold water and put on a stove, the frog will not jump out. He'll slowly boil to death as the temperature increases. It's not that the frog is dumb, but his nerve endings are becoming desensitized in the heated water. The hotter the water becomes, the more numb his nerve endings become—until finally he is cooked. The God that we adore does not want us to numb our spiritual nerve endings with careless communication. It can happen slowly…

Therefore each of you must put off falsehood and speak truthfully to his neighbor, for we are all members of one body. Do not let any unwholesome talk come out of your mouths, but only what is helpful for building others up according to their needs, that it may benefit those who listen. Get rid of all bitterness, rage and anger, brawling and slander, along with every form of malice. Be kind and compassionate to one another, forgiving each other, Justas in Christ god forgave you. Ephesians 4:25, 29, 31-32 (NIV)

With the tongue we praise our Lord and Father, and with it we curse men, who have been made in God's likeness. Out of the same mouth come praise and cursing. My brothers, this should not be. James 3:9-10 (NIV)

WORSHIP/OBEDIENCE

A transformed tongue must be a top priority for those who desire to grow in a relationship with God. If careless communication becomes acceptable, then our churches, homes, schools, and relationships will all be victimized, cooked to death like that frog by our lack of sensitivity!

Lord, help me to be more sensitive to bad speech patterns
and jump out before the water gets too hot.

"I promise to tell the whole truth and nothing but the truth!" Most of us have either been in a courtroom or seen one on television. When people take an oath and place their hand on the Bible, they are promising to tell the truth. The whole truth!

ADORATION/EXPLANATION

Truth has fallen on hard times these days. In sales jobs, we think that we are justified to lie for the company's good. It seems okay to take a little extra office supplies for home. We fill in time-cards untruthfully. Our culture seems to have shifted its ethics to self-advancement and falsehood. God tells us that there are serious spiritual consequences for tampering with the truth. God's intense concern for truthfulness comes from His very nature. He is a God of truth! God will not lie!

⁕

Into your hands I commit my spirit; redeem me, O Lord, the God of truth. Psalm 31:5 (NIV)

…a faith and knowledge resting on the hope of eternal life, which God, who does not lie, promised before the beginning of time… Titus 1:2 (NIV)

Do not lie to each other, since you have taken off your old self with its practices… Colossians 3:9 (NIV)

Surely you desire truth in the inner parts; you teach me wisdom in the inmost place. Psalm 51:6 (NIV)

WORSHIP/OBEDIENCE

Speaking the truth is the key to worship. Therefore, our commitment to the truth aligns our relationship with God, His nature, and His way of operating. Our conscience cannot be clear before God and our lives joyous if we get involved with that which is false. It is a matter of obedience! It is obvious!

Choose to tell the whole truth and nothing but the truth!

⁕

June 18

Kindness is not looked upon kindly by everyone. There are those who feel that being kind carries a cost they are not willing to pay. It is too time consuming, too demanding, and most likely to interfere with their private plans for self-indulgence. For many folks, kindness has no place in their world.

ADORATION/EXPLANATION

The Spirit-led life, however, insists that kindness is not an inconvenience to be avoided, but a characteristic to be embraced. The Hebrew word for kindness basically means "to bow the head". The example is to treat others carefully, courteously and appropriately. God deals with our stubborn hearts, minds, and souls with kindness. The prime example of God's kindness toward us is seen in His gift of the Lord Jesus.

And he passed in front of Moses, proclaiming, "The Lord, the Lord, the compassionate and gracious God, slow to anger, abounding in love and faithfulness…" Exodus 34:6 (NIV)

A kindhearted woman gains respect, but ruthless men gain only wealth. A kind man benefits himself, but a cruel man brings trouble on himself. Proverbs 11:16-17 (NIV)

Make sure that nobody pays back wrong for wrong, but always try to be kind to each other and to everyone else. 1 Thessalonians 5:15 (NIV)

Love is patient, love is kind. It does not envy, it does not boast, it is not proud. 1 Corinthians 13:4 (NIV)

WORSHIP/OBEDIENCE

Kindness often takes effort, but it is worth it. In fellowshipping with other believers, it is a necessary part of the Spirit-led life found in Christ! But kindness must extend past the church door to the unbeliever. Kindness to neighbors, strangers, or co-workers leaves a major calling card of who you really are.

No witnessing tool is more effective than genuine kindness to others, regardless of personal cost. Make the effort today!

I love honey. We purchase natural wildflower honey from local beekeepers who live in our area. It adds a wonderful taste to many recipes and also to our morning coffee and tea. It's amazing what a natural sweetener God enabled a small insect to make!

ADORATION/EXPLANATION

The delightful sweetness of God's precepts of goodness, light, and provision is often compared to honey in the Scriptures. The Israelites were promised a land flowing with milk and honey. The lover in Song of Songs describes his bride's lips as dripping sweetness like the honeycomb. The psalmist declares that God's promises are sweeter than honey. Honey…how sweet it is!

How sweet are your words to my taste, sweeter than honey to my mouth! I gain understanding from your precepts; therefore I hate every wrong path. Psalm 119:103-104 (NIV)

Eat honey, my son, for it is good; honey from the comb is sweet to your taste. Know also that wisdom is sweet to your soul; if you find it, there is a future hope for you, and your hope will not be cut off. Proverbs 24:13-14 (NIV)

The fear of the Lord is pure, enduring forever. The ordinances of the Lord are sure and altogether righteous. They are more precious than gold, than much pure gold; they are sweeter than honey, than honey from the comb. Psalm 19:9-10 (NIV)

WORSHIP/OBEDIENCE

When we begin to view God's plans, promises, and precepts as laid out in the Bible, we understand how sweet and beneficial they are for us. They are all-natural, no-preservative, just plain good food for our souls. Our obvious choice of worship and obedience is to seek God's words and apply them to today's schedule when we're driving, at our work place, and in our behavior with everyone that we come in contact with.

Pour on the honey! Let it flow!

Bearing children today is a choice, and in the face of much anti-family propaganda, this choice needs to be consciously worked out and even sometimes defended. The commitment to have children should certainly entail the commitment to love, nurture, and to give those children the very best hope of rising to their full potential. That requires an end to "me first" thinking—that is, if marriage hasn't taught you that already! Parenting ultimately requires cooperation with God's great plan for the family.

ADORATION/EXPLANATION
God has given us children to love, but it is important to remember that they don't always need to have the highest priority in our lives. Children need to know that while we have lives and interests that sometimes include them, sometimes they do not. We must be aware of our children's needs to develop and recognize their own gifts and calling under God. The family provides the framework of love, stability, and discipline.

Only be careful, and watch yourselves closely so that you do not forget the things your eyes have seen or let them slip from your heart as long as you live. Teach them to your children and to their children after them. Deuteronomy 4:9 (NIV)

If you, then, though you are evil, know how to give good gifts to your children, how much more will your Father in heaven give good gifts to those who ask him! Matthew 7:11 (NIV)

Train a child in the way he should go, and when he is old he will not turn from it. Proverbs 22:6 (NIV)

Fathers, do not exasperate your children; instead, bring them up in the training and instruction of the Lord. Ephesians 6:4 (NIV)

WORSHIP/OBEDIENCE
We can do our children the greatest of favors by helping them see themselves not as the center of any universe—including our own—but as important additions to our lives. Most of all, we need to treat our children as people, as individuals of worth and value, who are deeply loved and have a wonderful place in God's plan.

It is in letting go of our children that we find them and they discover themselves!

Our ability to part with our children reflects our confidence in God. It is not and never has been our job to hold onto them forever. If we just trust our children or our parenting methods, we will certainly be disappointed. If we claim the promises of God concerning our children, we will have His grace to let them go.

ADORATION/EXPLANATION
God loves our love for our children. In one sense He allows us the opportunity to never let them go. Like Job, we can pray for them daily, continuing the prayer vigil we had for them before their birth. We must respect their freedom, trusting a heavenly Father who loves them more than we do.

Discipline your son, and he will give you peace; he will bring delight to your soul. Proverbs 29:17 (NIV)

Her children arise and call her blessed; her husband also, and he praises her: Proverbs 31:28 (NIV)

"As a mother comforts her child, so will I comfort you; and you will be comforted over Jerusalem." Isaiah 66:13 (NIV)

He must manage his own family well and se that his children obey him with proper respect. (If anyone does not take care of his own family, how can he take care of God's church?) 1Timothy 3:4-5 (NIV)

Don't let anyone look down on you because you are young, but set an example for the believers in speech, in life, in love, in faith and in purity. 1Timothy 4:12 (NIV)

WORSHIP/OBEDIENCE
Only as we let our children go can they become the people that God fully intends them to be. By obeying this plan, we can fulfill our true commitment to them. More selfishly, it is only in letting them go that we can receive them back as friends. Choose today to commit to pray daily and faithfully for your children. That's how it's supposed to be.

*Letting our children go and grow in accordance with God's Word
means getting our children back.*

June 22

Every man and woman who walks on the face of the earth faces problems and trials of many kinds. They may occur in varying degrees, but no one can or will escape problems. What you do with your problems is what counts. Compare the thermometer to the thermostat. The thermometer is influenced by outside heat or cold. The thermostat controls the heat or cold. Choose to be a thermostat! In His prayer in John 17, Jesus did not ask the Father to remove us from this world of problems. Instead, He asked the Father to keep us safe in the midst of them.

ADORATION/EXPLANATION
God is not caught unaware or surprised at your difficulties. There is not a situation in life that Jesus cannot handle if you commit it to Him.

That is why I am suffering as I am. Yet I am not ashamed, because I know whom I have believed, and am convinced that he is able to guard what I have entrusted to him for that day. 2 Timothy 1:12 (NIV)

You then, my son, be strong in the grace that is in Christ Jesus. And the things you have heard me say in the presence of many witnesses entrust to reliable men who will be qualified to teach others. Endure hardship with us like a good soldier of Christ Jesus. No one serving as a soldier gets involved in civilian affairs—he wants to please his commanding officer. 2 Timothy 2:1-4 (NIV)

Endure hardship as discipline….Therefore, strengthen your feeble arms and weak knees. "Make level paths for your feet," so that the lame may not be disabled, but rather healed. Hebrews 12:7a, 12-13 (NIV)

WORSHIP/OBEDIENCE
Basically God is saying, dear kids, is your life full of difficulties? Then find joy because, when the way seems rough, your patience and faith have a chance to grow! Let them grow and don't try to quickly squirm out of your problems. Use the here and now and allow today's problems to teach you something. Don't let your problems control you.

Look for the lesson and refuse to let yourself over-heat or freeze to death.
Be a THERMOSTAT!

People are looking for spirituality in all the wrong places. They run the gamut from crystal healers, witches (no not the scary, craggy people in movies…but real bona fide witches), mediums, hypnotists, and just plain old meditative practices. Some openly reject Christ and turn to other gods, but many seek fulfillment in a variety of practices because they have never actually heard about Jesus—or what they've heard does not really represent the truth.

ADORATION/EXPLANATION
The Apostle Paul understood that these practices may be tempting to many folks who are searching. Instead of criticizing them, he pursued ways to open their eyes to the reality of the one true God. He understood that they were searching for spiritual fulfillment in all the wrong places! Great example, Paul.

On the last and greatest day of the Feast, Jesus stood and said in a loud voice, "If anyone is thirsty, let him come to me and drink. Whoever believes in me, as the Scripture has said, streams of living water will flow from within him." John 7:37-38 (NIV)

For the time will come when men will not put up with sound doctrine. Instead, to suit their own desires, they will gather around them a great number of teachers to say what their itching ears want to hear. They will turn their ears away from the truth and turn aside to myths. 2 Timothy 4:3-4 (NIV)

"The God who made the world and all things in it, since He is the Lord of heaven and earth, does not dwell in temples made with hands;" Acts 17:24 (NASB)

WORSHIP/OBEDIENCE
Our everyday environment is a lot like it was back in Paul's time. In fact, we are not much different at all. People are trying a great variety of religious practices, spiritual journeys, and other pursuits to fill a void in their lives. If you and I desire to be an effective witness to the truth, we need to acknowledge (not criticize) the spiritual need that drives people to seek other gods in the first place.

Live in such a way…that others want your God!

In the New Testament account, the Apostle Paul was called a common teacher by many of the religious leaders of the day. In the book of Acts, he was actually called a babbler. The Epicureans were convinced that even as a learned Jew, Paul must have gathered bits of useless information and pieces of philosophy to come up with this unsophisticated view of life. If what he was teaching was true, how could they not be aware of it?

ADORATION/EXPLANATION
Some towns and cities received Paul's message with eagerness and examined the Scriptures to see if what was being taught was true. They were not in competition or jealous of Paul's teaching. Instead of jumping to the conclusion that he was babbling, they studied and confirmed his information in their own hearts and minds. Paul did not give up on his first try at professing Christ's saving message to people and neither should we.

Now the Bereans were of more noble character than the Thessalonians, for they received the message with great eagerness and examined the Scriptures every day to see if what Paul said was true. When the Jews in Thessalonica learned that Paul was preaching the word of God at Berea, they went there too, agitating the crowds and stirring them up. Acts 17:11, 13 (NIV)

While Paul was waiting for them in Athens, he was greatly distressed to see that the city was full of idols. So he reasoned in the synagogue with the Jews and the God-fearing Greeks, as well as in the marketplace day by day with those who happened to be there. A group of Epicurean and Stoic philosophers began to dispute with him. Some of them asked, "What is this babbler trying to say?" Others remarked, "He seems to be advocating foreign gods." They said this because Paul was preaching the good news about Jesus and the resurrection. "You are bringing some strange ideas to our ears, and we want to know what they mean." Acts 17:16-18, 20 (NIV)

WORSHIP/OBEDIENCE
Our daily act of worship and obedience to God needs to be a willingness to explain our faith, belief, and hope to those who want to know. To the many people whom we will pass, mingle, or rub elbows with today, we should commit to being ready to share our personal story. Refuse to be a babbler!

Does God overlook ignorance in those that have never heard of His saving grace? The Bible tells us that God deals with people according to the revelation that He has given them. With further revelation comes further responsibility to act. The problem lies in the fact that many have heard of God's plan of salvation, yet still choose to act ignorant.

ADORATION/EXPLANATION

Ignorance is NOT bliss when it concerns the God of the universe. Jesus claimed to be the Light of the world, available for all. His life is not only recorded in the gospels but also mapped throughout history. His life, death, and resurrection shed the needed light on God's wonderful plan for mankind.

"The God who made the world and everything in it is the Lord of heaven and earth and does not live in temples built by hands. And he is not served by human hands, as if he needed anything, because he himself gives all men life and breath and everything else. From one man he made every nation of men, that they should inhabit the whole earth; and he determined the times set for them and the exact places where they should live. God did this so that men would seek him and perhaps reach out for him and find him, though he is not far from each one of us. 'For in him we live and move and have our being.' As some of your own poets have said, 'We are his offspring.'"

"For he has set a day when he will judge the world with justice by the man he has appointed. He has given proof of this to all men by raising him from the dead." When they heard about the resurrection of the dead, some of them sneered, but others said, "We want to hear you again on this subject." Acts 17:24-28, 31-32 (NIV)

WORSHIP/OBEDIENCE

Wow! In God we live and move and breathe. The Apostle Paul made it very clear, Jesus made it very clear, and we have the Bible available to study ourselves. The very fact that you are reading this daily devotional book is a great effort to destroy any remnants of ignorance to God's plan for your life.

Ignorance is not worship. Ignorance is not obedience. Ignorance is not bliss!

Sometimes we cry out to God for help as we complain and groan about our circumstances, yet we are not willing to change our ways. We have a tendency to bemoan the things that befall us and discount the fact that maybe if we followed God's commands and advice in the Bible, we could have avoided some of the pitfalls plaguing us.

ADORATION/EXPLANATION

The Old Testament book of Judges is filled with sensational stories of the Israelites, their disobedience to God, and their deliverance. These stories and accounts of the nation's heroes (called judges) still hold valuable lessons for us today.

Again the Israelites did evil in the eyes of the Lord, and for seven years he gave them into the hands of the Midianites. When the Israelites cried to the Lord because of Midian, he sent them a prophet, who said, "This is what the Lord, the God of Israel, says: I brought you up out of Egypt, out of the land of slavery. I snatched you from the power of Egypt and from the hand of all of your oppressors. I drove them from before you and gave you their land. I said to you, 'I am the Lord your God; do not worship the gods of the Amorites, in whose land you live.' But you have not listened to me." Judges 6:1, 7-10 (NIV)

WORSHIP/OBEDIENCE

Isn't it amazing how many times the Israelites would disobey God and then call out for help? We would never disobey that many times…or would we? Don't we do just about the same thing nowadays? God brings us through so many hard times, and we promise Him and ourselves that we will never behave like that again. "I'll shape up God…I really mean it!" Wow, what a wonderful personal Savior we have. He loves us no matter how much we mess up.

Lord, help me to read your Word, think about it and then act in your ways!

I doubt a lot of things that some people say and I doubt the validity of much information that is printed in the tabloids, but there is one source that I will never doubt, and that is God. He claimed to be the way, the truth, and the light, and His promises always pan out. His precepts guide my life and His plans are always perfect.

ADORATION/EXPLANATION

The story of Gideon is an amazing one. God had already assured him that He would help him to deliver the troubled Israelites from their problems, but Gideon doubted what God said and questioned His message. Gideon only thought about how weak his family was and how impossible the task was that God has set before him. This seems to be a lack of faith on Gideon's part, yet God in His infinite patience allowed Gideon to test Him, not once, but twice! When Jesus taught many years later about our faith, He commended those who believed without seeing. Sometimes our own view can get in the way!

"But sir," Gideon replied, "if the Lord is with us, why has all this happened to us? Where are all his wonders that our fathers told us about when they said, 'Did not the Lord bring us up out of Egypt?' But now the Lord has abandoned us and put us into the hand of Midian." The Lord turned to him and said, "Go in the strength you have and save Israel out of Midian's hand. Am I not sending you?" "But Lord," Gideon asked, "how can I save Israel? My clan is the weakest in Manasseh, and I am the least in my family." The Lord answered, "I will be with you, and you will strike down all the Midianites together." Gideon replied, "If now I have found favor in your eyes, give me a sign that it is really you talking to me." Judges 6:13-17 (NIV)

WORSHIP/OBEDIENCE

Never doubt what God says. His promises always come true and His mercies are new every morning. When our strength is weak, when the situation seems grim, or when our hope is faltering, that is when God is at His best. Just as in His promise to Gideon, God tells us, "Am I not sending you? I will be with you!"

Whatever happens today, Lord, help me walk by faith and not by sight!

June 28

Gideon not only questioned God's instructions but He also laid out a wool fleece to test God. Basically, Gideon already knew that God was instructing him but he chose to confirm it to himself by creating an experiment.

ADORATION/EXPLANATION
Gideon realized his own inadequacies and the thought of them made him reluctant to take the leadership role. God recognized Gideon's weaknesses also, but realized that Gideon had the potential for greatness if he chose to obey. God already sees our weaknesses, but He is in the business of doing the impossible with our lives if we just continue to trust.

Gideon said to God, "If you will save Israel by my hand as you have promised—look, I will place a wool fleece on the threshing floor. If there is dew only on the fleece and all the ground is dry, then I will know that you will save Israel by my hand, as you said." And that is what happened. Gideon rose early the next day; he squeezed the fleece and wrung out the dew—a bowlful of water. Then Gideon said to God, "Do not be angry with me. Let me make just one more request. Allow me one more test with the fleece. This time make the fleece dry and the ground covered with dew." That night God did so. Only the fleece was dry; all the ground was covered with dew. Judges 6:36-40 (NIV)

The crucible for silver and the furnace for gold, but the Lord tests the heart. Proverbs 17:3 (NIV)

WORSHIP/OBEDIENCE
God does not usually give us extraordinary signs to show us His will. Seeking amazing signs sometimes displays a lack of trust on our part. The Holy Spirit, along with prayer, the Bible, and counsel from trusted friends, can give us peace about decisions. As a faithful follower of Christ, I need to walk by faith and not by sight.

Stopping too long to figure things out or try to put God
in a logical little box will only get me off track in my obedience.

It is amazing how God shows up in our lives with direction and great displays of His all-knowing power right when we are at our weakest. The Bible, people, and circumstances can all point us to look directly into His wonderful face. I believe that God wants us to realize that we are weak and He is strong. Ughh…why do I have to be weak? It is in this position of pure weakness or helplessness that we truly, fully rely on God.

ADORATION/EXPLANATION

In the book of Judges, Gideon agrees that God is going to give him the victory over the Midianites. It took Gideon quite a while to be convinced of that fact and once he finally accepted it, God changed up the circumstances on him! I'm sure that Gideon was thinking, "Why God? What's the plan now? I don't get it!"

The Lord said to Gideon, "You have too many men for me to deliver Midian into their hands. In order that Israel may not boast against me that her own strength has saved her, announce now to the people, 'Anyone who trembles with fear may turn back and leave Mount Gilead.'" So twenty-two thousand men left, while ten thousand remained. But the Lord said to Gideon, "There are still too many men. Take them down to the water, and I will sift them for you there. If I say, 'This one shall go with you,' he shall go; but if I say, 'This one shall not go with you,' he shall not go." So Gideon took the men down to the water. There the Lord told him, "Separate those who lap the water with their tongues like a dog from those who kneel down to drink." Three hundred men lapped with their hands to their mouths. All the rest got down on their knees to drink. The Lord said to Gideon, "With the three hundred men that lapped I will save you and give the Midianites into your hands. Let all the other men go, each to his own place." Judges 7:2-7 (NIV)

WORSHIP/OBEDIENCE

Talk about bad odds! Gideon started with thirty-two thousand men, which were cut to ten thousand, and then cut again down to three hundred! What's going on with that! Well God very often allows the odds to stack against us, just like He did to Israel, so that there is no question on whose strength we need to rely on.

Lord, help me to accept the process of You doing the sifting in my life.
You can choose to sift out people, money, jobs, locations, relationships, addictions,
habits, and anything that distracts me from fully relying on you.

When I was a child, I was always enamored with the thought of a queen sitting on her throne and ruling her kingdom. One wave of her hand could change the course of someone's day. One point with her scepter and a major decision could be made. What a wonderful life it would be to sit high up on my velvet, padded, royal throne.

ADORATION/EXPLANATION

In real life, though, the only being that will remain forever on a throne is God. His term will never run out and He can never be removed. Talk about authority!

Your throne, O God, will last for ever and ever; a scepter of justice will be the scepter of your kingdom. Psalm 45:6 (NIV)

In putting everything under him, God left nothing that is not subject to him. Yet at present we do not see everything subject to him. Hebrews 2:8b (NIV)

Therefore let us draw near with confidence to the throne of grace, so that we may receive mercy and find grace to help in time of need. Hebrews 4:16 (NASB)

Let us fix our eyes on Jesus, the author and perfecter of our faith, who for the joy set before him endured the cross, scorning its shame, and sat down at the right hand of the throne of God. Consider him who endured such opposition from sinful men, so that you will not grow weary and lose heart. Hebrews 12:2-3 (NIV)

WORSHIP/OBEDIENCE

Wow! Today, let's fix our eyes, cast our gaze, and keep our focus on the one true God. He is the only authority that should be allowed to rule and reign over our daily decisions.

Remind me to keep my attention and royal respect for you,
Lord, as I go about my day. Thank you for loving me. Hail to the King!

The Bible tells us that God is seated on His throne in heaven. Jesus Christ, our Savior, is seated at His right hand. The way we choose to view God will ultimately determine our faith. If we see a King who is faithful, powerful, all knowing, and loving, then our faith will rise to that level. If we see God as distant, small, and unfamiliar, then that is how our faith will be lived out.

AWE/ADORATION

Faith in the face of trying circumstances, trials, and tribulation is a Hall-of-Fame kind of faith. The God that I claim to be a faithful follower of is a great, all-powerful King. I want to leave behind a legacy of Hall-of-Fame caliber faith for my children, grandchildren, family, and friends to remember.

Remember those earlier days after you had received the light, when you stood your ground in a great contest in the face of suffering. Sometimes you were publicly exposed to insult and persecution; at other times you stood side by side with those who were so treated. You sympathized with those in prison and joyfully accepted the confiscation of your property, because you knew that you yourselves had better and lasting possessions. So do not throw away your confidence; it will be richly rewarded. You need to persevere so that when you have done the will of God, you will receive what he has promised. Hebrews 10:32-36 (NIV)

Now faith is being sure of what we hope for and certain of what we do not see. Hebrews 11:1 (NIV)

WORSHIP/OBEDIENCE

I love the Apostle Paul's statement, "do not throw away your confidence." The life of faith is tough sometimes. Most people want to see some evidence before they put their faith into something or someone, but that is not genuine faith. That is logic. Our faith should soar high above logic, common sense, or human standards.

Choose to trust, worship, and obey our big, powerful God—
the same God who is higher than our thoughts and our understanding.

July 2

One of my favorite things about summer is how long light lingers in the evening. Long sunny days and blissfully long sunsets mark this season, and it is a real joy to sit on my back deck, having dinner alfresco into the early evening. I look around my beautiful yard and gardens while murmuring a heartfelt "Thank you" to God.

ADORATION/EXPLANATION

The Bible tells us that Jesus is the light of the world and the psalmist describes God as being wrapped in light. He is not just one long, beautiful summer day of light, He is resplendent with it! His Word provides light for our paths and wipes away all fear of the darkness. Light exposes truth!

Your word is a lamp to my feet and a light for my path.

The unfolding of your words gives light; it gives understanding to the simple. Psalm 119:105, 130 (NIV)

"This is the verdict: Light has come into the world, but men loved darkness instead of light because their deeds were evil. Everyone who does evil hates the light, and will not come into the light for fear that his deeds will be exposed. But whoever lives by the truth comes into the light, so that it may be seen plainly that what he has done has been done through God." John 3:19-21 (NIV)

Then Jesus told them, "You are going to have the light just a little while longer. Walk while you have the light, before darkness overtakes you. The man who walks in the dark does not know where he is going." John 12:35 (NIV)

He wraps himself in light as with a garment; he stretches out the heavens like a tent Psalm 104:2 (NIV)

WORSHIP/OBEDIENCE

Who would chose to live in darkness when we have the option of turning on the light?

Lord, I am thankful for the light!

I took an archery class in college because it was a requirement for the degree I was working toward. Shooting an arrow is a lot harder than it looks, and shooting an arrow accurately is even more difficult!

ADORATION/EXPLANATION

An arrow is only shot forward by pulling the string firmly in a backwards direction, and the amount of force that is exerted determines how well it will fly forward. God may be pulling or stretching you backward for a reason. He is preparing you for the most accurate flight of your life. Don't break and don't waver!

And when you pray, do not keep on babbling like the pagans, for they think they will be heard because of their many words. Do not be like them, for your Father knows what you need before you ask him. Give us today our daily bread. Matthew 6:7-8, 11 (NIV)

Who of you by worrying can add a single hour to his life? Therefore do not worry about tomorrow, for tomorrow will worry about itself. Each day has enough trouble of its own. Matthew 6:27, 34 (NIV)

Consider it pure joy, my brothers, whenever you face trials of many kinds, because you know that the testing of your faith develops perseverance. James 1:2-3 (NIV)

WORSHIP/OBEDIENCE

If you feel that life, children, marriage, your job, or relationships are pulling you strongly backward—hang on! Your act of pure obedience to God for today, just today, is to trust and keep your aim straight. Feel the pulling? Hang on…

Keep your focus on His promises for you and soon God will launch you forward, like a true arrow into something wonderful.

July 4

Happy Fourth of July! Today is our nation's birthday and a marvelous time for picnics, barbeques, and fireworks! It is also a time to remember the great sacrifices that have gone into forming this wonderful country. America is the land of the free and the home of the brave, a place where God certainly sheds His grace on you. Do you realize how fortunate we are to live here?

ADORATION/EXPLANATION
God in His infinite wisdom allowed you and me to be born and live in America. I could have been born in any third-world country or in the most desolate, disease-ridden land, yet God chose to place me here. Lord, help me to NOT take my country for granted. I am thankful!

The heavens declare the glory of God; the skies proclaim the work of his hands. Day after day they pour forth speech; night after night they display knowledge. Psalm 19:1-2 (NIV)

Blessed is the nation whose god is the Lord, the people he chose for his inheritance. From heaven the Lord looks down and see all mankind; from his dwelling place he watches all who live on the earth— Psalm 33:12-14 (NIV)

Taste and see that the Lord is good; blessed is the man who takes refuge in him. Psalm 34:8 (NIV)

WORSHIP/OBEDIENCE
Obviously, many people will be enjoying this holiday, but during this time of celebration, our act of worship to God will be lived out in joy, fun and thankfulness. With the correct attitude of our hearts, choose to realize and give God thanks for our country, our freedom, and our life.

Let the pyrotechnics begin!

Sometimes people can ruin your day! Have you ever noticed this? You can be enjoying a calm, peace-filled day, and then someone comes along and criticizes, yells, acts grouchy, or complains. It can send you into a downward spiral if you do not change its course.

ADORATION/EXPLANATION
Satan can use people to bring us down. If we are not completely aware and in control of our own attitude, we can start to let others' attitudes, tempers, and personalities cause us to act wrongly. When your mood starts to shift because of someone else, make a concerted effort to draw your focus back on the positive things that God is doing.

My tongue will speak of your righteousness and of your praise all day long. Psalm 35:28 (NIV)

Commit your way to the Lord; trust in him and he will do this: He will make your righteousness shine like the dawn, the justice of your cause like the noonday sun. Be still before the Lord and wait patiently for him; do not fret when men succeed in their ways, when they carry out their wicked schemes. Refrain from anger and turn from wrath; do not fret—it leads only to evil.

The mouth of the righteous man utters wisdom, and his tongue speaks what is just. Psalm 37:5-8, 30 (NIV)

WORSHIP/OBEDIENCE
Today we can choose to proceed through our day with the shield of God in front of us. Be on the alert for Debbie-downers, naysayers, and gossips. Watch and keep a check on your own attitude, and if you feel yourself start that downward slide, draw your focus right back towards God.

Pray for those Debbie-downers and praise our Lord!

While standing in a long line at my favorite discount store, the clerk opened a new register and called out, "Next in line?" The lady behind me quickly brushed past and basically ran to the register. I was next and this lady knew it, but I decided that it was not worth the fuss. When I got to the counter, the clerk said, "I knew that you were next." "No big deal," I replied. You see, that woman was simply subscribing to the trend of our culture. She was looking out for number one, even if it involved rudeness!

ADORATION/EXPLANATION

Self-fulfillment, selfishness, self-elevation, and self-advancement are common in the average behavior today, and they are evidence of the pride that the Bible warns us about. These behaviors are being sold as the truly successful way to live, but my God tells me otherwise!

Pride goes before destruction, a haughty spirit before a fall. Better to be lowly in spirit and among the oppressed than to share plunder with the proud. Proverbs 16:18-19 (NIV)

A man's wisdom gives him patience; it is to his glory to overlook an offense. Proverbs 19:11 (NIV)

Do nothing out of selfish ambition or vain conceit, but in humility consider others better than yourselves. Each of you should look not only to your own interests, but also to the interests of others. Philippians 2:3-4 (NIV)

WORSHIP/OBEDIENCE

Wow…I believe the Bible sums it up quite clearly when it tells us that true humility keeps God in His rightful place in our lives. You see, He is number one, the beginning and the end, the end-all and be-all ruler of the universe. A truly humble person will realize this. Our goal should be to keep God in His place. This will allow us to relate properly with those around us and getting rid of pride will allow us to live assertive, bold, and courageous lives that are yielded to God every day.

Do you trust God? Do you trust in His Word? When we really trust God to care for us, it frees us from self-interest and self-focus so that we are able to care for others. If we start to fall for the notion that we are in control and need to protect and preserve ourselves, then fear will begin to dominate us. Trusting in God to protect and provide dispels fear!

ADORATION/EXPLANATION

Why was there so much complaining from the Israelite nation in the wilderness as Moses led them toward the Promised Land? Twelve spies went in on a scouting mission and ten of them came out with fearful, pessimistic reports. Only the remaining two trusted God's promise that they were already going to own the land. They gave a thrilling report to their people of the land's wonderful bounty. Yet the people listened to the ten fearful pessimists and the trust factor went out the window!

Then Caleb quieted the people before Moses and said, "We should by all means go up and take possession of it, for we will surely overcome it." But the men who had gone up with him said, "We are not able to go up against the people, for they are too strong for us." Numbers 13: 30, 31 (NASB)

When I am afraid, I will put my trust in You. In God, whose word I praise, in God I trust; I shall not be afraid. What can mere man do to me?

Then my enemies will turn back in the day when I call; this I know, that God is for me. In God, whose word I praise, in the Lord, whose word I praise—In God I have put my trust; I shall not be afraid. What can man do to me? Psalm 56:3-4, 9-11 (NASB)

WORSHIP/OBEDIENCE

The kind of trust that dismisses fear is obviously a continual pursuit, not a one-time commitment. We must remain committed, not to our own power or strength, but to God's ever-present help in times of trouble.

Instead of hiding in fear, choose to dwell in the "trust factor" for your day!

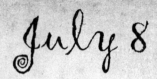

Because you belong to God's family of faith, the Bible tells us that He is very concerned for your life. The day that you confessed with your mouth and believed in your heart that Jesus died on the cross for you, you became a child of the most High God. He cares for you!

ADORATION/EXPLANATION

I am in awe of the God who is concerned with every detail of my life. He even has the hairs on my head numbered. He knows the grains of sand on the beach and yet He is concerned for my problems and needs. His mercies and love for me are too wonderful to fathom!

God is our refuge and strength, an ever-present help in trouble. Therefore we will not fear, though the earth give way and the mountains fall into the heart of the sea, though its waters roar and foam and the mountains quake with their surging. Psalm 46:1-3 (NIV)

Are not two sparrows sold for a penny? Yet not one of them will fall to the ground apart from the will of your Father. And even the very hairs of your head are all numbered. So don't be afraid; you are worth more than many sparrows. Matthew 10:29-31 (NIV)

He alone is my rock and my salvation; he is my fortress, I will never be shaken. Psalm 62:2 (NIV)

WORSHIP/OBEDIENCE

Today we can rest assured that God cares deeply and is concerned for us. Yes, that is hard to fathom at times, but we must choose to believe it. Our act of obedience to God during our comings and goings will be to live in confident assurance of His love and concern for us.

If put into daily practice, this assuring thought pattern will affect everyone that we come into contact with.

July 9

Every morning that you wake up and get out of bed, you are writing your life's secret story. Each day lived here on earth is another page penned in your book of life. You have about a thirty-page chapter for each month and at the end of a year, one sequel to the story is finished. Cherish every opportunity today because each day that you live reveals a blank page, clean and white. What will you write?

ADORATION/EXPLANATION
Our wonderful heavenly Father leaves the writing to us. What thoughts, words, actions, or events will cover your blank page by nighttime? He has given us His Word with some great tips for being a better writer. Have you opened it?

"I am the vine; you are the branches. If a man remains in me and I in him, he will bear much fruit; apart from me you can do nothing. If anyone does not remain in me, he is like a branch that is thrown away and withers; such branches are picked up, thrown into the fire and burned. If you remain in me and my words remain in you, ask whatever you wish, and it will be given you. This is to my Father's glory, that you bear much fruit, showing yourselves to be my disciples. John 15:5-8 (NIV)

You yourselves are our letter, written on our hearts, known and read by everybody. You show that you are a letter from Christ, the result of our ministry, written not with ink but with the Spirit of the living God, not on tablets of stone but on tablets of human hearts. 2 Corinthians 3:2-3 (NIV)

WORSHIP/OBEDIENCE
Wow…have you ever thought of your life as a letter or book? It can really change the way you go about your daily business.

Dear Lord, help me record beautiful, inspiring thoughts, words, and actions on my pages today. On some future day, You will write the word "finished" at the end of my story, and I want to be proud of the book that I give back to you!

July 10

Do you know that there is something called a laughter yoga class? They are actually taught by a certified laughter yoga instructor. There is usually a lot of simulated laughter, stretches, and breathing exercises, all in the effort to teach people to learn to relax and do the real thing. The man that invented this practice hit upon the idea that fake laughter could be as good as the real thing, and now this practice is a growing phenomenon!

ADORATION/EXPLANATION

This class would not be a surprising newsflash or brainstorm to the author of the book of Proverbs, because he mentions a merry heart and laughter often. God has told us about the ability of laughter to have important implications for our heart health and well being. In fact, people with heart disease have been encouraged to laugh more often to help their ailing organ. How is your laughter quotient?

A cheerful heart is good medicine, but a crushed spirit dries up the bones. Proverbs 17:22 (NIV)

A happy heart makes the face cheerful, but heartache crushes the spirit. All the days of the oppressed are wretched, but the cheerful heart has a continual feast. A cheerful look brings joy to the heart, and good news gives health to the bones. Proverbs 15:13, 15, 30 (NIV)

She is clothed with strength and dignity; she can laugh at the days to come. Proverbs 31:25 (NIV)

WORSHIP/OBEDIENCE

God knew when He created us that laughter had the ability to change the way we see the world. Negative, sad, fearful, and pessimistic thoughts cannot occupy the same psychological brain or heart space as humor. When we respond to humor the way God intended for His children, we can replace emotional distress, anxiety, depression, anger, and sometimes, even disease.

Learn to laugh! Love to laugh!

July 11

All winter long I composted and fertilized my vegetable garden with manure, egg shells, vegetable peels, coffee grounds, seaweed, and mulch. I planted in late May and am delighted to be harvesting already. Cucumbers, peppers, basil, squash, and zucchini have already graced my dinner table! My large crop of twenty-four tomato plants is still green though. I <u>can</u> wait!

ADORATION/EXPLANATION

Did you hear what I said? I said that I CAN wait. I will not be impatient because I know that all the labor and love that has gone into preparing my garden will definitely be worth the wait. I also know that rushing it could spoil all the hard work that I've put into it! That is exactly how it is with our Christian walk. We need to allow God to do all the prepping, fertilizing, and weeding, and then sit back and watch for the results. They are guaranteed!

And Jesus grew in wisdom and stature, and in favor with God and men. Luke 2:52 (NIV)

I planted the seed, Apollos watered it, but God made it grow. So neither he who plants nor he who waters is anything, but only God, who makes things grow. The man who plants and the man who waters have one purpose, and each will be rewarded according to his own labor. For we are God's fellow workers; you are God's field, God's building. 1 Corinthians 3:6-9 (NIV)

But grow in the grace and knowledge of our Lord and Savior Jesus Christ. To him be glory both now and forever! Amen. 2 Peter 3:18 (NIV)

WORSHIP/OBEDIENCE

We can wait! Our obvious act of obedience to God's plan for our lives will be patience in the process. Choose this day to have patience in the growing and maturing with confidence that the results will be beautiful and bountiful. No garden springs up and thrives immediately and those that do, die quickly on the first hot day.

Let's develop deep roots, a strong stem, and much fruit. We can wait!

Are you familiar with the man named Zacchaeus in the Bible? He was a Roman tax collector from Jericho. These positions were bid on and very coveted because most collectors extorted money from the citizens, over and above the usual amount. The position was bid on by how much money the collector would get for the Roman government, and anything collected beyond was kept by the tax collector himself. This system made tax collectors very rich, very dishonest, and very despised.

ADORATION/EXPLANATION
Jesus was walking and teaching as He went through Jericho one day. Zacchaeus was a man of short stature so he ran ahead of the crowd around Jesus to climb a sycamore tree, to observe from a better position. When Jesus passed by, he looked up and called to Zacchaeus to come down from the tree because He was going to stay at his house for dinner. What? Stay at the house of a corrupt tax collector? I'm sure that poor little man nearly fell out of the tree! My house? Now?

Jesus entered Jericho and was passing through. A man was there by the name of Zacchaeus; he was a chief tax collector and was wealthy. He wanted to see who Jesus was, but being a short man he could not, because of the crowd. So he ran ahead and climbed a sycamore-fig tree to see him, since Jesus was coming that way. When Jesus reached the spot, he looked up and said to him, "Zacchaeus, come down immediately. I must stay at your house today." So he came down at once and welcomed him gladly. Luke 19:1-6 (NIV)

WORSHIP/OBEDIENCE
Zacchaeus was a dishonest man whose curiosity led him to seek Jesus. Isn't that like many of us? We know that we have problems and maybe some dishonesty, but we want to seek Jesus. Having dinner with Jesus changed Zacchaeus' life for good. The Bible tells us he welcomed Christ gladly and that he was never the same again! Are we still the same?

Does spending time in the Bible and having a relationship with Jesus change us?

July 13

In yesterday's account of the dishonest tax collector, we saw that Zacchaeus was a seeker after the truth. Ironically, the meaning of the Hebrew name "Zacchaeus" can be loosely translated to mean "innocent" or "pure." To the outside community, Zacchaeus was anything but those things! He stole their money regularly, for Pete's sake!

ADORATION/EXPLANATION
The beauty of this account is the fact that Jesus, who should have been unaware of Zacchaeus' whereabouts, stopped to look up and tell him to come down! Isn't that the awesome nature of the God that we serve? Did he see into Zach's heart? Could Jesus have known that his name meant pure? Did Jesus know the potential of what a changed Zacchaeus could accomplish? I believe so! And even though there were grumblers and naysayers (how could Christ eat a meal with *him*, after all!), Zacchaeus didn't care in the least.

When Jesus reached the spot, he looked up and said to him, "Zacchaeus, come down immediately. I must stay at your house today." All the people saw this and began to mutter, "He has gone to be the guest of a 'sinner.'" But Zacchaeus stood up and said to the Lord, "Look, Lord! Here and now I give half of my possessions to the poor, and if I have cheated anybody out of anything, I will pay back four times the amount." Jesus said to him, "Today salvation has come to this house, because this man, too, is a son of Abraham. For the Son of Man came to seek and to save what was lost." Luke 19:5, 7-9 (NIV)

WORSHIP/OBEDIENCE
This account does not tell us anything about the conversation that went on at dinner between Jesus and Zacchaeus. Don't you wish you could have been a fly on the wall? Something happened that changed him and caused repentance immediately, right in front of a crowd of people. Zacchaeus must have felt Christ looking directly into his dishonest heart and loving him anyway. Our Savior does this for us and in spite of us! What can that concept cause you to change today?

July 14

If you ever feel small like Zacchaeus, trapped like the Israelites with the Red Sea in front of you, too weak like Gideon, threatened like Daniel in the lion's den, afraid like the disciples on the stormy sea, hopeless as you look on to your Promised Land with nothing but negativity and doubt ringing in your ears, praise God anyway! The conditions are always ideal for that!

ADORATION/EXPLANATION

"Conditions are ideal? Are you kidding me?" Nope. Start praising God because the situation is ideal for a miracle. Yes, a miracle! So many folks complain that God never does miracles anymore and they wish that they could see just one. Well, whenever a situation seems overwhelming and hopeless and your faith in God carries you through, you've seen a miracle.

Look to the Lord and his strength; seek his face always. Remember the wonders he has done, his miracles, and the judgments he pronounced, 1 Chronicles 16:11-12 (NIV)

When the Sabbath came, he began to teach in the synagogue, and many who heard him were amazed. "Where did this man get these things?" they asked. "What's this wisdom that has been given him that he even does miracles!" Mark 6:2 (NIV)

"Believe me when I say that I am in the Father and the Father is in me; or at least believe on the evidence of the miracles themselves. John 14:11 (NIV)

God did extraordinary miracles through Paul, Acts 19:11 (NIV)

WORSHIP/OBEDIENCE

We are alive and well today and must learn to say, "Thank you Lord, for the blessing of life."

Conditions are ideal today to observe a miracle. Look!

For some people, their religion is all business. Have you ever met anyone like this? They are serious, prim, proper, detailed, theologically spoken, and they sometimes give off the air that it is absolutely unattainable. Not available for the common folk… loftier than us, somehow? My faith and belief are different. It's not all business—it's personal!

ADORATION/EXPLANATION

When God sent Jesus down to earth to be the sacrifice for our sins, He never gave us the impression that salvation was unattainable. Jesus never displayed such pious, prim, or proper behavior that people felt shunned or excluded. As a matter of fact, He was just the opposite. People like tax collectors, lepers, and even prostitutes flocked to His company.

We put no stumbling block in anyone's path, so that our ministry will not be discredited. Rather, as servants of God we commend ourselves in every way: in great endurance; in troubles, hardships and distresses; in beatings, imprisonments and riots; in hard work, sleepless nights and hunger; in purity, understanding, patience and kindness; in the Holy Spirit and in sincere love; in truthful speech and in the power of God; 2 Corinthians 6:3-7a (TLB)

Pray for us. We are sure that we have a clear conscience and desire to live honorably in every way. Hebrews 13:18 (TLB)

WORSHIP/OBEDIENCE

Was Jesus all business? Yes! But it was the Father's business and He added the personal touch. God will take care of the business in our lives, but He desires us to make it personal. God has given some obvious advice…any questions?

Our way of worshipping and obeying His Word will be manifested
in how we relate and live our faith before others.

July 16

Did you know that most predatory animals circle their prey before attacking? They do not rush right in, but circle for a while, looking for a vulnerable moment. A shark circles and observes before it attacks, the hyenas on the plains circle a lone gazelle, and a lioness carefully approaches the zebra that it plans to separate from the herd. This slow approach is done to make sure the predator has the advantage. They wait, unseen by their prey, until the moment is just right for their attack. Danger is not obviously sensed.

ADORATION/EXPLANATION
Just like predatory animals, Satan is alive and well on planet Earth. The Bible warns us that he circles about like a lion looking for whom he can devour. This is not a scary, kid's ghost story scenario; this is the true nature of the one who does not want us to have a victoriously abundant, joyful life for Christ. Beware of the circling predator!

Yet I am not surprised! Satan can change himself into an angel of light, so is it no wonder his servants can do it too, and seem like godly ministers. In the end they will get every bit of punishment their wicked deeds deserve. 2 Corinthians 11:14-15 (NIV)

Be careful—watch out for attacks from Satan, your great enemy. He prowls around like a hungry, roaring lion, looking for some victim to tear apart. Stand firm when he attacks. Trust the Lord; and remember that other Christians all around the world are going through these sufferings too. 1 Peter 5:8-9 (NIV)

So give yourselves humbly to God. Resist the devil and he will flee from you. James 4:7 (NIV)

WORSHIP/OBEDIENCE
Our obvious act of obedience to God is to walk in awareness today and to be aware of the enemy's circling. Temptations toward addictions, unfaithfulness, lying, gossiping, meanness, frustration, depression, and anything that distracts us from a godly walk can be the circling of Satan.

Consciously be aware of "bad company," wrong acquaintances, or temptingly influential people that come into our life to pull us from our obedience to God. Beware of the circling!

Once we realize that our spiritual battle is against Satan, we can then live with authority over his temptations to do wrong. The Bible constantly reminds us that he is on the attack, but it also proclaims that he has no authority over us. Satan is counting on the fact that we are not reading the Bible and living daily by God's word. He hopes that we are ignorant.

ADORATION/EXPLANATION

We have power for living each and every day in victory. What do I mean by victory? Are we in some sort of fight? Yes! Our fight is against the sins and issues that may creep stealthily into our daily path if we are not vigilant. Satan loves to look for any chance to get us off track from listening to God. He wants us to remain ignorant of God's promises and awesome plans for our lives. But faith is our victory!

Run from anything that gives you evil thoughts that young men often have, but stay close to anything that makes you want to do right. Have faith and love, and enjoy the companionship of those who love the Lord and have pure hearts. Again I say, don't get involved in foolish arguments which only upset people and make them angry.

Be humble when you are trying to teach those who are mixed up concerning the truth. For if you talk meekly and courteously to them they are more likely, with God's help, to turn away from their wrong ideas and believe what is true. Then they will come to their senses and escape Satan's trap of slavery to sin which he uses to catch them whenever he likes, and then they can begin doing the will of God. 2 Timothy 2:22-23, 25-26 (TLB)

WORSHIP/OBEDIENCE

Obviously God is warning us to not remain naïve. We cannot stay naïve to the fact that Satan wants us to fail and will try to lure us from God's Word; or naïve to the fact that through our faith and trust in our Savior, we can have victory in every aspect of our lives. Today I will become a vigilante!

Wake up, look around, and stay vigilant!

What is the difference between an acquaintance and a companion? If you could go on a vacation to some wonderful place, would you take an acquaintance or choose to travel with a trusted companion? Would you consider yourself a good traveling companion and friend to others?

ADORATION/EXPLANATION

The beauty of our wonderful God is that He promises to never leave or forsake us and that is such a comforting promise to rely on! God, in His infinite care, also allows us to have earthly companions and friends. He knows that we need these relationships if we are to make it through life. Are you blessed with a companion or two? Be thankful!

Two can accomplish more than twice as much as one, for the results can be much better. If one falls, the other pulls him up; but if a man falls when he is alone, he's in trouble. Also on a cold night, two under the same blanket gain warmth from each other, but how can one be warm alone? And one standing alone can be attacked and defeated, but two can stand back-to-back and conquer; three is even better, for a triple-braided cord is not easily broken. Ecclesiastes 4:9-11 (TLB)

A true friend is always loyal, and a brother is born to help in time of need. Proverbs 17:17 (TLB)

There are "friends" who pretend to be friends, but there is a friend who sticks closer than a brother. Proverbs 18:24 (NIV)

WORSHIP/OBEDIENCE

Would you consider yourself a good companion to others? Can people count on you? Are you loyal and true to your word? Our worship to God can be played out in the way that we treat people. God calls us to have earthly friends and to stick close to them. We are to build them up and they are also to encourage us in our daily walk.

What companion will you see today? Smile and be thankful!

Has anyone ever told you to act your age? If I did something ridiculous or foolish, my parents would say this to me. When we were kids, there was a saying, "Act your age, not your shoe size!" As young teenage girls, we would yell this to the supposedly more immature teenage boys who followed us.

ADORATION/EXPLANATION
When it comes to our relationship with God, acting our age can sometimes be truly overrated. We assume that maturity means being pious, stodgy, and stoic about our beliefs. I want to live in such awe of my creator that I just cannot help but act like my shoe size, like a little kid filled with joy at a party, on Christmas morning, or at an all-you-can-eat ice cream buffet!

Once when some mothers were bringing their children to Jesus to bless them, the disciples shooed them away, telling them not to bother him. But when Jesus saw what was happening he was very much displeased with his disciples and said to them, "Let the children come to me, for the Kingdom of God belongs to such as they. Don't send them away! I tell you as seriously as I know how that anyone who refuses to come to God as a little child will never be allowed into his Kingdom." Then he took the children into his arms and placed his hands on their heads and he blessed them. Mark 10:13-16 (TLB)

Then he was filled with the joy of the Holy Spirit and said, "I praise you, O Father, Lord of heaven and earth, for hiding these things from the intellectuals and worldly wise and for revealing them to those who are as trusting as little children. Yes, thank you, Father, for that is the way you wanted it." Luke 10:21 (TLB)

WORSHIP/OBEDIENCE
Acting our age can sometimes be truly overrated! Today, look around through child-like eyes and see the beauty of God. We cannot afford to take God for granted. Do not act your age!

Help me to remember the joy of my youth and to keep that zeal and excitement for Your Word. Remind me today to appreciate Your love, Your creation, Your provisions, and Your plans for my life.

Stress prevention involves any activity that you love that tends to produce in you a calmer and more accepting attitude toward life. People who are able to find ways to do this are almost always able to bring a sense of peace into their relationships. They become more patient, kind, caring, and generous. Stress prevention makes people less critical, less defensive, jealous, judgmental, and much easier to be around.

ADORATION/EXPLANATION

Many folks think, "I don't have time to rest, practice yoga, meditate, go to church, get a massage, exercise or read." But if you get right down to it, God wants us to put it the other way around. You don't have time NOT to do one or more of these stress-relieving activities. God does not want us to be stubborn, tense, reactive, and stressed to the point of being useless to live for Him!

Yet the Lord pleads with you still: Ask where the good road is, the godly paths you used to walk in, in the days of long ago. Travel there, and you will find rest for your souls. But you reply, "No, that is not the road we want!" Jeremiah 6:16 (TLB)

"Come to me and I will give you rest—all of you who work so hard beneath a heavy yoke. Wear my yoke—for it fits perfectly—and let me teach you; for I am gentle and humble, and you shall find rest for your souls; for I give you only light burdens." Matthew 11:28-30 (TLB)

Give your burdens to the Lord. He will carry them. He will not permit the godly to slip or fall. Psalm 55:22 (TLB)

WORSHIP/OBEDIENCE

God has given us the mind to explore and investigate many stress-prevention options. One of the best activities is to make quiet time alone to read and think upon His words in the Bible. Reading this devotional book is a start to focusing your mind on Him and away from the minor things in life that cause tension.

Repeat His words out loud and just breathe!

The people of Israel often experienced defeat in the Old Testament because they sometimes refused to calm themselves in the presence of God and trust Him. Even though they had witnessed His mighty power to save, they sunk back into their old habits of doubting when the times got tough. Yikes…we seem to do the very same thing.

ADORATION/EXPLANATION

We should have such strong adoration for God because of His patience and love for us. He gives new opportunities to obey Him today even if we screwed up yesterday. His mercies are new every morning. We need to realize that He desires our obedience over sacrifices, money, or rituals.

The Lord of Hosts, the God of Israel says, Away with your offerings and sacrifices! It wasn't offerings and sacrifices I wanted from your fathers when I led them out of Egypt. That was not the point of my command. But what I told them was: Obey me and I will be your God and you shall be my people; only do as I say and all shall be well! But they wouldn't listen; they kept on doing whatever they wanted to, following their own stubborn, evil thoughts. They went backward instead of forward. Jeremiah 7:21-24 (TLB)

How happy I am to find some of your children here, and to see that they are living as they should, following the Truth, obeying God's command. 2 John 4 (TLB)

Samuel replied, "Has the Lord as much pleasure in your burnt offerings and sacrifices as in your obedience? Obedience is far better than sacrifice. He is much more interested in your listening to him than in your offering the fat of rams to him." 1 Samuel 15:22 (TLB)

WORSHIP/OBEDIENCE

Today I have a wonderful, new chance to live correctly. I will replace all of the doubts and fears from yesterday with a purpose driven heart. Yesterday is over!

Lord, help me calm myself in your presence today and trust you! Give me the strength not to sink back into old habits. When the going gets tough, I will still obey!

Scripture is filled with promises and glimpses of our eternal home, dwelling place, and role in eternity. In Jesus' day, the expectant early Christians were thrilled with the hope that one day God would come back and rule the earth. The question that puzzles many believers is whether the old earth as we know it will end after Christ returns or a thousand years later as talked about in the end of the Bible? It can get confusing…

ADORATION/EXPLANATION

Regardless of what thought you subscribe to, the fact of a life in heaven is the believer's inheritance. Salvation through Jesus Christ assures us of a home in heaven that can never rust, rot, or be destroyed! What a comforting future. Even if I am scared of death, I know that I can live secure in the hope and promise of an imperishable home someday with God.

And God has reserved for his children the priceless gift of eternal life; it is kept in heaven for you, pure and undefiled, beyond the reach of change and decay. And God, in his mighty power, will make sure that you get there safely to receive it, because you are trusting him. It will be yours in that coming last day for all to see. So be truly glad! There is wonderful joy ahead, even though the going is rough for a while down here. 1 Peter 1:4-6 (TLB)

Dear brothers, you are only visitors here. Since your real home is in heaven I beg you to keep away from the evil pleasures of this world; they are not for you, for they fight against your very souls. 1 Peter 2:11 (TLB)

But do not let this one fact escape your notice, beloved, that with the Lord one day is like a thousand years, and a thousand years like one day. 2 Peter 3:8 (NASB)

WORSHIP/OBEDIENCE

Lord, please give me the confidence to live one day at a time without fear of the future. Help me to thrive with a purpose of living and glorifying you with my actions and attitudes.

I do not know when my life here on earth will end but I do know that you have a place reserved for me in heaven. Keep the light on!

When I suffer the consequences of wrong behavior or decisions, I have two choices of how I react. I can get angry, upset, and yell that life is unfair (like Charlie Brown), or I can realize that God is faithful to discipline and chastise us in order to teach us a lesson. I can look dumbfounded and confused at the results of my choices, or I can choose to view them as a valuable life lesson that I do not want to repeat.

ADORATION/EXPLANATION
Our wonderfully sovereign God may chastise us, but He is also generous in compassion and comfort when we do foul up. He wants us to learn and learn well under His caring, loving hand.

Obey God because you are his children; don't slip back into your old ways—doing evil because you knew no better. But be holy now in everything you do, just as the Lord is holy, who invited you to be his child. 1 Peter 1:14-17 (TLB)

And have you quite forgotten the encouraging words God spoke to you, his child? He said, "My son, don't be angry when the Lord punishes you. Don't be discouraged when he has to show you where you are wrong. For when he punishes you, it proves that he loves you. When he whips you it proves you are really his child."

Our earthly fathers trained us for a few brief years, doing the best for us that they knew how, but God's correction is always right and for our best good, that we may share his holiness. Being punished isn't enjoyable while it is happening—it hurts! But afterwards we can see the result, a quiet growth in grace and character. Hebrews 12:5-6, 10-11 T(LB)

WORSHIP/OBEDIENCE
Today, let's determine to view punishment, chastisement, or consequences from God as a wonderful learning opportunity. If we are rebelling in any way against God, we can know that His goal is to curb our actions and not to condemn us.

We should not stay focused on the licking we're getting,
but instead on the lesson we're learning.

It is over ninety degrees outside today. On this typical hot July afternoon, the air is steamy and scorching. When it's this warm, even the sprinklers cannot seem to keep the grass green or the flowers perky. Working in my beloved vegetable garden has even become a sweaty chore, and I find myself longing to take a cool, refreshing plunge into my swimming pool.

ADORATION/EXPLANATION

There is a story in the Old Testament book of Daniel about three men who chose to be thrown into a fiery, roaring furnace instead of bowing down to other gods and idols. Their allegiance and love for the one true God of Israel gave them the courage to choose this hot, burning punishment with no sign of escape. They trusted God when there was no refreshing pool in sight.

"When the band strikes up, you are to fall flat on the ground to worship King Nebuchadnezzar's golden statue; anyone who refuses to obey will immediately be thrown into a flaming furnace."

"Is it true, O Shadrach, Meshach, and Abednego," he asked, "that you are refusing to serve my gods or to worship the golden statue I set up? I'll give you one more chance. When the music plays, if you fall down and worship the statue, all will be well. But if you refuse, you will be thrown into a flaming furnace within the hour. And what god can deliver you out of my hands then?" Shadrach, Meshach, and Abednego replied, "O Nebuchadnezzar, we are not worried about what will happen to us. If we are thrown into the flaming furnace, our God is able to deliver us; and he will deliver us out of your hand, Your Majesty. But if he doesn't, please understand, sir, that even then we will never under any circumstance serve your gods or worship the golden statue you have erected." Daniel 3:5-6, 14-18 (TLB)

WORSHIP/OBEDIENCE

Wow, talk about obedience unto death! These three young men knew that God could deliver them, but they also knew that He might choose not to. They confidently chose obedience, even though the outcome seemed like a fiery, painful death. I am not sure that I could do that.

Thank you, Lord, that I do not have to make a choice between worshipping you or a fiery furnace. Teach me to be brave and courageous to take a stand for you during my day today, no matter what the outcome may be.

July 25

Yesterday we read about the three men who were faced with the choice of worshipping idols or being thrown into a hot furnace for punishment. The weather outside reminded me of this fiery story. The temperature is well into the nineties and respite from the heat is sought by many. A swim in the ocean, pool, lake, or river is the way many folks choose to cool down when they're overheated, but what if there was no way of cooling down, no hope for a reprieve from the heat?

ADORATION/EXPLANATION

I am so amazed that these men knew what their final destination would be if they disobeyed the King, yet they remained true to God. They knew about the furnace and they knew that there would be no way of cooling down once they were thrown inside. Death would result. Yet they remained true!

Then Nebuchadnezzar was filled with fury and his face became dark with anger at Shadrach, Meshach, and Abednego. He commanded that the furnace be heated up seven times hotter than usual, and called for some of the strongest men of his army to bind Shadrach, Meshach, and Abednego, and throw them into the fire. So they bound them tight with ropes and threw them into the furnace, fully clothed.

But suddenly, as he was watching, Nebuchadnezzar jumped up in amazement and exclaimed to his advisors, "Didn't we throw three men into the furnace?" "Yes," they said, "we did indeed, Your Majesty." "Well, look!" Nebuchadnezzar shouted. "I see four men, unbound, walking around in the fire, and they aren't even hurt by the flames! And the fourth looks like a god!" Then Nebuchadnezzar came as close as he could go to the open door of the flaming furnace and yelled: "Shadrach, Meshach, and Abednego, servants of the Most High God! Come out! Come here!" So they stepped out of the fire. Daniel 3:19-21, 24-26 (TLB)

WORSHIP/OBEDIENCE

Sometimes, we just want to step out of the fires of life, don't we? We want to walk out unscathed from experiences that are hard, yet we do not always want to obey God without question. We're not sure that we want to be put to the test and we want the assurance that God will save us no matter what! But God tells us differently in the Bible. Ours must be a life lived by faith, not by sight, and worship and obedience are the keys!

Step into the flames, and trust that there will always be the fourth man there with you.

209

One of the reasons that we need to come through fires and trials is because it builds into our testimony of genuine belief in Christ. How we handle everyday fires, whether they are insignificant or monumental, will speak volumes of our trust in God. We are lights for Christ. Even if we escape the fiery furnace, we must never let the fire for Christ go out in our hearts!

ADORATION/EXPLANATION

I know that God was the fourth man in the fire with Shadrach, Meshach, and Abednego in the story from the Old Testament. Their trust in the face of a dire situation spoke volumes to all that observed. I want to be like that!

Then the princes, governors, captains, and counselors crowded around them and saw that the fire hadn't touched them—not a hair of their heads was singed; their coats were unscorched, and they didn't even smell of smoke! Then Nebuchadnezzar said, "Blessed be the God of Shadrach, Meshach, and Abednego, for he sent his angel to deliver his trusting servants when they defied the king's commandment, and were willing to die rather than serve or worship any god except their own. Daniel 3:27-28 (TLB)

Don't let anyone think little of you because you are young. Be their ideal; let them follow the way you teach and live; be a pattern for them in your love, your faith, and your clean thoughts. 1Timothy 4:12 (TLB)

Always be joyful. Always keep on praying. No matter what happens, always be thankful, for this is God's will for you who belong to Christ Jesus. Do not smother the Holy Spirit. 1Thessalonians 5:16-19 (TLB)

WORSHIP/OBEDIENCE

Obviously, neither you nor I will probably ever be thrown into a fiery furnace for our beliefs, but our behavior in the course of our daily schedule can carry a positive or negative impact for God. Is the fire for Christ still alive in our hearts when we're stressed, grouchy, irritable, moody, tired, or working?

Always be joyful. Always keep on praying. Do not smother the Holy Spirit!

It has been said that God places angels around us to accomplish His holy enterprises. Satan is alive and well on earth also, but angels have a much more important place in the Bible than the devil and his demons. An angel is a spiritual being created by God to further the purpose of Christ and the church.

ADORATION/EXPLANATION
We are not alone in this world! God's Holy Spirit has been given to empower and guide us. In addition, in almost three hundred places, the Bible teaches us that God has countless angels at His command. God has allowed these angels as secret agents to aid us in our struggles in this world. Wow!

How then can evil overtake me or any plague come near? For he orders his angels to protect you wherever you go. They will steady you with their hands to keep you from stumbling against the rocks on the trail. Psalm 91:10-12 (TLB)

God speaks of his angels as messengers swift as the wind and as servants made of flaming fire; but of his Son he says, "Your kingdom, O god, will last forever and ever; its commands are always just and right.

No, for the angels are only spirit-messengers sent out to help and care for those who are to receive his salvation. Hebrews 1:7-8, 14 (TLB)

"My God has sent his angel," he said, "to shut the lions' mouths so that they can't touch me; for I am innocent before God, nor, sir, have I wronged you." Daniel 6:22 (TLB)

WORSHIP/OBEDIENCE
Isn't that so cool? God has placed His own secret agents, or "James Bond" type of creatures around us to help with the impossible missions here on earth! We have our very own posse! What a wonderful feeling to know that we are never alone!

Our world and media is being increasingly bombarded with the existence of the occult and demonic powers. People pay attention to dramatic headlines and they flock to scary, satanic movies. The Bible tells us that through demonic influences, Satan will try to sway many people away from a life of faith in Christ. Shouldn't we as believers become more conscious of the awesome angelic powers who associate with God Himself and do His works on our behalf?

ADORATION/EXPLANATION

We must never fail to sense the operation of the angelic army. God has set them about His business and they are vigorous in delivering us in our time of need. When God sends them to do His work, they will not fail!

"In the same way there is joy in the presence of the angels of God when one sinner repents." Luke 15:10 (TLB)

Bless the Lord, you mighty angels of his who carry out his orders, listening for each of his commands. Yes, bless the Lord, you armies of his angels who serve him constantly. Psalm 103:20-21 (TLB)

"Beware that you don't look down upon a single one of these little children. For I tell you that in heaven their angels have constant access to my Father." Matthew 18:10 (TLB)

Continue to love each other with true brotherly love. Don't forget to be kind to strangers, for some who have done this have entertained angels without realizing it! Hebrews 13:1-2 (TLB)

WORSHIP/OBEDIENCE

If you are a believer, not only do you have the Holy Spirit living inside you, but expect powerful angels to accompany you in your life experiences. What a wonderful Savior we serve. He is the God of angel armies!

We can go about our business, looking for and obeying God's direction in every stop that we may make, peacefully knowing that our security staff is standing ready.

During this month, two dear Christian servants and friends passed away. I guess this is par for the course of life as we get older, but it is still a sobering fact each time it happens. Death is eminent! The beautiful thing about both of these deaths is that each person left a wonderful legacy of love and service for God. They left an awesome example of how to live life, love others, and love God, more extensive than any poster board or picture displays ever could. They left relationships!

ADORATION/EXPLANATION

The God that we adore has given us a wonderful life here on earth. The Bible does warn us that our days are fleeting, so we need to make the most of our relationships with others. What will we leave behind?

So get rid of all that is wrong in your life, both inside and outside, and humbly be glad for the wonderful message we have received, for it is able to save our souls as it takes hold of our hearts. And remember, it is a message to obey, not just to listen to. So don't fool yourselves.

Anyone who says he is a Christian but doesn't control his sharp tongue is just fooling himself, and his religion isn't worth much. James 1:21-22, 26 (TLB)

Dear brothers, what's the use of saying that you have faith and are Christians if you aren't proving it by helping others? Will that kind of faith save anyone? If you have a friend who is in need of food and clothing, and you say to him, "Well, good-bye and God bless you; stay warm and eat hearty," and then don't give him clothes or food, what good does that do? So you see, it isn't good enough just to have faith. You must also do good to prove that you have it. Faith that doesn't show itself by good works is no faith at all—it is dead and useless. James 2:14-17 (TLB)

WORSHIP/OBEDIENCE

Dear Lord, when I am saddened at the passing of dear friends, continually use this to teach me to realize that I need to leave a legacy of my own. I want to leave a legacy for you! My obvious act of worship for you today will be in making my faith a living, breathing advertisement for all to see. I do not want to have a dead and useless faith. Amen.

July 30

"Watch where you're going!" "Look up and pay attention!" These are things that our parents told us, that I told my own children, and I am sure things that they'll say to their children as well. As Christians, we need to look straight ahead and not become distracted by life. We cannot look backwards because we are not going in that direction. We might trip!

ADORATION/EXPLANATION

Remembering some mistakes in order to learn a lesson is a good thing. Satan, however, would love us to get so obsessed with the past that we refuse to move ahead. We cannot seem to forget and are not living freely now.

For I am convinced that nothing can ever separate us from his love. Death can't, and life can't. The angels won't, and all the powers of hell itself cannot keep God's love away. Our fears for today, our worries about tomorrow, or where we are—high above the sky, or in the deepest ocean—nothing will ever be able to separate us from the love of God demonstrated by our Lord Jesus Christ when he died for us. Romans 8:38-39 (TLB)

For God is not unfair. How can he forget your hard work for him, or forget the way you used to show your love for him—and still do—by helping his children? Hebrews 6:10 (TLB)

No, dear brothers, I am still not all I should be but I am bringing all my energies to bear on this one thing: Forgetting the past and looking forward to what lies ahead, Philippians 3:13 (TLB)

WORSHIP/OBEDIENCE

Do not get caught in staring, wondering, dwelling, or focusing backwards. You are NOT going in that direction. Onward Christian soldier!

Watch where you are going! Look up and pay attention! Lean into the wind and keep going, day by day by day.

July 30

"Watch where you're going!" "Look up and pay attention!" These are things that our parents told us, that I told my own children, and I am sure things that they'll say to their children as well. As Christians, we need to look straight ahead and not become distracted by life. We cannot look backwards because we are not going in that direction. We might trip!

ADORATION/EXPLANATION

Remembering some mistakes in order to learn a lesson is a good thing. Satan, however, would love us to get so obsessed with the past that we refuse to move ahead. We cannot seem to forget and are not living freely now.

For I am convinced that nothing can ever separate us from his love. Death can't, and life can't. The angels won't, and all the powers of hell itself cannot keep God's love away. Our fears for today, our worries about tomorrow, or where we are—high above the sky, or in the deepest ocean—nothing will ever be able to separate us from the love of God demonstrated by our Lord Jesus Christ when he died for us. Romans 8:38-39 (TLB)

For God is not unfair. How can he forget your hard work for him, or forget the way you used to show your love for him—and still do—by helping his children? Hebrews 6:10 (TLB)

No, dear brothers, I am still not all I should be but I am bringing all my energies to bear on this one thing: Forgetting the past and looking forward to what lies ahead, Philippians 3:13 (TLB)

WORSHIP/OBEDIENCE

Do not get caught in staring, wondering, dwelling, or focusing backwards. You are NOT going in that direction. Onward Christian soldier!

Watch where you are going! Look up and pay attention! Lean into the wind and keep going, day by day by day.

You are the greatest source of inspiration to your own life! I don't mean this to sound self-centered, but instead draw attention to the importance of the words that we speak to ourselves. Whether you mutter them under your breath, or proclaim them out loud, what you speak to yourself, you believe! It doesn't matter what anyone else says to you or about you, if you do not choose to believe it there is no benefit. How do you talk to yourself?

ADORATION/EXPLANATION
When we read the Bible, we should get in the habit of reading out loud to ourselves. I may read a scripture once in my head and then read it again out loud, with pauses, to really grasp what God is saying to me. I speak God's truths to myself for encouragement, for peace, and for comfort. It doesn't matter what the world is telling me.

Create in me a new, clean heart, O God, filled with clean thoughts and right desires. Restore to me again the joy of your salvation, and make me willing to obey you. Psalm 51:10, 12 (TLB)

In the crowd was a woman who had been sick for twelve years with a hemorrhage.

She had heard all about the wonderful miracles Jesus did, and that is why she came up behind him through the crowd and touched his clothes. For she thought to herself, "If I can just touch his clothing, I will be healed." And sure enough, as soon as she had touched him, the bleeding stopped and she knew she was well! Mark 5:25, 27-29 (TLB)

And I will tell everyone how great and good you are; I will praise you all day long. Psalm 35:28 (TLB)

WORSHIP/OBEDIENCE
The woman with the hemorrhage reminded herself of the promises and hope in Jesus. In fact, she inspired herself so much that she grew courageous enough to push through the crowd and touch Jesus' garment! We need to do that daily as well. We must meditate on God's awesome power and encouragement for our everyday lives.

Read out loud. Proclaim His truths out loud. Praise Him out loud.
This is one time that talking to yourself can be a good thing!

August 1

Being a single mother is tough. If you are there by divorce, death, or from never settling down, it is still a very rough and lonely position to be in. Most single moms also have to work, which in itself can be very stressful. Dinner time is when a dad is supposed to appear and help give the mother a few moments of peace so she can cook. The father can listen to the whining, hassles, and stories from the kids, or bring them outside to run around and toss the ball. Sounds great, huh?

ADORATION/EXPLANATION

Most single mothers have no one coming around while they are cooking. No one is helping to referee fights, discipline, bathe, or help put the kids to bed. The only father that will appear in times of need is our Heavenly Father. If you are a single mom, hang in there. Cry out to God, Abba Father! Ask God to restore your joy in life. He can!

With this news bring cheer to all discouraged ones. Encourage those who are afraid. Tell them, "Be strong, fear not, for your God is coming to destroy your enemies. He is coming to save you."

These, the ransomed of the Lord, will go home along that road to Zion, singing the songs of everlasting joy. For them all sorrow and all sighing will be gone forever; only joy and gladness will be there. Isaiah 35:3-4, 10 (TLB)

Oh, praise the Lord, for he has listened to my pleadings! He is my strength, my shield from every danger. I trusted in him, and he helped me. Joy rises in my heart until I burst out in songs of praise to him. Psalm 28:6-7 (TLB)

And so we should not be like cringing, fearful slaves, but we should behave like God's very own children, adopted into the bosom of his family, and calling to him, "Father, Father." Romans 8:15 (TLB)

WORSHIP/OBEDIENCE

The Bible tells us to cry out to God. Our simple act of obedience to Him is to do just that. Whether you are a single person or not, when everyday life gets overwhelming, call out, "Father, Father!" He hears.

When a young man or woman is physically fit or strong, they are often described as "able-bodied." Basically, that means they seem to have the ability to carry out a task or job that requires some labor or strength. So, are you an able-bodied faithful follower?

ADORATION/EXPLANATION

The Bible describes God as being able. Able to do, able to be, and able to save!

Our awesome love for our Lord should drive us to pursue an able-bodied life as a believer. We need to read, study, and meditate on His precepts to strengthen our feeble minds and bodies. If God is able, and He lives inside of us, then I can be able also!

Now glory be to God who by his mighty power at work within us is able to do far more than we would ever dare to ask or even dream of—infinitely beyond our highest prayers, desires, thoughts or hopes. Ephesians 3:20 (TLB)

But Jesus lives forever and continues to be a Priest so that no one else is needed. He is able to save completely all who come to God through him. Since he will live forever, he will always be there to remind God that he has paid for their sins with his blood. Hebrews 7:24-25 (TLB)

And he is able to keep you from slipping and falling away, and to bring you, sinless and perfect, into his glorious presence with mighty shouts of everlasting joy. Amen. Jude 1:25 (TLB)

WORSHIP/OBEDIENCE

Wow! We know we serve a God who is able to carry us through this life. Today, we have the strength and ability to carry on through work, kids, practice, car-pool, marriage, school and anything else that comes up. Let's look for opportunities to obey His word.

Today we can commit to being a more able-bodied, faithful follower of Christ.

Many people are after a cultural experience. They are convinced that this thing called "culture" will enhance their life and their intellect. They go to museums, read certain books, peruse fine art and sculpture galleries, and view foreign movies. There is a place in Lenox, Massachusetts called Seiji Ozawa Hall, and it is where the Boston Symphony Orchestra plays for the summer. Folks can relax and listen to the orchestral tunes drift out under the pines. If you really want a sense of culture, this is one place that you must visit.

ADORATION/EXPLANATION

Our world defines culture as "becoming enlightened by aesthetic training and activities." We go to all these venues of culture because we believe that they will somehow benefit us, and they usually do! But imagine if we placed just as much effort or importance on becoming enlightened with God's Word?

All scripture is inspired by God and profitable to teaching, for reproof, for correction, for training in righteousness; that the man of God may be adequate, equipped for every good work. 2 Timothy 3:16 (NASB)

Be diligent to present yourself approved to God as a workman who does not need to be ashamed, handling accurately the word of truth. 2 Timothy 2:15 (NASB)

I pray that the eyes of your heart may be enlightened, so that you may know what is the hope of His calling, what are the riches of the glory of His inheritance in the saints, Ephesians 1:18 (NASB)

As a result, we are no longer to be children, tossed here and there by waves, and carried about by every wind of doctrine, Ephesians 4:14a (NASB)

WORSHIP/OBEDIENCE

Dear Lord, thank you for all the beautiful, cultural things that you have created. Thank you for eyes to see and ears to hear the lovely objects and music of this earth.

Create in me the same desire to understand and worship You!

Do you ever overanalyze things, events, or people, replaying these things over and over and over again in your mind until it starts to drive you just a little crazy? This can be especially true if it is people that you are trying to understand. A spouse, a friend, relatives and especially in-laws can all fall prey? Do you constantly see their flaws or imagine their motives? Have you ever actually seen a motive?

ADORATION/EXPLANATION

If you look carefully enough, you're guaranteed to see that others are full of flaws. The problem with this tendency is that it virtually promises that your relationships will suffer. Our awesome God does not look at us in this way. Imagine if He only ever focused on our shortcomings? Yikes!

You were dead in sins, and your sinful desires were not yet cut away. Then he gave you a share in the very life of Christ, for he forgave all of your sins, and blotted out the charges proved against you, the list of his commandments which you had not obeyed. He took this list of sins and destroyed it by nailing it to Christ's cross. Colossians 2:13-14 (TLB)

Be gentle and ready to forgive; never hold grudges. Remember, the Lord forgave you, so you must forgive others. Colossians 3:13 (TLB)

He has removed our sins as far away from us as the east is from the west. Psalm 103:12 (TLB)

WORSHIP/OBEDIENCE

The next time you find yourself overanalyzing others, see if you can remember to stop and ask yourself this question: Is this really that big of a flaw or am I just caught up in my thinking? Does Christ focus on our flaws or does He see the best in us? Didn't He say as far as the east is from the west? That's pretty far!

One of the practices that can be very beneficial for our heart, soul, and mind is the confessing of our guilty habits and faults to someone. Not just anyone, but usually a trusted friend can help soothe our minds if something is weighing heavy upon them. Not only do we need people like that around us, but we need to BE a person like that.

ADORATION/EXPLANATION

The Bible is packed full of places that tell us to confess and pray with each other. God should be our first and foremost stop on the confession train, but other godly friends and family can help us not repeat mistakes, especially someone older and wiser. God in His infinite mercy provides us with relationships with others that will benefit us daily.

Admit your faults to one another and pray for each other so that you may be healed. The earnest prayer of a righteous man has great power and wonderful results.

Dear brothers, if anyone has slipped away from God and no longer trusts the Lord, and someone helps him understand the Truth again, that person who brings him back to God will have saved a wandering soul from death, bringing about the forgiveness of his many sins. James 5:16, 19 (TLB)

Timely advice is as lovely as golden apples in a silver basket. It is a badge of honor to accept valid criticism.

Putting confidence in an unreliable man is like chewing with a sore tooth, or trying to run on a broken foot. Proverbs 25:11-12, 19 (TLB)

I confess my sins; I am sorry for what I have done. Psalm 38:18 (TLB)

WORSHIP/OBEDIENCE

Obviously we can obey God by confessing our faults to one another. I have found that it is much simpler to quickly admit when I am wrong and then ask others to forgive me—you know, yanking off the Band-Aid, so to speak!

People cannot stay focused on your problems when
you readily admit them and ask for prayer.

During this hot month of August, whether you are poolside, lakeside, or just strolling through a woodland trail, think about what your conversations consist of. Do they mention others? Are they critical or backstabbing? Are they gossipy? Are they full of constant complaints? Are they truths or lies?

ADORATION/EXPLANATION
God wants us to temper and tame our tongue. I have definitely written about it during this year, but it bears repeating. The tongue and the damage it can do are mentioned many times in Scripture so we need to read and study about it again and again. Once is not enough!

I said to myself, I'm going to quit complaining! I'll keep quiet, especially when the ungodly are around me. Psalm 39:1 (TLB)

Anyone who says he is a Christian but doesn't control his sharp tongue is just fooling himself, and his religion isn't worth much. James 1:26 (TLB)

So also the tongue is a small thing, but what enormous damage it can do. A great forest can be set on fire by one tiny spark. And the tongue is a flame of fire. It is full of wickedness, and poisons every part of the body. And the tongue is set on fire by hell itself, and can turn our whole lives into a blazing flame of destruction and disaster. James 3:5-6 (TLB)

WORSHIP/OBEDIENCE
There is a simple way to obey God's word here, and it is obvious. Think before you speak! Is it true? Is it beneficial or gossip? Is it critical of someone? Is it damaging someone's reputation? Are we constantly complaining? We can enjoy summer recreation without the blazing flame of the tongue! Whether at the pool, lake, beach or boat, think before you speak!

August 7

I have always had great relationships with my grandparents and great-grandparents throughout my life. I recognized their potential wisdom and wellspring of good advice for everyday activities of life. One of the things my grandparents enjoyed in the summer was eating watermelon. Something that I took for granted they had learned to savor. Straight from the cooler, a crisp and dripping-down-your chin juicy slice of watermelon beats the scorch of a hot and humid day. It never felt quite like summer until we were spittin' seeds. They taught me simple lessons…and I listened and learned.

ADORATION/EXPLANATION
What does watermelon eating, and seed spitting have to teach us? Was it just a fun memory or a lesson in disguise? The apostle Paul writes to Titus with instructions on how to lead a troubled church in Crete. How we treat our older relatives and friends is a big indicator of our desire to learn. We can avoid trouble by giving correct respect, whether it is while enjoying a cool melon in the summer, just chatting and receiving some sage advice, or studying the Bible. Paul's same advice is available for us today.

Teach the older men to be temperate, worthy of respect, self-controlled, and sound in faith, in love and in endurance. Likewise, teach the older women to be reverent in the way they live, not to be slanderers or addicted to much wine, but to teach what is good. Then they can train the younger women to love their husbands and children, to be self-controlled and pure, to be busy at home, to be kind, and to be subject to their husbands, so that no one will malign the word of God. Similarly, encourage the young men to be self-controlled. In everything set them an example by doing what is good. Titus 2:2-8a (NIV)

Is not wisdom found among the aged? Does not long life bring understanding? Job 12:12 (NIV)

Apply your hearts to instruction and your ears to words of knowledge. Proverbs 23:12 (NIV)

WORSHIP/OBEDIENCE
I do not want my aging life to become wasted time… I want to go beyond the wedge of melon and savor some words of knowledge from my older friends and family. Help me to encourage them as I would want them to encourage me.

My memories…may be lessons in disguise!

Have you ever really wanted to spend time talking and praying to God, but then somehow always manage to put it off? I'll admit it—I have. Before I know it, I'm reading a magazine, running errands, or off to work. Sometimes when I do pray at night, my mind wanders off and I fall asleep! Can you imagine someone talking with you and falling asleep mid-sentence? How would that make you feel?

ADORATION/EXPLANATION

To fix this problem, I decided that I had to learn to multi-task. We women are supposed to be experts at multi-tasking, so why not walk while we pray? I like to try to commit to a forty-five minute to an hour walk each morning or evening for my physical health, so why not incorporate praying for my spiritual health? And if my mind wanders…I let it! I simply invite Jesus to go along for the ride.

We can justify our every deed but God looks at our motives. Proverbs 21:2 (TLB)

Because the Lord is my Shepherd, I have everything I need! Psalm 23:1 (TLB)

The Lord is my light and my salvation; whom shall I fear? Psalm 27:1 (TLB)

I will praise you, Lord, for you have saved me from my enemies. You refuse to let them triumph over me. Psalm 30:1 (TLB)

I will praise the Lord no matter what happens. I will constantly speak of his glories and grace. Psalm 34:1 (TLB)

WORSHIP/OBEDIENCE

Let's face it: God knows what your mind is doing all the time and He's not surprised to see your mind wandering. Ask Him to take charge of your thoughts while you walk and talk.

Remember that you're meeting with Someone who really cares about you.

August 9

Have you ever needed first aid? Maybe not a big medical emergency, but basic first aid to bandage a cut, wrap a sprained ankle, or receive cold water compresses to an over-heated body? Most of us have received first aid and also dispensed it to others at some time in our lives.

ADORATION/EXPLANATION

We should not wait until an emergency before investing in a few first-aid items. Bandages, wraps, salves, and ointments are only a few of these necessities. Likewise, we should not wait to heal ourselves with God's Word until an emergency happens. We need to make time to read and meditate on it daily and receive its wonderful rejuvenating benefits.

What happiness for those whose guilt has been forgiven! What joys when sins are covered over! What relief for those who have confessed their sins and God has cleared their record. There was a time when I wouldn't admit what a sinner I was. But my dishonesty made me miserable and filled my days with frustration. All day and all night your hand was heavy on me. My strength evaporated like water on a sunny day until I finally admitted all my sins to you and stopped trying to hide them. I said to myself, "I will confess them to the Lord." And you forgave me! All my guilt is gone. Psalm 32:1-5 (TLB)

WORSHIP/OBEDIENCE

I want to be rejuvenated!

Lord, please do not let me first suffer physically, mentally, emotionally, or spiritually before I learn the healing value of reading your Word. Help me repair my mind and soul with the encouraging nuggets of truth that come from Scripture. All my guilt is gone. You can set me free! Amen.

Last night, we experienced one of those crazy summer rainstorms. Lightning and loud thunder accompanied by high winds swirled through our area after dinner. Even though the Weather Channel predicted that storms would be moving through, I'm always amazed at how fast a summer weather change can occur. It can be beautiful and sunny one minute, dark and cloudy the next. Needless to say, I was thankful for shelter from the storm!

ADORATION/EXPLANATION

God wants to shelter us from the storms of life. Do you really understand what I just said? God wants to shelter us, but He allows the storms to come. Instead of sitting and wondering why the storm arrived so quickly, we must RUN, into His loving arms and find shelter. Only from here can we watch, learn, and observe what our mighty God can do.

You are my hiding place from every storm of life; you even keep me from getting into trouble! You surround me with songs of victory. I will instruct you (says the Lord) and guide you along the best pathway for your life; I will advise you and watch your progress. Psalm 32:7-8 (TLB)

Then he got into a boat and started across the lake with his disciples. Suddenly a terrible storm came up, with waves higher than the boat. But Jesus was asleep. The disciples went to him and wakened him, shouting, "Lord, save us! We're sinking!" But Jesus answered, "O you men of little faith! Why are you so frightened?" Then he stood up and rebuked the wind and waves, and the storm subsided and all was calm. Matthew 8:23-26 (TLB)

WORSHIP/OBEDIENCE

Here comes a storm! Yes, it may have been bright and sunny a couple of hours ago, but a storm is blowing in. Don't be afraid, but don't stay right out in the middle of it. Run for the shelter of the Most High God. Run to trusted godly companions. Delve into scripture that speaks about storms and what to do when you're caught in one, and earnestly pray for peace and safety. Then you will be able to shout confidently, "Here comes the Son!"

Near my home on the beach is a large red-and-white lighthouse. Did you ever notice that there are not two or three lighthouses in the same location, but there is only a singular structure? One is enough, though! There is one strong, powerful light that casts out many beams in all directions. Often there are reflectors around the light to help its glowing bulb shine out farther. It is a gorgeous sight to observe at night.

ADORATION/EXPLANATION

God placed His light in the world in the form of Jesus. He was the only true light of the world, a city set on a hill, a lighthouse on the shore. Now He calls us to be His reflectors. Our job is to reflect His light to all those around us. How is your reflecting going?

But we Christians have no veil over our faces; we can be mirrors that brightly reflect the glory of the Lord. And as the Spirit of the Lord works within us, we become more and more like him. 2 Corinthians 3:18 (TLB)

For God, who said, "Let there be light in the darkness," has made us understand that it is the brightness of his glory that is seen in the face of Jesus Christ. But this precious treasure—this light and power that now shine within us—is held in a perishable container, that is, in our weak bodies. Everyone can see that the glorious power within must be from God and is not our own. 2Corinthians 4:6-7 (TLB)

Anyone who says he is walking in the light of Christ but dislikes his fellow man, is still in darkness. But whoever loves his fellow man is "walking in the light" and can see his way without stumbling around in darkness and sin. 1 John 2:9-10 (TLB)

WORSHIP/OBEDIENCE

Can this message from the Bible be any clearer? To worship and obey the one true Light of the world, we cannot neglect to be reflectors. We might have to do some minor maintenance on our own lives to polish up if we are to be useful, but a little spit-shine can go a long way to dispelling the darkness!

Are you a gorgeous sight to observe?

August 12

I enjoy going fishing. The act of casting a line in the water with the expectation of feeling a fish bite is so exciting. Many times I'm lucky enough to catch a big stringer full of keepers, but other times I've gone home disappointed. Turns out, I'm not very fond of casting my line and just sitting for hours and hours on end. Boring! A friend once remarked to me, "You don't really like fishing, you like catching!"

ADORATION/EXPLANATION

The fishing industry was a large part of the disciples' lives. Jesus seemed to have fish at most meals and many of His miracles involved fish. I love the story in the book of Matthew where Jesus solves the problem of paying taxes with a fish. There never seemed to be a problem of catching when Jesus was around.

Pay everyone whatever he ought to have: pay your taxes and import duties gladly, obey those over you, and give honor and respect to all those to whom it is due. Romans 13:7 (TLB)

On their arrival in Capernaum, the Temple tax collectors came to Peter and asked him, "Doesn't your master pay taxes?" "Of course he does," Peter replied. Then he went into the house to talk to Jesus about it, but before he had a chance to speak, Jesus asked him, "What do you think, Peter? Do kings levy assessments against their own people, or against conquered foreigners?" "Against the foreigners," Peter replied. "Well, then," Jesus said, "the citizens are free! However, we don't want to offend them, so go down to the shore and throw in a line, and open the mouth of the first fish you catch. You will find a coin to cover the taxes for both of us; take it and pay them." Matthew 17:24-27 (TLB)

WORSHIP/OBEDIENCE

I would have loved going fishing with Jesus! You never knew what or who He was going to catch. It was certainly never boring! How can we not worship and obey a risen savior who can do these kinds of miracles? He always did what He said He would do, and He still will in our lives today.

Lord, you have caught my heart and soul.
Give me the zeal to live for you in my travels today.

I am convinced that when we feel the least like praying, we should. When we think that we need to get up and do something, then that is the perfect time to stay put for a moment and pray. Sometimes we need to ask for guidance or advice from God, and other times we just need to weep in frustration with life.

ADORATION/EXPLANATION
In the Old Testament book of 1 Samuel, there is a woman named Hannah who is childless. She wouldn't eat and couldn't stop crying bitter tears over her situation. Also, the other women who had children taunted her. Even her husband, Elkanah, couldn't console her. Then Hannah realized that the only place for her to go was to the Tabernacle to pray.

"What's the matter, Hannah?" Elkanah would exclaim, "Why aren't you eating? Why make such a fuss over having no children? Isn't having me better than having ten sons?" One evening after supper, when they were at Shiloh, Hannah went over to the Tabernacle. Eli the priest was sitting at his customary place beside the entrance. She was in deep anguish and was crying bitterly as she prayed to the Lord. And she made this vow: "O Lord of heaven, if you will look down upon my sorrow and answer my prayer and will give me a son, then I will give him back to you, and he'll be yours for his entire lifetime, and his hair shall never be cut."

The entire family was up early the next morning and went to the Tabernacle to worship the Lord once more. Then they returned home to Ramah, and when Elkanah slept with Hannah, the Lord remembered her petition; in the process of time, a baby boy was born to her. She named him Samuel (meaning "asked of God") because, as she said, "I asked the Lord for him." 1 Samuel 1:8-11, 19-20 (TLB)

WORSHIP/OBEDIENCE
I am sure that Hannah had petitioned God before to be able to bear children. Quite possibly she had been praying for many, many years. But when she finally could handle it no more, when she could not eat or handle the taunts from others, she knew that she had to try again. Her act of worship was the fact that instead of turning away from God in her time of sorrow, she turned to Him.

We can learn from Hannah's example. Run to the Tabernacle!

August 14

The amazing fact about the life of Hannah from yesterday's devotional lesson is that she kept her vow to God. Hannah had been barren for many years and she promised God that if He gave her a son, she would give him back to serve the Lord in the Tabernacle. She would take her treasured son and leave him with the priest. Can you imagine waiting all that time for a child, only to have to give him back? How many of us would honor that promise once God answered our prayer?

ADORATION/EXPLANATION
Hannah knew what an awesome God she believed in. Her true faith was demonstrated by the fact that she was willing to give her beloved child up so he could live in the temple. It wasn't like she could just drop in for a visit whenever she wanted, but she trusted God anyway.

Then, though he was still so small, they took him to the Tabernacle in Shiloh, along with a three-year-old bull for the sacrifice, and a bushel of flour and some wine. After the sacrifice they took the child to Eli. "Sir, do you remember me?" Hannah asked him. "I am the woman who stood here that time praying to the Lord! I asked him to give me this child, and he has given me my request; and now I am giving him to the Lord for as long as he lives." So she left him there at the Tabernacle for the Lord to use. 1 Samuel 1:24-28 (TLB)

This was Hannah's prayer: "How I rejoice in the Lord! How he has blessed me! Now I have an answer for my enemies, for the Lord has solved my problem. How I rejoice!" 1 Samuel 2:1 (TLB)

WORSHIP/OBEDIENCE
Do we rejoice? How long has it been since you rejoiced in the Lord? Hannah rejoiced in the Lord, even after taking her toddler son to the temple to live. Wow…a tough promise to keep! Even more difficult would be to rejoice while dropping him off. Today, let's find some reason to rejoice!

August 15

Did you ever notice that situations that seemed so dire last year (or even last week!) can change in an instant? A problem that has given us much grief can seem so insignificant once God's will falls on it. Our light and momentary affliction will all pass away when we see the blessings that God has for the ones that He loves. Something wonderful may be just up ahead!

ADORATION/EXPLANATION
When I continue to read in the book of 1 Samuel, I see the result of Hannah's obedience to God. The childless woman with no hope of having heirs, who was bitterly sobbing at the altar of the Tabernacle a couple of years earlier, was now a changed lady. This was the result of rejoicing!

Samuel, though only a child, was the Lord's helper and wore a little linen robe just like the priest's. Each year his mother made a little coat for him and brought it to him when she came with her husband for the sacrifice. Before they returned home Eli would bless Elkanah and Hannah and ask God to give them other children to take the place of this one they had given to the Lord. And the Lord gave Hannah three sons and two daughters. Meanwhile Samuel grew up in the service of the Lord. 1 Samuel 2:18-21 (TLB)

No one is as holy as the Lord! There is no other God, nor any Rock like our God. 1Samuel 2:2 (TLB)

WORSHIP/OBEDIENCE
What? The crying, sobbing, weeping, praying woman who had to give up her child is now blessed with three more sons and two daughters? Isn't it astounding how God can change circumstances? There is NO rock like our God! Today, lean fully on Him.

Do not give up hope because of what is happening today,
for something wonderful may be right around the corner.

August 16

Nothing happens in this world by chance or luck. Do you believe this…or do you just feel that your life is in the hands of fate, or karma? God is at work in the lives of his people, and He governs and guides all circumstance. I find this concept very reassuring! Someone much greater than all of creation is caring for us.

ADORATION/EXPLANATION

God is the God of providence. He upholds and watches over us. Sometimes this is difficult to see, but Paul teaches us in Ephesians that God works out everything according to His perfect will. Do you believe it's perfect? Your stance on this teaching will make a very big difference on how you daily live.

***

Now all praise to God for his wonderful kindness to us and his favor that he has poured out upon us, because we belong to his dearly loved Son. So overflowing is his kindness towards us that he took away all our sins through the blood of his Son, by whom we are saved; and he has showered down upon us the richness of his grace—for how well he understands us and knows what is best for us at all times.

Moreover, because of what Christ has done we have become gifts to God that he delights in, for as part of God's sovereign plan we were chosen from the beginning to be his, and all things happen just as he decided long ago. Ephesians 1:6-8, 11 (TLB)

For who in all of heaven can be compared with God? What mightiest angel is anything like him? Psalm 89:6 (TLB)

WORSHIP/OBEDIENCE

If our thinking about God and His nature is not correct then every other teaching, verse or precept that we try to apply to our minds and hearts will be incorrect. We cannot…we must not…we dare not reduce God to terms and descriptions that are acceptable to us.

He is a mighty God and He is not like anything else that mankind
has ever known or experienced. He deserves our worship!

Can you honestly say that when God calls or leads you in a certain direction, that you reply cheerfully, "Yes, I'm listening!" and really mean it? Do you seriously want to listen or do you try to ignore what you think God is telling you? What about when you read verses or passages in the Bible that ask you to refrain from certain things or do specific actions that are difficult and may take some adjustment? Why do some folks seem to hear God speaking and other do not?

ADORATION/EXPLANATION

We cannot fool God! If you are able to say, "Speak, for your servant is listening," as Samuel did, than you really need to listen up. Our awesome God has much to say to us through His Word, through people, and through the circumstances of our lives. Things are not happening just by chance or by luck…

So he said to Samuel, "Go and lie down again, and if he calls again, say, 'Yes, Lord, I'm listening.'" So Samuel went back to bed. And the Lord came and called as before, "Samuel! Samuel!" And Samuel replied, "Yes, I'm listening." 1 Samuel 3:9-10 (TLB)

Don't be misled; remember that you can't ignore God and get away with it: a man will always reap just the kind of crop he sows! Galatians 6:7 (TLB)

My sheep recognize my voice, and I know them, and they follow me. John 10:27 (TLB)

WORSHIP/OBEDIENCE

We should listen carefully for God's voice in our lives—not an audible, mysterious, Wizard of Oz kind of voice, but His gentle prodding in our hearts. We need to read the Bible and be aware that He is speaking to us. If we listen closely during the day, we'll know and feel how He would have us behave in all situations. No other voice should matter.

Lord, yes, I'm listening!

August 18

What kind of hands do you have? Even though I'm a woman, I have my father's large hands. Perhaps not the most desirable look for a girl, but they sure did come in handy while I was playing sports, carrying groceries, paddling a surfboard, or swimming! Are yours long and slender? Are they rough and calloused or plump and smooth? Soft, weak, shaky, full of arthritis? Go ahead, take a look.

ADORATION/EXPLANATION
I cannot see your hands, but odds are if you are a mother, I can safely say that your hands are full! Mothers use their hands to feel their child's forehead for a fever, to stroke their small faces, to scratch their backs, and to give them hugs. Mothers also use their hands to pack school lunches, make dinner, comb hair, lace up sport cleats, and juggle schedules. The Bible has much to say about our hands.

***

And to make it your ambition to lead a quiet life and attend to your own business and work with your hands, just as we commanded you; so that you may behave properly toward outsiders and not be in any need. 1 Thessalonians 4:11-12 (NASB)

Therefore I want the men in every place to pray, lifting up holy hands, without wrath and dissension. 1Timothy 2:8 (NASB)

O clap your hands, all peoples; shout to God with the voice of joy. Psalm 47:1 (NASB)

Give her the product of her hands, and let her works praise her in the gates. Proverbs 31:31 (NASB)

WORSHIP/OBEDIENCE
"There is a Heavenly Father up above, looking down in love," so be careful how you use your hands. Today, choose to find ways to worship God with your hands. What kind of hands do you have?

***

August 19

This morning as I was sipping my coffee on my back deck, I noticed a small ant dragging a leaf. The leaf was at least twenty times the size of the ant and I sat amazed at the resilience of this little insect. It did not give up. Even if the leaf got stuck on something, the ant kept pulling and pushing until it got its load moving in the right direction. Then came the daunting task of trying to drag the leaf down into the ant's hole. Well, he never gave up, but he eventually did receive the assistance of a few comrades. What a scene!

ADORATION/EXPLANATION
What a marvelous God we serve! He not only created us, but all the creatures in the world, including the smallest of insects. Even with their tiny size, they are amazing and sometimes quirky creations. God even teaches us lessons in His Word using the ant as an example.

Go to the ant, O sluggard, observe her ways and be wise, which, having no chief, officer or ruler, prepares her food in the summer, and gathers her provision in the harvest. Proverbs 6:6-8 (NASB)

Four things are small on the earth, but they are exceedingly wise: The ants are not a strong folk, but they prepare their food in the summer; the badgers are not a mighty folk, yet they make their houses in the rocks; the locust have no king, yet all of them go out in ranks; the lizard you may grasp with the hands, yet it is in king's palaces. Proverbs 30:24-25 (NASB)

WORSHIP/OBEDIENCE
Our obedience to God needs to be in our resolve of not giving up. Even if our load seems much too large for us, we need to persevere. The Bible tells us that perseverance produces godliness in our character. Truthfully then, we should be thankful when we have large difficult loads to bear. We should prepare, push, pull, and call on comrades if need be, but always continuing to work.

Lord, help me to have the determination of the ant today. I've got high hopes!

August 20

We are all different for a reason. Did you ever look at people (maybe your own family) and think, "How could those children have all come from the same parents?" How can one family be raised with the same set of values and still the members all behave differently? God has certainly had fun with creating us all differently!

ADORATION/EXPLANATION
God has gifted us with differing gifts, talents, dispositions, and temperaments. Satan's goal is to get us to focus on the differences and the negatives in each personality, thereby causing dissension. When we read about the early church in the Bible, they had many differences but shared everything and seemed to glorify the various abilities each person had. Why do we seem to struggle with that now?

Day by day continuing with one mind in the temple, and breaking bread from house to house, they were taking their meals together with gladness and sincerity of heart, praising God and having favor with all the people. And the Lord was adding to their number day by day those who were being saved. Acts 2:46-47 (NASB)

And the congregation of those who believed were of one heart and soul; and not one of them claimed that anything belonging to him was his own, but all things were common property to them. Acts 4:32 (NASB)

To sum up, all of you be harmonious, sympathetic, brotherly, kindhearted, and humble in spirit; 1 Peter 3:8 (NASB)

WORSHIP/OBEDIENCE
How do you live, work, or put up with others who have so many annoying traits? How would you want others to live and work with you? God wants us to focus on the good. He wants us to adapt ourselves to others, be sympathetic, and learn to function in harmony.

The body of Christ might be made up of different parts,
but when we sing together, we create a beautiful sound!

Have you ever seen a pressure cooker? They're wonderful tools and can produce tasty dishes, but they can also explode if they're not functioning properly. How do you behave under pressure? The proof of who you really are and the characteristics that really define you can only be seen under pressure. Pressure situations are continuing opportunities for others to see the real you.

ADORATION/EXPLANATION

I have learned not to become upset when pressure situations come. Even if I blow up, flip out, or act unbecoming, I can realize that God has just shown me where I need to do some work in my personality. In reality, I should be thrilled for these trials. Although I usually feel bad, I can learn to ask for forgiveness and focus on doing better next time. It really is all about perseverance, after all.

And do not be conformed to this world, but be transformed by the renewing of your mind, so that you may prove what the will of God is, that which is good and acceptable and perfect. Romans 12:2 (NASB)

Consider it all joy, my brethren, when you encounter various trials, knowing that the testing of your faith produces endurance. And let endurance have its perfect result, so that you may be perfect and complete, lacking in nothing.

But if any of you lacks wisdom, let him ask of God, who gives generously and without reproach, and it will be given to him. James 1:2-5 (NASB)

WORSHIP/OBEDIENCE

Obviously we have to learn to control our tempers. God does not want us to explode under pressure (even if we have the right to) but to call on His strength to muddle through. We must rely on His peace, His calm, and His steadfast nature in times when our human nature is failing.

God can enable us to learn to let the steam out of our hearts and minds little by little—before the lid blows off!

Many Christians' chief complaint is that they have just lost the excitement of being a believer. Years ago when they asked Jesus into their lives, it was all bubbly, emotional and exciting. Perhaps they joined a new church, got involved with a Bible study, or hung with others who were on fire for God. So as hard as it might be to admit, perhaps it was more about the emotional high than about making a commitment to God. It was kind of like joining a club, the excitement was contagious.

ADORATION/EXPLANATION

If someone does not feel the excitement or the emotional swell of their faith could it have all been a farce? If you do not feel total, rapturous love for your spouse during every single moment, does that make you not married? Obviously not! If you genuinely received Christ, just as if you genuinely got married, His promise to be your heavenly Father and love you forever is not null and void— even if it feels less than thrilling.

For He himself has said, "I will never desert you, nor will I ever forsake you," so we confidently say, "The Lord is my helper, I will not be afraid. What can man do to me?" Remember those who led you, who spoke the word of God to you; and considering the result of their conduct, imitate their faith.

Jesus Christ is the same yesterday, today and forever. Hebrews 13:5b-8 (NASB)

But prove yourselves doers of the word, and not merely hearers who delude themselves. James 1:22 (NASB)

WORSHIP/OBEDIENCE

Most people will go through a case of the blahs sometime after their conversion, just like a married couple might go through the doldrums after time passes by. But the relationship does not change and we can't let the communication break down.

Keep talking to God! Tell Him your struggles. Continue to worship and obey.
Repair the communication!

Why is it so important to dedicate our whole lives to Christ? Our thoughts, our actions, our relationships, and even our future plans should belong to Him? Why would we want to get neurotic worrying about every little detail? How hard do we have to try before it's enough for God? Doesn't He tell us not to worry?

ADORATION/EXPLANATION

God calls us to be a whole person, and you have to decide if you are all in for Christ. You can only grow into the wonderful person that God desires by completely yielding to Him. You sacrifice everything, yes, but you gain everything in return! Halfway committed is no relationship at all! Would you accept that from a spouse? No!

⟞⟝

"Why do you call Me, 'Lord, Lord,' and do not do what I say? Everyone who comes to Me and hears My words and acts on them, I will show you whom he is like: he is like a man building a house, who dug deep and laid a foundation on the rock; and when a flood occurred, the torrent burst against that house and could not shake it, because it had been well built. But the one who has heard and has not acted accordingly, is like a man who built a house on the ground without any foundation; and the torrent burst against it and immediately it collapsed, and the ruin of that house was great." Luke 6:46-49 (NASB)

Only conduct yourselves in a manner worthy of the gospel of Christ, Philippians 1:27a (NASB)

So then, my beloved, just as you have always obeyed, not as in my presence only, but now much more in my absence, work out your salvation with fear and trembling; Philippians 2:12 (NASB)

WORSHIP/OBEDIENCE

Again and again the Bible refers to Christ as "Lord." That means He is in charge of everything in your life. Totally! No worries!

Take one thing, one event, and one problem at a time to God and say,
"Here it is. You are in charge, Lord. Guide me!"

⟞⟝

Have you ever been in pain? I guess that is a really dumb question, because who hasn't been in pain? But I am talking about immobilizing, life-threatening pain. Some people live their lives in constant, excruciating pain from a chronic or terminal illness. If this is your story then you have realized that we need more than human help. Talk show hosts like Dr. Phil or Dr. Oz and your own family physician would be enough if this were not so. We need our heavenly Father's help!

ADORATION/EXPLANATION

Pain and suffering can keep us from having a life filled with abundance and joy. God does not always choose to remove our pain, but He can give us the spiritual strength and comfort to continue living. If you are in pain right now, decide that you will not waste this time of suffering. Learn from it. Open the Bible, pray, and jot down thoughts to God. He cares!

Do you not know? Have you not heard? The Everlasting God, the Lord, the Creator of the ends of the earth does not become weary or tired. His understanding is inscrutable. He gives strength to the weary, and to him who lacks might he increases power. Though youths grow weary and tired, and vigorous young men stumble badly, yet those who wait for the Lord will gain new strength; they will mount up with wings like eagles, the will run and not get tired, they will walk and not become weary. Isaiah 40:28-31 (NASB)

Blessed be the God and Father of our Lord Jesus Christ, the Father of mercies and God of all comfort, who comforts us in all our affliction so that we will be able to comfort those who are in any affliction with the comfort with which we ourselves are comforted by God. 2 Corinthians 1:3-4 (NASB)

WORSHIP/OBEDIENCE

Where is God in all this pain? He is there. We don't just snap our fingers and get healed, but He is there to provide spiritual calmness through the pain. If you personally are not dealing with major affliction at the moment, find someone who is to comfort and love. Don't know how? Read 1 Corinthians 13:4-8.

The same principles of love can be applied to the person dealing with pain.

When Jesus encountered pain and suffering and faced imminent death on the cross, he reacted like many of us would. He begged God three times for any other way to accomplish the task. He did not want the pain, but He endured it for us. The history of Jesus' life on earth will forever answer the provoking question, "How does God feel about our pain?" The answer is that He gave us Himself. His only Son! He gave us the cross!

ADORATION/EXPLANATION
The cross is not just a piece of jewelry to be worn around our necks, but rather a universal symbol by which to remember Jesus. The cross offers proof that God cares about our own suffering and pain. Christ endured the floggings, whippings, spitting, insults, nails, crown of thorns, the spear in his side, and the agony of death on the cross. For *us!* No, not just a symbol to be worn around our neck!

What then shall we say to these things? If God is for us, who is against us? He who did not spare His own Son, but delivered Him over for us all, how will He not also with Him freely give us all things? Romans 8:31-32 (NASB)

For you have been called for this purpose, since Christ also suffered for you, leaving you an example for you to follow in his steps, who committed no sin, nor was any deceit found in His mouth; and while being reviled, He did not revile in return; while suffering, He uttered no threats, but kept entrusting himself to Him who judges righteously; and He himself bore our sins in His body on the cross, so that we might die to sin and live to righteousness; for by his wounds you were healed. 1 Peter 2:21-24 (NASB)

WORSHIP/OBEDIENCE
Remind yourself today of the reason we wear the cross. How do you view this symbol? Do you ever look at it, think about it, or give thanks for it? Think…really think long and hard about the cross. Wow!

Do not take it lightly…Jesus didn't!

Have you ever put out a call for praise? We place calls to 911, to the gas company, to the electric company, to the doctor's office, and to the fire department. We place a call to the police if there's a traffic accident, we call the school principal to complain, we call the church pastor or priest for counsel, and the florist to order flowers. But have you ever put a call out for praise to God?

ADORATION/EXPLANATION

Psalm 98 entices us to rejoice in God's goodness to us. It describes His triumphs, His marvelous works, and encourages us to shout joyfully. It sends the call out for praise, and the verses volley back and forth like a game of praise to God. Can you imagine a game like that?

O sing to the Lord a new song, for He has done wonderful things, His right hand and His holy arm have gained the victory for Him. The Lord has made known His salvation; He has revealed His righteousness in the sight of the nations. He has remembered His loving kindness and His faithfulness in the house of Israel; all the ends of the earth have seen the salvation of our God.

Shout joyfully to the Lord, all the earth; break forth and sing for joy and sing praises. Sing praises to the Lord with the lyre, with the lyre and the sound of melody. With trumpets and the sound of the horn, shout joyfully before the King, the Lord. Psalm 98:1-6 (NASB)

WORSHIP/OBEDIENCE

The last three verses of this psalm (which are not included here) state the reason why all creation should praise God. The Lord is coming to judge the world someday with righteousness and truth. Put out a call for praise!

Do not wait! Find a friend, co-worker, or spouse and volley back and forth the awesome things that God has done for you.

Do you take time to think about the Lord and about how He saved us, helps us, comforts us, provides for us, guides us, lifts us up to solid ground, and forgives our sins daily? Ponder the achievement of what God has done and is doing in our lives. He doesn't condone our sin or compromise on His supreme standard of justice, but He did send His only begotten Son to pay the ultimate sacrifice in our place.

ADORATION/EXPLANATION

When I think about the Lord, it makes me want to shout, "Hallelujah!" I am in awe of His wonderful, benevolent gift of grace. I do not deserve it one little bit nor can I even imagine trying to earn it. That is exactly why we must think about the Lord and dwell on Him…

For while we were still helpless, at the right time Christ died for the ungodly.

But God demonstrates his own love toward us, in that while we were yet sinners, Christ died for us. For if while we were enemies we were reconciled to God through the death of His Son, much more, having been reconciled, we shall be saved by His life. Romans 5:6, 8, 10 (NASB)

Therefore there is now no condemnation for those who are in Christ Jesus. Romans 8:1 (NASB)

Therefore you are no longer a slave, but a son; and if a son, then an heir through God. Galatians 4:7 (NASB)

WORSHIP/OBEDIENCE

When we think about the Lord, isn't it amazing that He looks at us through the lens of Jesus Christ and views us as perfect? Flailing through life with no hope and eternal death are not options anymore. God's gracious gift of Jesus Christ has paid the penalty if we have accepted the free gift of salvation.

When you think about the Lord, think about saying, "Thank you!"

August 28

Sometimes when Christians share their faith, it tends to sound negative. They paint God and the Christian walk as gloomy and guilt ridden. They use harsh words and desire to have others feel ashamed of their so-called performance as believers. There is always an unseen measuring stick somewhere. Well, I'm here to tell you that this example of the life they're showing is like a drudge, not a delight. A kind of drag…

ADORATION/EXPLANATION

Our awesome God has given us the Bible as a playbook for life. Many people see it as a finger-pointing book, but this is just not true. Whenever Jesus spoke of His crucifixion, He automatically tied it in to His resurrection. When sin is mentioned, the Bible provides the way out through grace. This is not a drag, but instead a super-abounding book of delight. This is not depressing or discouraging! In fact, it is the most wonderful, positive outlook on life!

For all have sinned and fall short of the glory of God, being justified as a gift by His grace through the redemption which is in Christ Jesus; Romans 3:23-24 (NASB)

So now, since we have been made right in God's sight by faith in his promises, we can have real peace with him because of what Jesus Christ our Lord has done for us. For because of our faith, he has brought us into this place of highest privilege where we now stand, and we confidently and joyfully look forward to actually becoming all that God has had in mind for us to be. Romans 5:1-2 (TLB)

"For God so loved the world, that He gave His only begotten Son, that whoever believes in Him shall not perish, but have eternal life. For God did not send the Son into the world to judge the world, but that the world might be saved through Him." John 3:16-17 (NASB)

WORSHIP/OBEDIENCE

Many folks believe that God is angry with them. They avoid the Bible and church because they'd rather avoid the supposed feeling of God's wrath. Of course life comes with pain and sacrifice. Lots of it! But God also meant for the Christian walk to be joyful and fun! Why not? Start believing today that God likes you. He really, really likes you!

As a matter of fact, He loves you!

August 29

If my mind is to be rested and relaxed during the summer, it will be because I have made myself determined to see my time as God's gift. Warm, enjoyable, outdoor time is very seasonal where I live, and as a teacher who has a limited summer vacation it is cherished like gold. My time is worthy of careful investment. Sometimes I must clear my schedule to do…wait…wait for it…NOTHING!

ADORATION/EXPLANATION

If our time is limited and we want to accomplish some activities such as relaxing, going to the beach, or reading some favorite novels, the first step to take is a truthful self-appraisal about our habits of time use. Are we organized or not?

God is not a God of chaos. He wants us to have some leisure time to just think, meditate, and enjoy. Take back some lost time today!

And Jesus said to him, "Today salvation has come to this house, because he, too, is a son of Abraham. "For the Son of Man has come to seek and save that which was lost." Luke 19:9-10 (NASB)

My times are in your hand; deliver me from the hand of my enemies and from those who persecute me. Psalm 31:15 (NASB)

'For six days work may be done, but on the seventh day there is a Sabbath of complete rest, holy to the Lord; whoever does any work on the Sabbath day shall surely be put to death. Exodus 31:15 (NASB)

WORSHIP/OBEDIENCE

That last verse from the book of Exodus sounds harsh, but God knew what He was doing when He set up time restraints on man. He knew that we could get distracted and "busy" ourselves to death. Even Jesus sought time in solitude and He was never caught short on time. He never seemed to feel guilty about taking a break, either!

We need to commit to free ourselves of the fever pitch of daily activity. Today!

Most people think of money whenever stewardship is mentioned, but being a good steward is about a lot more than just our money. Handling our hours, days, weeks, months, and years in a calm, organized way is also considered under the mantle of stewardship. As faithful followers of Christ, we cannot be total masters of our daily schedule, purpose, time, and destiny. We need to draw on that beautiful strength from within to make outward decisions about our time.

ADORATION/EXPLANATION

For instance, how do I budget my time? I have learned to put activities in proper perspective. I call my system the three T's: Trash, Trinkets, and Treasures. Time invested in wrongful activity is labeled TRASH. Activity that is fun but not necessarily edifying is labeled TRINKETS. Valuable relationships and soul strengthening time is labeled TREASURE.

"He must increase, but I must decrease. He who comes from above is above all, he who is of the earth is from the earth and speaks of the earth. He who comes from Heaven is above all. John 3:30-31 (NASB)

Sow with a view to righteousness, reap in accordance with kindness; break up your fallow ground, for it is time to seek the Lord until He comes to rain righteousness of you. Hosea 10:12 (NASB)

"Be dressed in readiness, and keep your lamps lit. You too, be ready; for the Son of Man is coming at an hour that you do not expect." Luke 12:35, 40 (NASB)

WORSHIP/OBEDIENCE

We may be intelligent, multi-faceted, a good communicator, kind, caring, and have a beautiful heart and soul, yet we will end up squandering it all because of our inability to make good stewardship choices with our time. Not sure how to do this? John's advice in his gospel is right on the mark. He must increase, and I must decrease. Breathe calmly and re-organize your schedule. Drop some activities out…it's really okay!

More of Him in my time spent, and less of me. Wake up Christian!

August 31

I have been married for many years, and I am still deeply in love with my husband. Lots of people have one or the other—I'm blessed beyond measure to have both and I believe that to be married for many, many years and still love the same person requires God in the mix. For a marriage to last, I believe that both people have to love God first, and then have a total, selfless commitment to really love each other through thick and thin.

ADORATION/EXPLANATION

God is so wonderful that He even includes marriage counseling in the Bible. He certainly knows what He is talking about because He created men and women especially for one another. It is amazing, though, how many couples in relationships will not honor God's direction. Yes...ideally...both people must be onboard for it to work as intended; but if you are reading this now, it can begin with you. YOU!

***

In the same way, you wives, be submissive to your own husbands so that even if any of them are disobedient to the word, they may be won without a word by the behavior of their wives, as they observe your chaste and respectful behavior. Your adornment must not be merely external—braiding the hair, and wearing gold jewelry, or putting on dresses; but let it be the hidden person of the heart, with the imperishable quality of a gentle quiet spirit, which is precious in the sight of God. 1 Peter 3:1-4 (NASB)

Love is patient, love is kind and is not jealous; love does not brag and is not arrogant, does not act unbecomingly; it does not seek its own, is not provoked, does not take into account a wrong suffered, does not rejoice in unrighteousness, but rejoices with the truth; bears all things, believes all things, hopes all things, endures all things. 1 Corinthians 13:4-7 (NASB)

WORSHIP/OBEDIENCE

God's instructions are very clear here and He is not mincing words. Let love start with YOU...in marriage, in friendships and life. Enough said? Obviously!

Don't wait for others to be the LOVERS first!

***

September 1

How do you think of the elderly in your life? What about the older people in your family, the supermarket, church or your neighborhood—do you tend to ignore them and act like they are non-existent, or do you try to engage them and glean some wonderful gems of knowledge from them? One day, if not now, you and I will be the elderly folks.

ADORATION/EXPLANATION
We need to see the older friends in our circles as valuable people. We need to have intimate relationships with friends of all ages, including the older ones. God gives some very wise advice on how to treat people of age. Respect them! One of the ways we can adore our God is to show love, care, and patience towards the older generation in our lives. What does God have to say about this?

Never speak sharply to an older man, but plead with him respectfully just as though he were your own father. Talk to the younger men as you would to much loved brothers. Treat the older women as mothers, and the girls as your sisters, thinking only pure thoughts about them. The church should take loving care of women whose husbands have died, if they don't have anyone else to help them. But if they have children or grandchildren, these are the ones who should take the responsibility, for kindness should begin at home, supporting needy parents. This is something that pleases God very much. 1 Timothy 5:1-4 (TLB)

Young men, listen to me as you would to your father. Listen, and grow wise, for I speak the truth—don't turn away. Proverbs 4:1-2 (TLB)

WORSHIP/OBEDIENCE
Touch is wonderful—reach out when you pass people, hold a hand, grab a shoulder. If there are older people in your social circle, church, or job, they may be longing for a hug. Embrace them! Chat with them! Show respect! This is our obvious act of obedience to God's Word.

Listen, HUG, and grow wise!

September 2

Are you afraid of physical contact from people? Do you tend to only touch those in your family, or maybe none at all? Do you cringe when someone comes too close within your "personal space?" Or, are you very comfortable with touch, hugs, and handshakes?

It may depend on how you were raised and how you felt as a child.

ADORATION/EXPLANATION

Figuring out what makes you react the way that you do to physical contact is an important discovery. People need touch, but this does not necessarily mean someone who barges right up close to your face and breathes on you. It means the kind of touch that comforts and calms; the kind of touch that assures and reassures; the kind of touch that demonstrates that you are loved. We must also keep in close consideration that many friends may have been violated or harmed by physical contact in their pasts. Allow God to help you proceed and discern these situations with caution and love. God created touch, and we can help relay that to a hurting world.

❧❧❧

So stop evaluating Christians by what the world thinks about them or by what they seem to be like on the outside. Once I mistakenly thought of Christ that way, merely as a human being like myself. How differently I feel now! When someone becomes a Christian he becomes a brand new person inside. He is not the same any more. A new life has begun! 2 Corinthians 5:16-17 (TLB)

For she thought, "If I only touch him, I will be healed." Matthew 9:21 (TLB)

I close my letter with these last words: Be happy, Grow in Christ. Pay attention to what I have said. Live in harmony and peace. And may the God of love and peace be with you. Greet each other warmly in the Lord. 2 Corinthians 13:11-12 (TLB)

WORSHIP/OBEDIENCE

Beyond your most intimate circle of family and friends, what lives do you touch? Do you greet anyone warmly in the Lord? Our obvious way to obey God's Word and show the world we care is to love people, touch people, and influence them for Jesus. Shake someone's hand, hug them, touch an arm or even give a squeeze.

Walk out the front door…someone may need your loving touch today!

❧❧❧

September 3

Do you care about your reputation with others? Of course you do. Anyone who says that they do not care at all about what people think is usually lying. They pretend that they are not concerned because it takes any responsibility off of them to act correctly. The Apostle Paul throughout Scripture talks about our behavior and how it can and should point others to Christ. When I allow God to shape my personal reputation with obedience to His word, I can rest assured that I am moving in the right direction.

ADORATION/EXPLANATION

If our lives and our actions were of no importance to God, then why would He allow so much Scripture to be focused on that topic? We are repeatedly given an example from Paul and others on how to conduct ourselves. God can give us the strength to take daily assessment of how we are living out our faith to the world.

As God's partners we beg you not to toss aside this marvelous message of God's great kindness. We try to live in such a way that no one will ever be offended or kept back from finding the Lord by the way we act, so that no one can find fault with us and blame it on the Lord. In fact, in everything we do we try to show that we are ministers of God. We patiently endure suffering and hardship and trouble of every kind. We stand true to the Lord whether others honor us or despise us, whether they criticize us or commend us. We are honest but they call us liars. 2 Corinthians 6:1, 3-4, 8 (TLB)

You can see that I am not trying to please you by sweet talk and flattery; no, I am trying to please God. If I were still trying to please men I could not be Christ's servant. Galatians 1:10 (TLB)

WORSHIP/OBEDIENCE

The Apostle Paul explained it beautifully. We stand true to the Lord, no matter what! That is the key. It wasn't Paul's own personal, prideful reputation that he cared about, but rather that he did not want his behavior to keep anyone from knowing God. When we CARE about our reputation for Christ, most of the time it will lead us in a way of behaving that will draw others to us.

Today I will choose to care. It does matter!

September 4

Do you desire to know God more? Not to just simply know about Him, but to really gain a better understanding of Him? Do you believe it is important to intimately seek Him in your daily life, to allow Him to influence everything that you do? The Bible tells us that we should, and that God KNOWS us! We can trust Him to guide our lives because He is the one who knit them together for His purposes!

ADORATION/EXPLANATION

From studying Scripture, I am in such awe of God and His mighty ways, and I do not want to waste a day without trying to seek Him more. Just spending time reading the Bible and applying it to my life is the beginning of KNOWING Him better. I wrote this devotional to help guide you on your way. Make a habit to practice being in His presence and to live consciously before Him.

"Let not your heart be troubled. You are trusting God, now trust in me. There are many homes up there where my Father lives, and I am going to prepare them for your coming. When everything is ready, then I will come and get you, so that you can always be with me where I am. If this weren't so, I would tell you plainly. And you know where I am going and how to get there." John 14:1-4 (TLB)

I am always thinking of the Lord; and because he is so near, I never need to stumble or to fall. Psalm 16:8 (TLB)

WORSHIP/OBEDIENCE

What is a simple way to live this in daily worship and obedience to God? Choose to live your life consciously before God, moment by moment, and trust Him to help you do it. Make a choice to line all your daily decisions and actions up against God's Word. Remain alert to His leading. The King James Version of Psalm 16:8 states, "I have set the Lord always before me." Always!

Keep your eyes on the target and you will not miss.

I set out to write this devotional to encourage people to make time for a daily quiet reflection with God. Even if for a few moments, we can stop our activity to read His Word and learn how to apply them; life will run more smoothly. I have always believed that it is basically obvious as to how God wants us to live the Christian life. We do not need to search for opportunities—they happen right in front of us every day. Look around!

ADORATION/EXPLANATION
God adores us. The Bible says that He desires a relationship with us and wants us to seek Him. We need to jealously guard the small chances that we get to spend a few quiet moments alone with Him. Oh, come let us adore HIM!

Lord, how merciful you are to those who are merciful. And you do not punish those who run from evil. You give blessings to the pure but pain to those who leave your paths. You deliver the humble but condemn the proud and haughty ones. You have turned on my light! The Lord my God has made my darkness turn to light. Now in your strength I can scale any wall, attack any troop. What a god he is! How perfect in every way! All his promises prove true. He is a shield for everyone who hides behind him. For who is God except our Lord? Who but he is as a rock? He fills me with strength and protects me wherever I go. Psalm 18:25-32 (TLB)

WORSHIP/OBEDIENCE
Everyone has the same twenty-four hours in their day. What are you doing with yours? An obvious way to obey God would be to set aside a few minutes each day to spend time with Him—just Him! Read the Bible and pray about how you can apply it wisely to today's, tomorrow's, or even next week's schedule.

Everyone has twenty-four little hours…how will you spend a few minutes of yours?
It will pay great dividends!

September 6

Now that you are gaining ground on the idea of setting aside a few minutes for God in quiet devotion, why not seek an occasionally longer chunk of time? Jesus did! In the Gospel of Luke it tells us that He spent an entire night in prayer because He felt it was needed. What? The Son of God felt the need for more than just a few moments of prayer and reading? Yes! Well if He did, then this should be our example to try to find more than a few minutes of each day to grow with God. You may need to schedule it in, but the rewards will be well worth the cost.

ADORATION/EXPLANATION
Our awesome God is thrilled with any conversation and prayer time that we dedicate to Him. But as the mother of sons, I have to admit that I was thrilled when my boys decided that they wanted to chat and share their thoughts for more than just a cursory "Hello, Mom." I love them no matter what, but I cherish those longer conversations and so does their father. Likewise, our heavenly Father craves those long, thought-provoking conversations with us.

At this, the enemies of Jesus were wild with rage, and began to plot his murder. One day soon afterwards he went out into the mountains to pray, and prayed all night. Luke 6:11-12 (TLB)

One day as he was alone, praying, with his disciples nearby, he came over and asked them, "Who are the people saying I am?"

Then he asked them, "Who do you think I am?" Luke 9:18, 20 (TLB)

Cling to wisdom—she will protect you. Love her—she will guard you. Proverbs 4:6 (TLB)

Then afterwards he went up into the hills to pray. Matthew 14:23 (TLB)

WORSHIP/OBEDIENCE
A few ways to accomplish longer chunks of time with God might be to set aside time in the morning (or evening, if you work night shift). Get up an hour earlier, or maybe even spend your lunch break once a week alone in prayer and meditation. Talk about all your struggles, worries, and blessings. You will not believe how fast the time goes when you really start to commune with God. Plus, He will never think that you talk too much!

Do you attend church or Bible study? How often do you go? Twice a week? Once a week? Once a month? Or maybe just once in a while with Easter and Christmas thrown in? I don't ask to bug you or make you feel guilty, but only because there are some pretty clear directives from God about meeting together for worship. And while there are a few folks who announce to everyone that they can worship from home, or their bed, or a mountain top if they want, it's very rarely that people who don't go to a place of worship (with other believers) keep up the actual time and act of worship. God wants us to be there mingling with other people, not via television or the Internet.

ADORATION/EXPLANATION
God knows that it is better to gather together to worship and learn. He gives us so many choices of churches, congregations, and denominations to choose from. He allows us to pick our style of teaching and singing, which is fine, as long as it is truly based on His Word. Mark your calendar to wake up and go to church this week. Bring a friend…you will be glad that you did!

<hr>

In response to all he has done for us, let us outdo each other in being helpful and kind to each other and in doing good. Let us not neglect our church meetings, as some people do, but encourage and warn each other, especially now that the day of his coming back again is drawing near. Hebrews 10:24-25 (TLB)

When he came home to the village of Nazareth, his boyhood home, he went as usual to the synagogue on Saturday, and stood up to read the scriptures. Luke 4:16 (TLB)

I will instruct you (says the Lord) and guide you along the best pathway for your life; I will advise you and watch your progress. Psalm 32:8 (TLB)

WORSHIP/OBEDIENCE
Don't go to church out of guilt. Let's go because we need and desire the teaching and the worship time. Go because, as a faithful follower of Christ, we want to imitate His example. Don't make church attendance an "unusual" event in your life.

If Jesus went as usual…shouldn't we also?

<hr>

September 8

The Bible is revelation—God revealing Himself to man, disclosing His will and His plan for the world. The Bible brings man the gospel, or "good news," about how God has acted in history in order to communicate to man, to save him, and to help him out of the fatal dilemma called sin. Again and again, we must come back to the importance of Scripture. The Christian faith rests on the facts of the life, death, and resurrection of Jesus Christ.

ADORATION/EXPLANATION
To want reasonable answers from the Bible is no disgrace, nor is it something to feel guilty about asking. God loves our seeking hearts. We should search, study and understand. But God tells us in the Bible itself, some thoughts are mine and you will never make logic of them. Some ways are mine and you will never see the sense in them. I am God, you are not! This is where faith really steps in.

You can never please God without faith, without depending on him. Anyone who wants to come to God must believe that there is a God and that he rewards those who sincerely look for him. Hebrews 11:6 (TLB)

For the truth about God is known to them instinctively, God has put this knowledge in their hearts. Since earliest times men have seen the earth and sky and all God made, and have known of his existence and great eternal power. So they will have no excuse when they stand before God at Judgment Day. Romans 1:19-20 (TLB)

For all God's words are right, and everything he does is worthy of our trust. Psalm 33:4 (TLB)

WORSHIP/OBEDIENCE
Every person who is confronted with the Truth in the Bible and the life of Christ must weigh the evidence for himself. We then must decide if we will place our faith in what we find or if we will reject it and seek truth elsewhere.

Seek and you will find…

Start knocking…

September 9

Do you know yourself well? Are you intimately familiar with your own quirks, foibles, and fumbles? Do you really know your own best traits? Taking the occasional time away from others can teach you reams of information about yourself. This is important because if you are a stranger to yourself, then you are usually estranged from others as well.

ADORATION/EXPLANATION

Sometimes God wants us to spend some time with me, myself, and I. He longs for us to re-connect with our own inner core, our inner spring that feeds the soul. Women especially pour out from their life's cup all day long to their family and friends. Also, in this day and age, many women have full-time jobs outside the home. We need times of reflection, peace, and solitude to fill our water bottles back up to the brim. How can "my cup runneth over" if there is no water?

Thou preparest a table before me in the presence of mine enemies; thou annointest my head with oil; my cup runneth over. Surely goodness and mercy shall follow me all the days of my life; and I will dwell in the house of the Lord for ever. Psalm 23:5, 6 (KJV)

For the Lord God, the Holy One of Israel says: Only in returning to me and waiting for me will you be saved; in quietness and confidence is your strength; but you'll have none of this, Isaiah 30:15 (TLB)

And out of justice, peace. Quietness and confidence will reign forever more. Isaiah 32:17 (TLB)

WORSHIP/OBEDIENCE

If women could convince themselves that time alone would be worth it for their mental growth and stability, they would do it. Certain rejuvenating springs start to flow through the soul when we are alone. We begin to hear our inner voice start to speak. We also start to discern the sound of God's direction for our lives. Painters can paint, writers write, musicians play, composers create, and saints can pray.

Start learning who you are!

September 10

A copy of the latest fashion magazine just arrived in the mail. Big beautiful pictures on the cover, big, bold titles, and a large neon pink headline screaming, "All Access Pass to All the Greatest Insider Style Tips that You'll Ever Need to Know!" Wow…all we'll ever need to know? Really?

ADORATION/EXPLANATION
God has got to be amazed when we fall for headlines such as this. It is not that the magazine itself is wrong, more that the empty promises seem to catch us every time. Our world is full of magazines, media, politicians and strange practices that offer empty promises year after year. The person of Jesus Christ is the only promise that is not empty. Imagine if we cared as much about the tips that His Word offers? Now that really is all we'll ever need to know!

❦

Run from anything that gives you evil thoughts that young men often have, but stay close to anything that makes you want to do right. Have faith and love, and enjoy the companionship of those who love the Lord and have pure hearts. 2 Timothy 2:22 (TLB)

You know how, when you were a small child, you were taught the holy Scriptures; and it is these that make you wise to accept God's salvation by trusting Christ Jesus. The whole Bible was given to us by inspiration from God and is useful to teach us what is true and to make us realize what is wrong in our lives; it straightens us out and helps us do what is right. It is God's way of making us well prepared at every point, fully equipped to do good to everyone. 2 Timothy 3:15-17 (TLB)

WORSHIP/OBEDIENCE
Today we should choose to be aware of all the false promises that the world tries to lure us with. We should remember Scripture and realize that God's promises and life tips are never false advertising. He does not need bold, colorful headlines to attract our attention.

He is TRUTH! We are privileged to worship and obey a God like that!

❦

I know a crazy lady. Well, she's not really insane she's just an annoying nuisance of a person that I have to deal with every once in a while. If I had my druthers, I would rather not be involved with her at all; but, because of my job, I have to. Then one day I decided that God may have put her in my path for a reason. Was the reason to help her? To set her straight? To tell her off? Was it because she annoyed everyone else and I was the only one that could handle her? Or…

ADORATION/EXPLANATION

…did God decide that I was the one who needed the lesson? Did God in His infinite mercy and love want this woman in my life because of what she could teach me? Was I looking deeper than the surface of the situation, or was I just getting annoyed? So I had to ask God…do I need to learn more? Do you, dear reader have someone like this in your world?

"The second is: 'You must love others as much as yourself.' No other commandments are greater than these." Mark 12:31 (TLB)

If anyone refuses to live by these rules he is not disobeying the rules of men but of God who gives his Holy Spirit to you. But concerning the pure brotherly love that there should be among God's people, I don't need to say very much, I'm sure! For God himself is teaching you to love one another. 1 Thessalonians 4:8-9 (TLB)

If anyone says, "I love God," but keeps on hating his brother, he is a liar; for if he doesn't love his brother who is right there in front of him, how can he love God whom he has never seen? 1 John 4:20 (TLB)

WORSHIP/OBEDIENCE

If you are struggling to deal or love someone in your own daily life; pray this prayer today.

Dear Lord, please do not tell me that this person is considered my brother. What? They are? This is my neighbor, brother, and the "others" that you teach us to love? This is difficult. It's easy to love someone who is loveable—I figured that one out! Wow…I have been failing! Help me view them through your eyes and not my own. I'll do better, Lord. Amen

---

September 12

Love is a mysterious force imparted by God to His human creation. This emotion goes far beyond our reasoning and comprehension. No wonder Christ said to his disciples that people would recognize believers by their love for others. But loving your enemies? C'mon…let's get real! Who can do that?

ADORATION/EXPLANATION

We've all had people who have hurt us emotionally, maybe even physically. It's people like that who make the second most important commandment (loving our neighbors as ourselves) difficult to follow, because we want to choose who our neighbors are. We want to love only the very nice, pretty, fun, and loveable folks. That doesn't take God's strength though. To love enemies or difficult people means that we will continually have to call on God for help. Do you think He knew this?

"There is a saying, 'Love your friends and hate your enemies.' But I say: Love your enemies! Pray for those who persecute you! In that way you will be acting as true sons of your Father in heaven. For he gives his sunlight to both the evil and the good, and sends rain on the just and on the unjust too. If you love only those who love you, what good is that? Even scoundrels do that much. If you are friendly only to your friends, how are you different from anyone else? Even the heathen do that."
Matthew 5:43-47 (TLB)

WORSHIP/OBEDIENCE

This passage does not take a brain surgeon to figure it out! Loving others as yourself means to LOVE others. All others! God is not necessarily talking about effusive hugging, kissing, emotional love here, but instead the kind of love that teaches kindness, courtesy, and prayer for difficult people. We mix up the directive and say, "How can I feel love and affection for a mean person?" Simple—call on God's strength for His kind of love. Pray, don't argue with them, and do not repay evil for evil

September 13

Victory in life comes when we remember how much we mean to God. We are the creation of a Father who is fully capable of meeting all our needs. But we must cease acting as if He is poor, or has limited resources, or is unaware of what is going on in our lives. He knows! He may be waiting for us to get some of our priorities in order before He answers us. We may be glad that He doesn't always give us what we ask for.

ADORATION/EXPLANATION
When we read the Bible, it helps us have a clearer memory of God's past actions and blessings that keep us from panicking at the thought of our present day problems. He is still the same God and can handle any emergency. Your life can present NO problems that Christ can't solve!

Jesus looked at them intently and said, "Humanly speaking, no one. But with God, everything is possible." Matthew 19:26 (TLB)

God is our refuge and strength, a tested help in times of trouble. And so we need not fear even if the world blows up, and the mountains crumble into the sea. Let the oceans roar and foam; let the mountains tremble! Psalm 46:1-3 (TLB)

For God hath not given us the spirit of fear; but of power, and of love, and of a sound mind. 2 Timothy 1:7 (KJV)

WORSHIP/OBEDIENCE
The average person spends more time with his fears than he does with his beliefs. Yet God's Word is very clear about trusting in God for the solution for our fears. Weigh your problem against God's promises and believe for the answer. Don't press the panic button.

Today, all things are possible!

September 14

Are you a sinner? Most people do not like this question. They will skirt around the issue and try to tell you what a "good" person they basically are, based on the charities they donate to, the church they attend, the services they do for the poor, etc. And when they are done, the question still remains: "Are you a sinner?"

ADORATION/EXPLANATION
I am a sinner! There, I said it…and you can too! We all are, and it is okay to admit it. As a matter of fact, we have to admit it. Don't rely on your own righteousness or good works to save you. The Bible tells us that outside of Christ, there is no chance. No man is good enough to save himself, yet no one is bad enough that God will not do it for him. So go ahead…admit it!

If we say that we have no sin, we are only fooling ourselves, and refusing to accept the truth. But if we confess our sins to him, he can be depended on to forgive us and cleanse us from every wrong. And it is perfectly proper for God to do this for us because Christ died to wash away our sins. For if we claim we have not sinned, we are lying and calling God a liar, for he says we have sinned. 1 John 1:8-10 (TLB)

God is my shield; he will defend me. He saves those whose hearts and lives are true and right. Psalm 7:10 (TLB)

For it is by believing in his heart that a man becomes right with God; and with his mouth he tells others of his faith, confirming his salvation. For the scriptures tell us the no one who believes in Christ will ever be disappointed. Romans 10:10,11 (TLB)

WORSHIP/OBEDIENCE
Cheer up! There is no fine print that we may have missed in His promise. We are all sinners. The obvious thing to do would be to accept God's free gift and be saved. Then as forgiven sinners, we can keep doing all those wonderful deeds, charities, church services, etc., that never were able to redeem us, because we NOW realize how much God loves us and that we are free in Him!

September 15

Sometimes we forget that our lives are only a prelude to greater things to come. We get caught up in our own agendas, in activities, jobs, and family ties. We are on our way though, with every breath we take, to a full and complete life with God. In a very real sense, we are pilgrims in the here and now, working, trudging, and seeking our way toward the very face of God.

ADORATION/EXPLANATION
God has given us fellow pilgrims called "friends" on this journey. As we fumble and grope around this crazy world, let us take care not to get lost. Friends can help us along this saga called life and give us encouragement. Let us keep in mind the prize that we are striving for and uplift our friends to do the same.

Give your burdens to the Lord. He will carry them. He will not permit the godly to slip or fall. Psalm 55:22 (TLB)

A good man is known by his truthfulness; a false man by deceit and lies. Proverbs 12:17 (TLB)

Anxious hearts are very heavy but a word of encouragement does wonders! Proverbs 12:25 (TLB)

A true friend is always loyal, and a brother is born to help in time of need. Proverbs 17:17 (TLB)

WORSHIP/OBEDIENCE
If we want the best for our friends and ourselves, our lives will begin and end with God. Our job as faithful followers of Christ needs to be that of an encourager, especially to those who are the closest to us in our own journey.

Look around today for someone who may need an emotional boost.
Press on fellow pilgrim…

When the concept of free will comes up in a conversation, many people are confused. Some say, "If we have God-given free will, then we can do whatever we want." Another person may add, "We must deny our self-will completely and let Christ do the work in our lives." Both extremes seem to be dangerous. If you totally deny your own God-given will, you are nothing but a big blob of protoplasm in a petri dish. If you strive for you own total self-will, you have now ceased to be led by the Spirit.

ADORATION/EXPLANATION

Our awesome God has given us a combination of wills: His and ours. When we become Spirit-filled and led as a true Christian, we don't lose our personalities! Instead, God uses them. God has chosen to work through YOU to accomplish His will. God does not handle our daily tasks such as wash dishes, go to work, pack lunches, or do the homework. He does not speak audibly from Heaven, either. He allows us to live our daily lives with His spirit as a guide and a helper. He uses men and women to accomplish His work on this planet. You and I…

But when the Holy Spirit controls our lives he will produce this kind of fruit in us; love, joy, peace, patience, kindness, goodness, faithfulness, gentleness and self-control; and here there is no conflict with Jewish laws. Those who belong to Christ have nailed their natural evil desires to the cross and crucified them there. If we are living now by the Holy Spirit's power, let us follow the Holy Spirit's leading in every part of our lives. Galatians 5:22-25 (TLB)

WORSHIP/OBEDIENCE

Obviously we all want to live a joyous, Spirit-led life. Who wouldn't? Thus, we need to use our God-given free will to obey His directives for our lives. We need to read His word and apply it to our everyday plans. It is at this point when we step out in faith and choose to live for Christ that God meets us and His will begins to guide us. How exciting!

September 17

In the past man has been seen as a victim of his subconscious, his upbringing, or his environment. The power he had to change himself seemed to be minimized. But, why? We have choices over the direction of our lives, after all. The real problem is that we so often choose to pretend that we have no power over our lives. We make excuses. But the influence that others use to manipulate us in relationships can be overcome by ourselves. We can even choose to be happy. Wow!

ADORATION/EXPLANATION

I am responsible for myself. What is presently wrong with me as well as right with me is a result of my own choices. Our wonderful God wants to be a participant in these choices. Once we really understand that we are loved and have worth in the eyes of the ultimate Supreme Being, we can have the faith to live a radically courageous life, even with its pitfalls and pot-holes.

In my distress I prayed to the Lord and he answered me and rescued me. Psalm 118:5 (NASB)

The Lord is my light and my salvation; whom shall I fear? When evil men come to destroy me, they will stumble and fall! Yes, though a mighty army marches against me, my heart shall know no fear! I am confident that God will save me. Psalm 27:1-3 (NASB)

I will bless the Lord who counsels me; he gives me wisdom in the night. He tells me what to do. Psalm 16:7 (TLB)

WORSHIP/OBEDIENCE

Obviously God knows that we need to start at the beginning, especially if we feel powerless to change the direction that our lives are traveling. Go back to the basics of simple, humble prayer. Ask for directions. Put one foot in front of the other…even Kindergartners need to work on the alphabet and number counting before they learn to read. No hiker conquers a mountain unless he starts at the bottom. Start in making small choices, and then move up to a worthy goal.

God can and will make a way!

September 18

Some friends just returned from camping and told how their tent was on a hill and ended up being flooded with water during a storm. Whenever pitching a tent, a flat, level spot should be chosen, if possible. However, they were on a mountain and had no choice of location. The Bible talks about setting up camp or pitching our tent, so to speak, in the correct spot.

ADORATION/EXPLANATION

If life could be compared to a campground, where would you pitch your tent? What spot would you choose? Flat? Rocky? Hilly? Muddy? Our awesome God has enough beautiful, perfectly flat and level camp-sites available for all. Go pick your spot!

O Lord, who may abide in Your tent? Who may dwell on Your holy hill? Psalm 15:1 (NASB)

For you have been a refuge for me, a tower of strength against the enemy. Let me dwell in Your tent forever; let me take refuge in the shelter of your wings. Psalm 61:3, 4 (NASB)

"Is not the whole land before you? Please separate from me; if to the left, then I will go to the right; or if to the right, then I will go to the left." Abram settled in the land of Canaan, while Lot settled in the cities of the valley, and moved his tents as far as Sodom. Now the men of Sodom were wicked exceedingly and sinners against the Lord. Genesis 13:9, 12, 13 (NASB)

WORSHIP/OBEDIENCE

If you get the chance, read Genesis chapter thirteen all the way through. The difference between the fate of Abram and Lot was the place that they chose to set up their tents. We can all remember Sodom and Gomorrah, right? Lot chose to set his tents in a bad place. Sometimes we choose hilly, muddy, rocky, slippery, or sinful places to erect our tents, and then wonder why trouble is happening.

Look around…the problem may be your tent site!

Have you ever lain down in a green lawn full of clover? Many of us haven't done so since we were children. Most of the time, we just mow over the clover and do not pay much attention to its insignificant flower, but you should really stop and take notice. The flower might be small, but the intricate beauty up close is amazing. Its fragrance is also so powerful that now most major candle companies are making their products with the scent of clover. Size does not matter!

ADORATION/EXPLANATION

Oh, the beautiful aroma of a clover! Stop and smell one if you get the chance and let it remind you that our awesome God took such care with even the smallest and over-looked of all the flowers. He cared enough to give it a beautiful fragrance, even if most do not take the time to appreciate it. Could you be a clover in the field of life? Do you feel over-looked? Are people missing your value and aroma? Keep blooming, even if you get mowed over. Keep popping up! Someone will notice.

As far as God is concerned there is a sweet, wholesome fragrance in our lives. It is the fragrance of Christ within us, an aroma to both the saved and the unsaved all around us. 2 Corinthians 2:15 (TLB)

How fragrant your cologne, and how great your name! No wonder all the young girls love you! Song of Solomon 1:3 (TLB)

Be full of love for others, following the example of Christ who loved you and gave himself to God as a sacrifice to take away your sins. And God was pleased, for Christ's love for you was like sweet perfume to him. Ephesians 5:2 (TLB)

WORSHIP/OBEDIENCE

God desires our lives to be lived in such a way that, even if we are overlooked or mowed over, we will still bloom and give off a beautiful fragrance. We may not be the biggest; we may not be the most flamboyant of all the flowers; we may not be the tallest or the prettiest; however, we can remain steady in our position until the day when someone gets close enough to see our true value. But never forget—God always sees it! So hang tough, little clover!

September 20

Moses went up to the top of the mountain to hear from God. He received the Ten Commandments and delivered them to the people of Israel. The second commandment is a tricky one: do not have or worship idols. Most folks today would say that they would never have an idol or graven image, but this is because they are thinking of statues, ivory images, or sculptures. But an idol is really anything that we make more important or essential to our daily living than God. What? Does that mean that our kids, television shows, our jobs, money, our homes, our sports, or our hobbies can be idols? Yes!

ADORATION/EXPLANATION

If anything comes before our love and devotion to Christ, it is considered an idol. If anything becomes so important, essential, time consuming, or thought provoking, attention grabbing, and worthy of my time before God, that is an idol! Think about it—do you have an idol?

Never worship any god but me. Never make idols; don't worship images, whether of birds, animals, or fish. Deuteronomy 5:7, 8 (TLB)

Nor worship idols as they did. The Scriptures tell us, "The people sat down to eat and drink and then got up to dance" in worship of the golden calf. 1 Corinthians 10:7 (TLB)

Dear children, keep away from anything that might take God's place in your hearts. Amen. 1 John 5:21 (TLB)

WORSHIP/OBEDIENCE

Today we might not have golden calves or statues that we bow down to, but we have many other obvious things that take precedence in our lives over God. Television, money, work, home, hobbies, sports, kids, boat, security, and countless other things can be considered idols.

Choose today to focus on God first!

September 21

Do you remember….? The twenty-first day of September? (A popular song from the 1970s asked this question.) Truthfully, unless there is a special event planned or some occasion to look forward to, this date is no more of a memory than any other. Summer is over and autumn is on the horizon. School has started for children. Quite mundane really!

ADORATION/EXPLANATION

Often people ask the question, "Why do I even get up in the morning? Nothing is new, there are no special plans, nothing to look forward to…." In answering this question, we need to remind ourselves daily that our purpose is to get up, set our hearts, minds, and souls before the Lord, and walk through this day yielding (not stubbornly being dragged) to His plan for our lives.

Since, then, you have been raised with Christ, set your hearts on things above, where Christ is seated at the right hand of God. Set your minds on things above, not on earthly things. For you died, and your life is now hidden with Christ in God. Colossians 3:1-3 (NASB)

Therefore be careful how you walk, not as unwise men, but as wise, making the most of your time, because the days are evil. So then do not be foolish, but understand what the will of the Lord is. Ephesians 5:15-17 (NASB)

WORSHIP/OBEDIENCE

How does this pan out in our everyday, sometimes mundane life? Does this mean we don't like life when we're hurt, upset, when people don't act or behave the way we think they should, when there is nothing exciting to do, to see, to get up in the morning for?

We must choose to stay focused on the things that are eternal: God, His Word, and people. That is the key to understanding our purpose each day. It is not our purpose or our lives to remember—it is God's plan and purpose for our lives! *This* is why we get up in the morning!

September 22

We should get up each morning striving to keep our minds focused on the things above and to be conformed to the image of Christ. We should have the compassion, kindness, and boldness of Christ in relating to other people throughout our day. What will we give (or what will we give up), in order for God to accomplish His purpose in us?

ADORATION/EXPLANATION

What a God we serve. He has a mighty plan and purpose for our lives. My life! Your life! If we just sit and meditate on this fact for a few moments, we can't help but feel awestruck that God has such an interest in our personal, individual lives. And we know this to be true because God's word speaks volumes to us...

However, I consider my life worth nothing to me, if only I may finish the race and complete the task the Lord Jesus has given me—the task of testifying to the gospel of God's grace. Acts 20:24 (NASB)

But whatever was to my profit I now consider loss for the sake of Christ. What is more, I consider everything a loss compared to the surpassing greatness of knowing Christ Jesus my Lord, for whose sake I have lost all things. I consider them rubbish, that I may gain Christ and be found in him, not having a righteousness of my own that comes from the law, but that which is through faith in Christ—the righteousness that comes from God and is by faith. Philippians 3:7-9 (NASB)

WORSHIP/OBEDIENCE

Do our lives testify to God's grace? Are we willing to follow God's eternal purpose for our lives? Bow your head at this moment and tell Him.

Father, I want the very best that You have to offer me in each day of my life,
and I want to offer You my very best,
no matter what my circumstances might be.
I am WILLING, Lord!

September 23

If we truly want to follow God's purpose for our lives, then we must use some practical tips to guard our hearts. Guard our hearts? What does this mean and how do we do this? How do we keep God's ways from departing from our lives?

ADORATION/EXPLANATION
We have a heavenly Father who is personally involved in accomplishing His purpose through us! This image should provide us with hope and peace for our futures. This view on life is not easily explained or understood, but it is God's precious gift to those who choose to deeply love and trust Him above all else.

"Only give heed to yourself and keep your soul diligently, lest you forget the things which your eyes have seen, and lest they depart from your heart all the days of your life." Deuteronomy 4:9 (NASB)

Fix these words of mine in your hearts and minds; tie them as symbols on your hands and bind them on your foreheads. Teach them to your children, talking about them when you sit at home and when you walk along the road, when you lie down and when you get up. Deuteronomy 11:18-19 (NIVB)

WORSHIP/OBEDIENCE
Wow…obviously, we are supposed to read, study, meditate on, and put into practice the precepts and advice of the Bible. Love, joy, peace, and much needed advice on kindness, anger, patience, humility, money, sorrow, relationships, marriage, and every other pursuit on this earth are to be "fixed" on our hearts! This means that they are made important…a priority! Like Nike says, "Just do it!"

God is always at work in our temporal (earthly/every day) circumstances to bring about HIS eternal (heavenly) purposes. So, am I saying that this will all be made clear to us? Shown, demonstrated, explained, and laid bare before our eyes so that we are never doubting or confused? No. Absolutely not! As a matter of fact, it is usually just the opposite with God.

ADORATION/EXPLANATION
Do not yield to the temptation of trying to figure it all out. Trust in the Lord. God's ways are not our ways. Our own understanding is usually faulty. Our thoughts are not His...

But GOD...He is GOD!

Jesus told His disciples that night in the vineyard...

"Remain in me, and I will remain in you. No branch can bear fruit by itself; it must remain in the vine. Neither can you bear fruit unless you remain in me.

I am the vine; you are the branches. If a man remains in me and I in him, he will bear much fruit; apart from me you can do nothing."

"If you obey my commands, you will remain in my love, just as I have obeyed my Father's commands and remain in his love." John 15:4-5, 10 (NASB)

WORSHIP/OBEDIENCE
He is God! He owes no explanation, no demonstration, nothing! But what He does offer is love, joy, peace, and purpose for our lives if we choose to hang on to the vine. Hold fast, remain in, continue in, abide! Hang on to that one true vine for all you're worth, and put your trust in the words of Christ. Sometimes, just sometimes, God allows us to recognize and actually see His perfect plan at work! Wow!

September 25

God has made it very clear in the Bible that we have been thoughtfully and purposefully made. If this is so, than why do we sometimes wonder "Who am I" and "What in the world am I doing here?" We'd all like a quick, easily understood explanation. A simple, cheap "fast food" directive from God! But thankfully, God is not in the "fast food" business…

ADORATION/EXPLANATION

What is amazing is that not only are we thoughtfully made, but God desires a relationship with us and wants us to reflect His glory. Yes, us!! Many people know about Jesus, but do not have a personal kinship with him. Do you?

And they were calling to one another:

"Holy, holy holy is the Lord Almighty;

the whole earth is full of his glory." Isaiah 6:3 (NASB)

So, whether you eat or drink or whatever you do, do it all for the glory of God. 1 Corinthians 10:31 (NASB)

For it is by grace you have been saved, through faith—and this not from yourselves, it is the gift of God—not by works, so that no one can boast. For we are God's workmanship, created in Christ Jesus to do good works, which God prepared in advance for us to do. Ephesians 2:8-10 (NASB)

WORSHIP/OBEDIENCE

No simple, "fast food" answers here: we are complex, beautiful creations of God, and a valuable project requires more than a quick, one step instruction guide. It involves study, meditation, desire, and most of all trust—a veritable lifetime of trust in the Creator himself. So whether we are eating, drinking, sleeping, working, or just plain living life, we should choose to pursue God's game plan in order to honor Him. Because that is exactly why in the world we are here!

September 26

As a small child, my parents always made us take naps on Sunday afternoons. When I attended kindergarten, the class was required to have nap time each day. Why? Because parents and teachers seemed to know that children need rest times in order to function properly. Without rest, children become cranky, grouchy and more prone to disobedience. I never liked nap times, or rest periods. I would always fight the urge to sleep during the day, unless I was forced to lie down and relax. Sometimes trials in our life can be the driving force to make us learn to "rest" as adults. What we may view as a stop in the road, a detour or a bump, may really be a required "nap time" from God. He knows what we need to function properly.

ADORATION/EXPLANATION
When you learn to trust God fully, there is an internal rest that takes place. This rest is a calm peacefulness that can only come from a total trust and reliance on His plan for your life. You know that He is going to do something…but you don't know what. You don't know how. You don't know when. And…you don't care! You trust that He is a mighty, awesome God who can handle it all. Done deal!

Commit your way to the Lord, trust also in Him, and He will do it. Rest in the Lord and wait patiently for Him; Psalm 37:5, 7a (NASB)

"Come to me, all who are weary and heavy-laden, and I will give you rest. Take my yoke upon you and learn from Me, for I am gentle and humble in heart, and you will find rest for your souls. For My yoke is easy and My burden is light." Matthew 11:28-30 (NASB)

WORSHIP/OBEDIENCE
Our rest in God may not be the physical naps that we had as children, but rather the spiritual, emotional rest that our souls crave—a calm sense of trust in a future that may seem uncertain and a peace of mind that only comes from obedience to a Creator who has promised to provide rest for our souls. God wants us to allow Him to get into the yoke, come along side, and do all the pulling. His promise is secure that He will never leave or forsake us. Why would we not call upon His name?

"Resting, resting…sweetly resting!"

September 27

The average person spends more time going over his worries than he does his faith. Why? We ponder, mull, ruminate, and just plain dwell on the things that bother and scare us instead of focusing on the mighty power of God. We need to forget the formalities and just tell God how we feel. He already knows our hearts and sees our fears, but He wants us to communicate with Him. We need to ponder and ruminate on the promises in His Word. Don't worry whether you are getting through or not. God hears!

ADORATION/EXPLANATION
"My ear is not heavy that it cannot hear," Jesus said. If you are facing a situation and there seems to be no way out, look up. We have an awesome God! Ask Him, seek Him for comfort from your fears, and apply His Word to your worry. Hold up your fearful situation to the mirror of the Bible…and believe for the answer! Money, security, relationships, job or health…

And looking at them Jesus said to them, "With people this is impossible, but with God all things are possible." Matthew 19:26 (NASB)

"So I say to you, ask, and it will be given to you; seek, and you will find; knock, and it will be opened to you. For everyone who asks, receives; and he who seeks, finds; and to him who knocks, it will be opened." Luke 11:9-10 (NASB)

For God has not given us a spirit of timidity, but of power and love and discipline. 2 Timothy 1:7 (NASB)

WORSHIP/OBEDIENCE
With the kind of resource that we have in Christ, isn't it regrettable that we continue to live with our fears? The God that we worship knows everything and can do anything. Why do we tend to wait until the last resort to call upon Him? We can confidently look to Him daily for the answers and solutions to our fears. Start today to begin to let go of your distressing thoughts, attitudes or feelings, and realize that God is up to handling any emergency that may come upon you. Wow!

September 28

Why read the Bible daily? Why even have a devotional book or guide to turn to each morning? God himself tells us that His Word is living, breathing, and useful to guide us through our life. The Bible is a great deal more than cold print. It is not just a best seller to be quickly read and then discarded to a shelf. It is charged with the power of the Holy Spirit to bring into our lives power, might, teaching, joy, comfort, assurance, and the salvation message. Not just the salvation from Christ's death on the cross of Calvary, but salvation from the daily grind of life!

ADORATION/EXPLANATION

What a wonderful reward we can receive in our daily lives by the keeping of His Word! There is advice for our every want or need, problem or purpose, fear or failure, delight or desire. What love God has for us in leaving the Bible as a daily resource for living. When we spend time in the Word, we realize how much adoration our marvelous Creator deserves.

***

"He who has My commandments and keeps them is the one who loves Me; and he who loves Me will be loved by My Father, and I will love him and will disclose Myself to him." Jesus answered and said to him, "If anyone loves Me, he will keep My Word; and My Father will love him, and We will come to him and make Our abode with him. He who does not love Me does not keep My words; and the word which you hear is not Mine, but the Father's who sent Me." John 14:21, 23-24 (NASB)

But God demonstrates His own love toward us, in that while we were yet sinners, Christ died for us. Much more then, having been justified by His blood, we shall be saved from the wrath of god through Him. Romans 5 8-9 (NASB)

WORSHIP/OBEDIENCE

Today you can choose to read and trust God's Word. Do not be shaken by what you observe and feel around you, at home, work, or play. Emotions and feelings are not always real indicators of truth. There is Someone standing beside you and desiring to guide you through, if only you consider trusting Him. "No good thing will he withhold from them that walk uprightly."

Dear Father, guide us today in the beautiful plans that you teach us about in your Word.

***

September 29

It amazes me that respect and courtesy seem to be missing from the general population these days. We wonder why many children fail to possess these traits, yet we need not look much further than at the home and the parents. Children do not know enough at a young age to fake respect and courtesy. They are quick to mimic and copy what they observe from their parents. When we adults monitor our words, tone of voice, and body language, compliment and encourage and build positive manners in relationships, we are instilling a wonderful legacy in our children. We are teaching respect for themselves as well as others.

ADORATION/EXPLANATION

More than reading scripture, more than lip service, more than church attendance, God desires our lives to be an example of His love in us. How can we adore a wonderful Savior if we are not following His example? Like children following our example, we need to seek Jesus' life as a living, breathing guide on how to treat people.

———

The Lord is gracious and merciful; slow to anger and great in lovingkindness. The Lord is good to all, and His mercies are over all His works. Psalm 145:8-9 (NASB)

And let us consider how to stimulate one another to love and good deeds, Hebrews 10:24 (NASB)

Through Him then, let us continually offer up a sacrifice of praise to God, that is, the fruit of lips that give thanks to his name. And do not neglect doing good and sharing, for with such sacrifices God is pleased. Hebrews 13:15-16 (NASB)

So, as those who have been chosen of God, holy and beloved, put on a heart of compassion, kindness, humility, gentleness and patience... Colossians 3:12 (NASB)

WORSHIP/OBEDIENCE

The best way to compliment anyone is to follow his or her example. Do we want our children to follow our example of respect and courtesy toward others? As children of God, we can show our love and honor towards Him by living in such a way that demonstrates love, courtesy, and respect. Not just to those that deserve it, but to those that may be rude, unkind, and unappreciative of our efforts.

Remember…children may be watching, people may be listening,
and God most certainly is cheering us on!

———

Do you thank God for every event that happens to you? Do you trust that He, in His infinite love and mercy, may have allowed the very event that you are fretting about to teach you some wonderful lesson? When you choose to view your life in this manner, it will produce a beautiful trait of continual thankfulness. You will begin to view all things as coming down from your heavenly Father for a spiritual purpose. It doesn't mean that you will necessarily like or enjoy every event that occurs, but you will be better able to accept, deal, and learn from them.

ADORATION/EXPLANATION
Our awesome God knows precisely what we need to grow closer to Him. He sees our needs before we even ask. And when we do ask for Him to remove some trials and tribulations, His answer is often a resounding, "NO!" because He understands the situation far better than we do. We need to continue on with a thankful attitude, believing that God will show up in each situation with a valuable lesson for us. Open our eyes Lord…

Beyond all these things put on love, which is the perfect bond of unity. Let the peace of Christ rule in your hearts, to which indeed you were called in one body; and be thankful. Let the word of Christ richly dwell within you, with all wisdom teaching and admonishing one another with psalms and hymns and spiritual songs, singing with thankfulness in your hearts to God. Whatever you do in word or deed, do all in the name of the Lord Jesus, giving thanks through him to God the Father. Colossians 3:14-17 (NASB)

Devote yourselves to prayer, keeping alert in it with an attitude of thanksgiving; Colossians 4:2 (NASB)

WORSHIP/OBEDIENCE
So God is telling us to pray with an attitude of thanksgiving at all times? What if I don't like my situation? What if I want to beg God to remove my trial? The Bible is very clear in telling us that we can bring anything and everything to the feet of our heavenly Father in prayer. But when we really grasp God's omnipotence (all powerful strength), and His love, mercy, and abounding grace toward us, we can still learn to be thankful in His answers to us. If a trial remains, we can believe that is for our ultimate good.

Look for the lesson. Father knows best…

October 1

"Blue skies...nothing but blue skies, do I see!" Isn't it wonderful looking up at clear, bright blue skies? Sucking crisp air into our lungs makes us wish it would stay that way all the time. Summer is over and fall has arrived!! Leaves are turning, grass is browning—change is everywhere! So what is changing in this season of your life? Anything? Many things? Everything?

ADORATION/EXPLANATION

Praise the Lord, He never changes! When life is NOT consistent? When friends, jobs, relationships, come and go? We can count on our one Redeemer, our one true Friend, our one Provider, on the little finger of just one hand. But that is enough. We don't need to be able to list many things to count on. One finger is all we need. That is good enough!

And, "Lord, in the beginning you laid the foundation of the earth, and the heavens are the work of your hands, even they will perish, but you remain forever. They will wear out like old clothing. You will roll them up like an old coat. They will fade like old clothing. But you are always the same. You will never grow old" Hebrews 1:10-12 (NIV)

Listen, I tell you a mystery: We will not all sleep, but we will all be changed---in a flash, in the twinkling of an eye, at the last trumpet. For the trumpet will sound, the dead will be raised imperishable, and we will be changed. 1 Corinthians 15:51-52 (NIV)

Jesus Christ is the same yesterday and today and forever. Hebrews 13:8 (NIV)

WORSHIP/OBEDIENCE

Wow...stop and look around. Fall has really arrived! Leaves are turning and seasons are changing. But there is one thing in this world of changing times and seasons that we can count on—God and His word! He stays the same, He never grows old, and He NEVER changes. If we have put our trust in God, then we need to learn to worship and obey Him in <u>every</u> season of our lives.

Look up! I bet there is a blue sky!

The Bible is not simply a collection of words from God. It is living, life changing, and dynamic in its potential power for our lives. With the sharpness of a surgeon's scalpel, it cuts back and reveals who we are and what we are not. This scalpel carves away to reveal both good and evil in our lives, if we only allow it!

ADORATION/EXPLANATION

What an awesome, mighty Savior we have. Nothing can be hidden from God. He knows about everyone everywhere, and everything that we think is hidden about our personal lives is "splayed" open before His all-seeing eyes. To some folks, that thought is scary and to others, it is a comfort.

For the word of God is full of living power. It is sharper than the sharpest knife, cutting deep into our innermost thoughts and desires. It exposes us for what we really are. Nothing in all creation can hide from him. Everything is naked and exposed before his eyes. This is the God to whom we must explain all that we have done. Hebrews 4:12-13 (NIV)

"Behold, I am coming soon! Blessed is he who keeps the words of the prophecy in this book." Revelation 22:7 (NIV)

Heaven and earth will pass away, but my words will never pass away. Mark 13:31 (NIV)

WORSHIP/OBEDIENCE

God's Word requires decisions. Like a skilled surgeon's knife, we need to allow God's Word to penetrate and change our daily living. We can have no secrets from God. Isn't it such a beautiful concept that although God knows us intimately, privately, and personally, He still loves us? He isn't upset with the diseases in our lives that may need removal. He just wants us to allow him to operate.

"Who can I talk to?" "Who can understand me in these changing seasons of my life?" "Does God really hear me and understand what I am going through?" Aren't these questions that many of us have asked? Isn't this a place or position that we find ourselves in, over and over again, during the year?

ADORATION/EXPLANATION

Like a high priest, Jesus mediates between God and us. As God's representative, as well as our counselor and advocate, He assures us of God's forgiveness. Jesus has more authority than any Jewish high priest did because He is truly God and truly man. High priests went before God once a year, but our high priest, Christ, is always at God's side interceding for us. Isn't it awe inspiring that our legal counsel is Christ himself? This should eradicate any doubts from our minds!

Therefore, since we have a great high priest who has gone through the heavens, Jesus the Son of God, let us hold firmly to the faith we profess. For we do not have a high priest who is unable to sympathize with our weaknesses, but we have one who has been tempted in every way, just as we are—yet was without sin. Let us then approach the throne of grace with confidence, so that we may receive mercy and find grace to help us in our time of need. Hebrews 4:14-16 (NIV)

WORSHIP/OBEDIENCE

Jesus understands us! He experienced many temptations and problems throughout his life as a human being. He can and does sympathize with us. We can talk to him, complain to him, confess and commiserate with him. Jesus faced temptation without giving in to sin. He understands our plight as flawed human beings, but lived as an example that we do not have to give in to sin.

Wonderful Counselor!

If we understand the concept of needing Jesus as our High Priest and Counselor, then wouldn't it be obvious that we also need to spend time getting to know Him personally? Who chooses legal counsel that they know nothing about? Jesus has left this earth and is sitting at God's righteous, right hand. He is watching us and the beautiful fact is that He has given us His story, His reputation, and His references, creating a wonderful "resume" in His Word! Have you looked at His resume yet?

ADORATION/EXPLANATION

A story, a reference list, or even a resume is of no value unless they are read. We should want to make every effort to pursue the character of the one we call "Lord." Why not have a "meet and greet?" Open your Bible…

Do your best to present yourself to God as one approved, a workman who does not need to be ashamed and who correctly handles the word of truth. 2 Timothy 2:15 (NIV)

Oh, how I love your law! I meditate on it all day long. Your commands make me wiser than my enemies, for they are ever with me.

Your word is a lamp to my feet and a light for my path.

Accept, O Lord, the willing praise of my mouth, and teach me your laws. Psalm 119:97-98, 105, 108 (NIV)

"For there is nothing hidden that will not be disclosed, and nothing concealed that will not be known or brought out into the open." Luke 8:17 (NIV)

WORSHIP/OBEDIENCE

Earlier it was asked, "Who chooses legal counsel that they know nothing about?" Poor, pitiful prisoners who can afford no one else, that's who! Praise God that we are NOT those prisoners. Praise God that we have been set free and that our chains are gone! But now we have a whole lot of reading to do.

October 5

Like cookies and milk…learning about God daily goes better with prayer.

Dear Lord, help me to make it my goal and longing desire to study your Word, to actually study with a true plan to apply your precepts to my everyday living even if this goal means an awful lot of reading and in-depth thought. Do you want to know the really cool thing though? I realize that you have given me a whole lifetime! No rush…

ADORATION/EXPLANATION
A whole lifetime—that sounds long, doesn't it? But is it, really? Are we sure that we have many, many long years ahead? Lord, help us not to worry or dwell on the amount of days ahead. Help us not to comfortably count on a hundred years either. May we be good workmen in our study of Your Word!

Accept, O Lord, the willing praise of my mouth, and teach me your laws. Though I constantly take my life in my hands, I will not forget your law. The wicked have set a snare for me, but I have not strayed from your precepts. Your statutes are my heritage forever; they are the joy of my heart. My heart is set on keeping your decrees to the very end. Psalm 119:108-112 (NIV)

Your statutes are wonderful; therefore I obey them. The unfolding of your words gives light; it gives understanding to the simple. Psalm 119:129-130 (NIV)

Lord, how I love you! For you have done such tremendous things for me. Psalm 18:1 (TLB)

WORSHIP/OBEDIENCE
It gives understanding to the simple? Are we simple? We'd like to think not, but the way we live and behave on many occasions in everyday life demonstrates that we still have a long way to go. Here is the good news, though: the <u>unfolding</u>, opening, reading, and searching of God's word gives light. Turn the light on!

October 6

Have you ever had every light turned on, searching the whole house, but still cannot seem to find what you're looking for? Have you ever done this and then later in the day come across exactly what you were seeking, and it is right in front of your face the entire time?

ADORATION/EXPLANATION
Sometimes finding something requires us to slow down, look carefully, and wait! We need to be still, calm ourselves, and clear our heads.

But, you may say, "I am in a rush, in a hurry! I have an agenda to my day! There are many things that I have to accomplish on my ever-growing list!"

But seek first his kingdom and his righteousness, and all these things will be given to you as well. Therefore do not worry about tomorrow, for tomorrow will worry about itself. Each day has enough trouble of its own. Matthew 6:33-34 (NIV)

And you, my son Solomon, acknowledge the God of your father, and serve him with wholehearted devotion and with a willing mind, for the Lord searches every heart and understands every motive behind the thoughts. If you seek him, he will be found by you; but if you forsake him, he will reject you forever. 1 Chronicles 28:9 (NIV) (*King David, speaking to his son Solomon*)

In my distress I screamed to the Lord for his help. And he heard me from heaven, my cry reached his ears. Psalm 18:6 (TLB)

WORSHIP/OBEDIENCE
If we think that we cannot find God's plan, path, or directive for our lives, we need to stop, slow down, cease striving, and stop looking. Wait, what?

Stop looking?

Yes. Stop looking, take a break, and pray!

No agenda here!

October 7

Sometimes it is very hard to wait on God. Or is it? Are we actually waiting on God or are we just impatient for some clear-cut arrows, directions, and easy "fast-food" rules to follow? If God would just give some easy steps...then we could actually accomplish something...and get down to this business of living for God. Hurry up God...

ADORATION/EXPLANATION
To be loved by God and be a part of His kingdom is an awesome privilege, but when I fail to trust God with my life or when I doubt His wisdom in the affairs of this world (yes, even when there are no clear cut arrows, signs, etc.), I presume that He is not really almighty God! I want to rush and do things my own way.

But you are a chosen people, a royal priesthood, a holy nation, a people belonging to God, that you may declare the praises of him who called you out of darkness into his wonderful light. Once you were not a people, but now you are a people of God; once you had not received mercy, but now you have received mercy.

Dear friends, I urge you, as aliens and strangers in the world, to abstain from sinful desires, which war against your soul. Live such good lives among the pagans that, though they accuse you of doing wrong, they may see your good deeds and glorify God on the day he visits us. 1 Peter 2:9-12 (NIV)

I waited patiently for God to help me; then he listened and heard my cry. Psalm 40:1 (TLB)

WORSHIP/OBEDIENCE
We have the choice of living as secure, beloved sons or daughters of the King, or living as anxious, upset, frustrated children whose God is not all-powerful. Today, choose to view yourself as part of a royal priesthood, a Holy nation! Even if you are waiting on something that you're asking of God, choose to obey and live your life today in obvious ways that point to your King.

Who is your KING?

October 8

We have all heard the statement that God is sovereign. We may even shake our head in agreement to this, but do we actually even know what this means? A sovereign person is one who exercises supreme authority or acts as an acknowledged leader. As a quality or characteristic of God, it means that He reigns with supreme power of the most exalted kind; it means that He is over and above, excellent, having undisputed ascendancy, ABSOLUTE.

In other words, God is in control!

ADORATION/EXPLANATION
In what ways do we sometimes overlook God's sovereignty in our understanding of how He works in our everyday lives? When we are scared, unsure, stressed, and confused, we very often start questioning and complaining because we have forgotten the security of having an ABSOLUTE GOD. Nothing will ever happen to us that God does not permit to happen.

Remember this, fix it in mind, Take it to heart, you rebels. Remember the former things, those of long ago; I am God, and there is no other; I am God, and there is none like me. I make known the end from the beginning, from ancient times, what is still to come. I say: My purpose will stand, And I will do all that I please. From the east I summon a bird of prey; from a far-off land, a man to fulfill my purpose. What I have said, that will I bring about; what I have planned, that will I do. Isaiah 46:8-11 (NIV)

WORSHIP/OBEDIENCE
When we believe that God is in control, we do not mean that God is controlling everything that is happening like a master puppeteer. He allows us to do what we want, but trusting in Him is an option! When He says that "I am God, and there is none like me," we should believe it!

Today I will trust in God's sovereignty…not my own!

I know that I cannot rule my own life and find true fulfillment. How do I know this? Well, as a matter of confession, I've tried! But eventually I had to throw in the towel, cry "uncle," and surrender to the fact that I do not have all the answers. I have to rest in God's wisdom to accomplish real lasting fulfillment in my life. REST…what a secure and beautiful concept!

ADORATION/EXPLANATION
We should decide to thank the Lord today, right now, in this very moment, because His love and concern for us never wears out and never grows old.

But the plans of the Lord stand firm forever, the purposes of his heart through all generations. Blessed is the nation whose God is the Lord, the people he chose for his inheritance. From heaven the Lord looks down and sees all mankind; from his dwelling place he watches all who live on earth— he forms the hearts of all, who considers everything they do.

No king is saved by the size of his army; no warrior escapes by his great strength. A horse is a vain hope for deliverance; despite all its great strength it cannot save.

But the eyes of the Lord are on those who fear him, on those whose hope is in his unfailing love, Psalm 33:11-18 (NIV)

WORSHIP/OBEDIENCE
No king, warrior, horse, or anything here on earth (especially ourselves!) can save us! Whew— what a relief that is! We can rest in God's love and trust. Understanding His wonderful grace will help us to confidently trust, obey, and hope in a wonderful, caring, and unfailing God.

Sounds like a plan…a mighty good plan!

There is nothing about us that Jesus does not understand. We are His children; He has claimed us for His own! He loves us, sees us, and hears us when we call.

Basically he "gets" each one of us! He has come to live inside us and wants the best for our lives! Jesus knows us…

ADORATION/EXPLANATION

But what if you do not feel like this? What if you don't feel like God understands, loves you, sees you, and hears you when you pray?

Luckily for us, the way we feel doesn't change the promises of His word! He is faithful! He loves when we choose to obey…even when we do not feel like it. Especially when we don't feel like it!

This is genuine adoration for our Lord.

Remain in me, and I will remain in you. No branch can bear fruit by itself; it must remain in the vine. Neither can you bear fruit unless you remain in me.

I am the vine; you are the branches. If a man remains in me and I in him, he will bear much fruit; apart from me you can do nothing. John 15:4-5 (NIV)

And we know that in all things God works for the good of those who love him, who have been called according to His purpose. Romans 8:28 (NIV)

No, in all things we are more than conquerors through him who loved us. Romans 8:37 (NIV)

WORSHIP/OBEDIENCE

Oh, how He loves you and me…

Do we have to feel things before we put our trust and hope in Him?

Not if it is God who is making the promises. As a matter of fact, we have to choose to remain, stay attached, and abide in Christ, the true vine, especially when we don't feel like it. This demonstrates real worship and obedience!

October 11

God wants to reveal truth to us. He uses people, circumstances, and, most importantly, His Word! God desires obedience from anyone who claims to be His child. He speaks and we should obey. He explains…maybe? Does God owe me an explanation for anything? No. Why? Because He is God! He is all-powerful, all-knowing, and all-present!

ADORATION/EXPLANATION
We have to read God's word with the intent to obey. We have to study, meditate, and NOT forget what He is telling us. And then maybe, just maybe, we will get a glimpse of His wonderful plan for our lives.

Do not merely listen to the word, and so deceive yourselves. Do what it says. Anyone who listens to the word but does not do what it says is like a man who looks at his face in a mirror and, after looking at himself, goes away and immediately forgets what he looks like.

But the man who looks intently into the perfect law that gives freedom, and continues to do this, not forgetting what he has heard, but doing it—he will be blessed in what he does. James 1:22-25 (NIV)

Trust in the Lord with all your heart and lean not on your own understanding… Proverbs 3:5 (NIV)

WORSHIP/OBEDIENCE
Am I staring intently into God's mirror, the Bible, for my life? As the New Testament book of James reminds us, we need to look intently at God's perfect Word and follow the advice. I can measure my reflection accurately through the mirror of the Bible. What can I work on?

I need to make the obvious choice of continuing to examine myself and NOT forget what I look like, NOT forget what I have heard, and do it!

No explanations needed!

October 12

What are you planning to do today? Where are you going in this crisp, blue sky, autumn air? Are you off to work? School? Grocery shopping? Appointments? It may seem of utmost importance…but does it really matter to God where you are going? No!

ADORATION/EXPLANATION

When we realize that our destination is not of big importance to God, but more importantly is how we get there; then our travels can take on a new purpose. It isn't our mode of travel but our mode of operating that matters most! Our way of keeping His teachings daily wherever we go, wherever we are, and whoever we are with. God is concerned with how we are operating our vehicle…

My son (*daughter*), do not forget my teaching, but keep my commands in your heart, for they will prolong your life many years and bring you prosperity. Let love and faithfulness never leave you; bind them around your neck, write them on the tablet of your heart. Proverbs 3:1-3 (NIV)

Oh, the depth of the riches of the wisdom and knowledge of God! How unsearchable his judgments, and his paths beyond tracing out! Who has known the mind of the Lord? Or who has been his counselor? Who has ever given to God, that God should repay him? For from him and through him and to him are all things. To him be the glory forever! Amen. Romans 11:33-36 (NIV)

WORSHIP/OBEDIENCE

We should strive for the wisdom and knowledge of God for everyday living. What is my mode of operation? How am I traveling?

Are love and faithfulness written on your heart? Is anything bound around your neck wherever you go? Are you consulting the driver's manual?

Today is the day to begin!

Leaves are just starting to change their colors: reds, yellows, greens, and brilliant oranges. This process cannot be stopped! Changing, growing, aging, and turning will continue through each season of every year whether we want it or not!

ADORATION/EXPLANATION

God in His infinite wisdom has set this world spinning on its axis in a continual motion. And it will keep on going until He decides that it is time to stop. We live in an awesomely ordered world. God is the master of continuity, order, authority and perfect submission of even the seasons. The autumn leaves are a visual reminder of His power and control!

"I the Lord do not change. So you, O descendants of Jacob, are not destroyed. Ever since the time of your forefathers you have turned away from my decrees and have not kept them. Return to me, and I will return to you," says the Lord Almighty. Malachi 3:6-7 (NIV)

Don't be deceived, my dear brothers. Every good and perfect gift is from above, coming down from the Father of the heavenly lights, who does not change like shifting shadows. James 1:16-17 (NIV)

There is a time for everything, and a season for every activity under heaven... Ecclesiastes 3:1 (NIV)

WORSHIP/OBEDIENCE

Changing leaves, changing lives, changing world...does anything ever stay the same? YES!! God! We can always count on Him. What a comforting thought.

Praise the Lord, He never changes!

October 14

I am choosing this day to look around my environment, my yard, my home, my life and embrace the changes that are occurring. Not just the falling leaves but all the other obvious changes that are out of my control. People, health, job, finances, age…even my "slightly" graying hair!

ADORATION/EXPLANATION
In the Bible it tells us to extol the Lord with all our hearts. To extol something or someone basically means to lift up or praise highly! Our adoration for God should still be present even when changes occur that we may not like. Extol the Lord!

Praise the Lord. I will extol the Lord with all my heart in the council of the upright and in the assembly. Great are the works of the Lord; they are pondered by all who delight in them. Glorious and majestic are his deeds, and his righteousness endures forever. He has caused his wonders to be remembered; the Lord is gracious and compassionate. Psalm 111:1-4 (NIV)

For, "All men are like grass, and all their glory is like the flowers of the field; the grass withers and the flowers fall, but the word of the Lord stands forever." 1 Peter 1:24-25 (NIV)

WORSHIP/OBEDIENCE
Is this bit of scripture supposed to cheer me up about the changes that are taking place in my daily life? We are fading, falling, and withering?

Absolutely! Face it! These are the facts…

We just need to stop fretting about life and rest on the fact that God's word NEVER changes and neither does He! Let's extol Him greatly for that!

It is hard to praise and extol God when we struggle with what is happening in our daily existence: the here and now, the present, the right-this-second circumstances that seem to distract us! We don't always seem to like the hand of cards that we believe we are dealt. What I see is what I get? This is a difficult concept to grasp. Ugh!

ADORATION/EXPLANATION

This is where we need to let our faith in God take over. Now is when we have to let go of the things that we can see (our own resources, abilities, and feelings) and rely on the things that we cannot see…God and His promises! And although this is true, it is easier said than done! And it does not come naturally to us.

Now faith is being sure of what we hope for and certain of what we do not see. Hebrews 11:1 (NIV)

Let us hold unswervingly to the hope we profess, for he who promised is faithful.

So do not throw away your confidence; it will be richly rewarded. You need to persevere so that when you have done the will of God, you will receive what he has promised. Hebrews 10:23, 35-36 (NIV)

WORSHIP/OBEDIENCE

An inner conviction or feeling alone does not define our faith. Faith proves itself by our obedience to the Lord's words. We may come across a confusing or scary situation at work today that overwhelms us. Our confidence needs to be placed on God's promises and provisions, even when we cannot see them immediately. What we see is NOT always what we get. We must trust what we cannot see!

Are you holding on unswervingly?

October 16

Oh what a beautiful morning! Once again the crispness of the fall air wakes me out of my reverie. This is NOT just another day, but another wonderful day that the LORD has made for me. Yes, for all His children, but especially for me! When I realize fully that God cares specifically for me and my needs, I can live with excitement. He is powerful enough to take on the whole world's cares; but intimately concerned enough to specifically care for even me! Wow!

ADORATION/EXPLANATION
When we look to God with assurance and expectation each new day, only then will we begin to understand His plan for our daily living.

Therefore, holy brothers, who share in the heavenly calling, fix your thoughts on Jesus, the apostle and high priest whom we confess. He was faithful to the one who appointed him, just as Moses was faithful in all God's house. Jesus has been found worthy of greater honor than Moses, just as the builder of a house has greater honor than the house itself. For every house is built by someone, but God is the builder of everything. Hebrews 3:1-4 (NIV)

"For I know the plans I have for you," declares the Lord, "plans to prosper you and not to harm you, plans to give you hope and a future." Jeremiah 29:11 (NIV)

He has made everything beautiful in its time. He has also set eternity in the hearts of men; yet they cannot fathom what god has done from beginning to end. Ecclesiastes 3:11 (NIV)

WORSHIP/OBEDIENCE
This day was created for me, for you, for all of us!

God has plans for our lives, but the construction schedule must be the Lord's and not our own. He holds the architectural prints in His hands and is ready to guide us. All He needs us to do is show up with our tool belts on and be ready for instructions!

Are you leaving the building process up to the master builder?

October 17

My fig tree finally produced figs! Yes, ripe delicious figs that I can actually eat and enjoy! For the past few years I've been wondering what good it was to have fig trees if I could only get one or two fruits from them each year. I have plenty of trees for shade and other shrubs for flowers…I wanted figs!

ADORATION/EXPLANATION

To make matters worse, I had given my mother the same kind of tree for her yard and she was reaping baskets of figs. What was the matter with my trees? What was the difference? Could it be sun, climate, yard placement, or fertilizing?

Blessed is the man who does not walk in the counsel of the wicked or stand in the way of sinners or sit in the seat of mockers. But his delight is in the law of the Lord, and on his law he meditates day and night. He is like a tree planted by streams of water, which yields its fruit in season and whose leaf does not wither. Whatever he does prospers. Psalm 1:1-3 (NIV)

He cuts off every branch in me that bears no fruit, while every branch that does bear fruit he prunes so that it will be even more fruitful.

I am the vine; you are the branches. If a man remains in me and I in him, he will bear much fruit; apart from me you can do nothing. John 15:2, 5 (NIV)

WORSHIP/OBEDIENCE

I chose to trouble shoot, investigate, prune, and put into action some new fertilizers and watering amounts for my tree. I also had to remove some other problem trees that were blocking sunlight to my precious fig tree. People are a lot like my little fig tree—we often bear little fruit because we haven't given ourselves the proper growing conditions.

Lord, help us this day to put into action some new and right practices
for our lives so that we can also bear much fruit!

Self-examination is a good thing—a very good thing! Without it, I would never have to look, think, or critique my life and purpose here on earth. But many people find this to be a difficult and scary process. They would much rather NOT know the areas that they need to change in, maybe because it is easier that way. But is ignorance really bliss?

ADORATION/EXPLANATION

Do not let the worldview of gaining self-esteem allow you to be complacent in your self-examination and evaluation. Motivational speakers and teachers will say that it is all about YOU! Only you matter!

Look out for number one! Why change for anyone… But the truth is that our lives aren't about us at all—they're about God!

Watch out for false prophets. They come to you in sheep's clothing, but inwardly they are ferocious wolves. By their fruit you will recognize them. Do people pick grapes from thornbushes, or figs from thistles? Likewise every good tree bears good fruit, but a bad tree bears bad fruit. A good tree cannot bear bad fruit, and a bad tree cannot bear good fruit. Thus, by their fruit you will recognize them. Matthew 7:15-19 (NIV)

Enter through the narrow gate. For wide is the gate and broad is the road that leads to destruction, and many enter through it. Matthew 7:13 (NIV)

Test me, O Lord, and try me, examine my heart and my mind. Psalm 26:2 (NIV)

WORSHIP/OBEDIENCE

God is not trying to make life more difficult for us or add a load of guilt. Quite the contrary! He is warning us that the road of faithful living requires self-denial, change, growth, and trust. Too bad this is usually not the easiest, widest, or most traveled path!

We should daily commit to self-examination so that others may see Christ in us.

Ask yourself, do they recognize your fruit?

October 19

Have you heard the idea of preparing for the storm or saving for a rainy day? How about "batten down the hatches," "close the barn door," or "buckle up because it's going to be a bumpy ride?" I have and I am trying to prepare daily for the trouble, trials, and storms that will befall me in this life here on earth. This is not a doomsday attitude, but rather a confident preparedness!

ADORATION/EXPLANATION

This is not meant to be a scary prediction from God. No! Actually a wonderful lesson from our awesome God, on the fact that there will be difficulties and we obviously need to prepare. How do we prepare for what we can't see coming? We study the Bible and fill the pantry of our minds with all the necessary provisions for any unexpected visits from life!

"Therefore everyone who hears these words of mine and puts them into practice is like a wise man who built his house on the rock. The rain came down, the streams rose, and the winds blew and beat against that house; yet it did not fall, because it had its foundation on the rock. But everyone who hears these words of mine and does not put them into practice is like a foolish man who built his house on sand. The rain came down, the streams rose, and the winds blew and beat against that house, and it fell with a great crash." Matthew 7:24-27 (NIV)

"I have told you these things, so that in me you may have peace. In this world you will have trouble. But take heart! I have overcome the world." John 16:33 (NIV)

WORSHIP/OBEDIENCE

So how do we batten down and buckle up? Fill your mind with God's promises and place your life, your house, your daily living, on the Rock!

Today my choices, my language, my behavior, my friendships and my thoughts will remain firm. So let the storms come, let the winds blow, let the waters rise—God is our shelter.

Our hope can be built on nothing less!

I am daily choosing to build my life on the rock of Jesus Christ. I have placed my faith in what He did for me on the cross at Calvary. But why then do I not always feel secure? Why do I sometimes have doubts about my life, my hope, my faith?

ADORATION/EXPLANATION

When we place our faith in Jesus Christ as the way, the truth, and the path to life, the Holy Spirit becomes our spiritual Sherpa or guide. We need to trust its inner leadings, guiding, and convictions when we read the Bible. My human nature will always have doubts and fears, but the spirit can always be my trusted guide. God gave us a spiritual Sherpa!

"I have much more to say to you, more than you can now bear. But when he, the spirit of truth, comes, he will guide you into all truth. He will not speak on his own; he will speak only what he hears, and he will tell you what is yet to come. He will bring glory to me by taking from what is mine and making it known to you. All that belongs to the Father is mine. That is why I said the spirit will take from what is mine and make it known to you." John 16:12-15 (NIV)

"And I will ask the Father, and he will give you another Counselor to be with you forever—the Spirit of truth. The world cannot accept him, because it neither sees him nor knows him. But you know him, for he lives with you and will be in you." John 14:16-17 (NIV)

WORSHIP/OBEDIENCE

A Sherpa is a high altitude mountain guide. They live in the Himalayas and are often used to lead people on expeditions because they know the territory so well. No one would think of climbing without a Sherpa!

Likewise, Jesus has left us with a guide for our heart and soul—the Holy Spirit, our spiritual Sherpa.

We should not think of climbing without Him!

October 21

Wow! I have not only been left a handbook (the Bible), but also a spiritual guide for my very own life journey (the Holy Spirit). As I travel through this life, I must make it a daily priority to consult the handbook and then listen closely to my "tour guide." I must admit that this is tough sometimes. I want to wander off on my own and not stick with the guide. I want to move faster, see more sights…

ADORATION/EXPLANATION

Lord, this world is not my permanent home. I am just passing through.

I am walking through my life on earth with the hope of obeying and bringing you glory in my daily living. Teach me not to rush and set out on my own. Help me listen closely to your voice so that I do not miss any coming attractions. You have so many sights, sounds and bits of information for me. You know best!

Jesus replied, "If anyone loves me, he will obey my teaching. My Father will love him, and we will come to him and make our home with him. He who does not love me will not obey my teaching. These words you hear are not my own; they belong to the Father who sent me.

All this I have spoken while still with you. But the Counselor, the Holy Spirit, whom the Father will send in my name, will teach you all things and will remind you of everything I have said to you. Peace I leave with you; my peace I give to you. I do not give to you as the world gives. Do not let your hearts be troubled and do not be afraid. John 14:23-27 (NIV)

WORSHIP/OBEDIENCE

Following the leader was a fun game to play as a child, but very often as an adult, I struggle with the "following" position and try to move to the front. I am so thankful that I have a God that has "been there, done that" in this life! We need to be thankful for a spiritual guide that gets the instructions for our life directly from the Father. Choose to rely on the perfect tour guide for your journey. He created you, He knows you…He's been down this road before.

"He is leading…will you follow?"

Sometimes I feel like my life is very simple. Other times I feel it is very complex, like a tapestry of colors. Many hues of red, orange, green, blue, and yellows are swirling around in complicated pictures and stories. How can God even begin to understand me? My incoherent ranting and raving about life even disturbs me on occasion.

ADORATION/EXPLANATION

The beautiful fact is that God does know who I am. How can this be? Most of my friends and family barely know the authentic person behind the image I let them see. But the Bible tells us that God knows the reality of our inner life. He knows the "me" that the world doesn't see!

O Lord, you have searched me and you know me.

You know when I sit and when I rise; you perceive my thoughts from afar. You discern my going out and my lying down; you are familiar with all my ways. Before a word is on my tongue you know it completely, O Lord. You hem me in behind and before; you have laid your hand upon me. Such knowledge is too wonderful for me, too lofty for me to attain. Psalm 139:1-6 (NIV)

"I am the good shepherd; I know my sheep and my sheep know me—just as the Father knows me and I know the Father—and I lay down my life for the sheep." John 10:14-15 (NIV)

WORSHIP/OBEDIENCE

My life may be a tapestry of complex and rich design, far too wonderful for me to even fathom at times, but I've been given the opportunity to have a relationship with the tailor of this fine fabric. He has stitched my life together with His own hands! I trust you, Lord, to figure out the various hues of my life. I will allow YOU to be the tailor of my day!

Today, I will choose to let all my various colors be used for your purposes.

October 23

Even though I believe that God knows my every need and loves me, I still feel weak and unqualified to live for Him on some days. This weak feeling pushes me to study His words and strive to put His commandments into practice. So I can truthfully yell hip-hip-hooray for lack of human strength, especially when it pushes us closer to the Father.

ADORATION/EXPLANATION

I am not celebrating a lack of desire or effort on my part to live for Christ. I am acknowledging that even with all of my human fleshly effort, I will not be strong enough for every battle that comes my way. My weakness points me to my need for God!

You then, my son, be strong in the grace that is in Christ Jesus.

Endure hardship with us like a good soldier of Christ Jesus. No one serving as a soldier gets involved in civilian affairs—he wants to please his commanding officer. Similarly, if anyone competes as an athlete, he does not receive the victor's crown unless he competes according to the rules. The hardworking farmer should be the first to receive a share of the crops. Reflect on what I am saying, for the Lord will give you insight into all this. 2 Timothy 2:1, 3-7 (NIV)

All scripture is God-breathed and is useful for teaching, rebuking, correcting and training in righteousness, so that the man of God may be thoroughly equipped for every good work. 2 Timothy 3:16-17 (NIV)

WORSHIP/OBEDIENCE

We should want to sincerely please our commanding officer. Have we placed our trust in human strength or in our heavenly Father's words of wisdom? Today, Lord, help us to call on your grace and strength for every good work that we need to accomplish. While we are at work, in school, driving the car, with the kids, or alone, we will count on you.

"I may be weak, but He is strong!"

I desire to be a good worker, a faithful employee, a loving parent, loyal spouse, kind friend, trusted confidant, and faithful workman in whatever circumstance I find myself. I need some basic, obvious ways to navigate as a trusted child of God.

ADORATION/EXPLANATION

Teach us, dear Lord! Our eyes and ears are open, our arms and legs are on the alert, and our hearts are ready, willing and waiting. Any part of us that you need to use is available today. This is difficult Lord…help us!

Keep reminding them of these things. Warn them before God against quarreling about words; it is of no value, and only ruins those who listen. Do your best to present yourself to God as one approved, a workman who does not need to be ashamed and who correctly handles the word of truth. Avoid godless chatter, because those who indulge in it will become more and more ungodly. 2 Timothy 2:14-16 (NIV)

Do not let any unwholesome talk come out of your mouths, but only what is helpful for building others up according to their needs, that it may benefit those who listen.

Get rid of all bitterness, rage and anger, brawling and slander, along with every form of malice. Ephesians 4:29, 31 (NIV)

WORSHIP/OBEDIENCE

Dear God, let this be our prayer together for this day. Mold me…make me!
I want to be a workman who does not need to be ashamed.
I want to control my tongue, my emotions, and my actions.
Help me keep your thoughts and precepts throughout this day. I love you. Amen.

As I look out my window, I notice that the leaves are continuing to yellow and turn brown. Time is marching on, and I cannot stop the fall season from passing. This can be a wonderful day if I realize that God has given it to me to enjoy. I cannot focus on the passing of time, but need to live in the here and now!

ADORATION/EXPLANATION

Today is just an ordinary day to work, to walk, to love, to exercise, and to laugh; it's just an ordinary day to live with Jesus Christ as our Lord and personal Savior. Ordinary? When we grow comfortable in His love and grace…ordinary takes on a whole new meaning. It really is extra-ordinary! We shouldn't want to waste a minute of it!

This is the day that the Lord has made; let us rejoice and be glad in it. Psalm 118:24 (ESV)

"My command is this: Love each other as I have loved you. Greater love has no one than this: that he lay down his life for his friends. You are my friends if you do what I command. I no longer call you servants, because a servant does not know his master's business. Instead, I have called you friends, for everything that I learned from my Father I have made known to you. John 15:12-15 (NIV)

Do not boast about tomorrow, for you do not know what a day may bring forth. Proverbs 27:1 (NIV)

WORSHIP/OBEDIENCE

Today—is it just an ordinary day? Maybe not! Commit to look and live for God today. Do NOT waste a moment for we know not what tomorrow may bring. Let the colors change, let the foliage come tumbling down…it will not disturb us, but instead, remind us of our reliable Savior.

Wow! What a lesson from the season! Let the leaves fall!

Sometimes events or circumstances that seem like big mistakes turn out to be miracles that happen right before our eyes. What we consider to be a big *disappointment* turns out to be an actual *appointment* orchestrated by God! If we are astute and perceptive, we may just have the privilege of seeing God's plan unfold in front of our eyes. Wow!

ADORATION/EXPLANATION

Trusting God means walking away from our problems or situations and letting God work on the answer. It doesn't mean that He can't use us in the solution...it just means that we are not the ones in control!

To you, O Lord, I lift up my soul; in you I trust, O my God. Do not let me be put to shame, nor let my enemies triumph over me. Psalm 25:1-2 (NIV)

Please, Lord, rescue me! Quick! Come and help me! Psalm 40:13 (TLB)

And without faith it is impossible to please God, because anyone who comes to him must believe that he exists and that he rewards those who earnestly seek him. Hebrews 11:6 (NIV)

Jesus looked at them and said, "With man this is impossible, but not with God; all things are possible with God." Mark 10:27 (NIV)

WORSHIP/OBEDIENCE

I have never known the Lord to back down on His promises. We serve an amazingly creative God who can adjust to every problem that we will ever have. My act of worship and obedience is to learn to "see"…really see events in my life as divine acts from God.

Lord, help us to keep our appointments with you today!

I want to remember to be thankful and pray today. I do not want to wait until I am backed into a corner with no other option but to pray. I am deciding at this moment to talk with God and be grateful for my life: the big things, the little things, and all the things that take up space in the middle!

ADORATION/EXPLANATION

I trust in the fact that my Savior cares for me. If there are any anxious hours ahead today, I believe that God already knows them. He is never surprised or shocked at the future. I sit in awe at the foresight that God has on my life. It may be scary to me, but I can rest in His care.

***

Call to me and I will answer you and tell you great and unsearchable things you do not know. Jeremiah 33:3 (NIV)

"Though the mountains be shaken and the hills be removed, yet my unfailing love for you will not be shaken nor my covenant of peace be removed," says the Lord, who has compassion on you. Isaiah 54:10 (NIV)

For this reason I kneel before the Father.... Ephesians 3:14 (NIV)

I love the Lord, for he heard my voice; he heard my cry for mercy. Because he turned his ear to me, I will call on him as long as I live. Psalm 116:1-2 (NIV)

WORSHIP/OBEDIENCE

I may be nervous, anxious or scared about what today may hold, but I can put my trust in God's almighty providence. He loves me!

Lord, I am thanking you and trusting you ahead of time.
Whether I get backed into a corner or find myself in a jam that I cannot handle,
I will still rest in your strength. "Great is your faithfulness!"

***

October 28

We are "overcomers" with Christ on our side. We hear this phrase all the time, but do we actually stop to think about its meaning? If we are overcomers, doesn't it make sense to study and learn about it? What are we trying to overcome? What personal issue are you trying to get past in your own life?

ADORATION/EXPLANATION

I have given up trying on my own power. God has let me know through His Word that I am already an overcomer in this journey called life. These troubles, issues, relationships, hardships, illnesses, and even physical deaths have all been handled by trusting in Christ. The definition of an overcomer is someone who surmounts difficulties, overwhelms, overpowers, gains superiority over—basically, someone who WINS!

"I have told you these things, so that in me you may have peace. In this world you will have trouble, but take heart! I have overcome the world." John 16:33 (NIV)

Do not be overcome by evil, but overcome evil with good. Romans 12:21 (NIV)

This is love for God: to obey his commands. And his commands are not burdensome, for everyone born of God overcomes the world. This is the victory that has overcome the world, even our faith. Who is it that overcomes the world? All of us who choose to believe that Jesus is the Son of God. 1 John 5:3-5 (NIV)

WORSHIP/OBEDIENCE

Wow—it's a done deal! God tells us that we're already overcomers if we place our faith and trust in Him. You can stake your life on these odds. This doesn't mean that difficulties will not arise; but it does assure us that we have the power to SURMOUNT the problems. Believe!

We are more than conquerors!

October 29

We are more than conquerors! The Bible tells us we are. But if you're like me, there are some days that I do not feel like being a Christian soldier. I do not feel like an overcomer, a victor, or anything remotely resembling a winner in this journey called life. I am tired, weak and weary.

ADORATION/EXPLANATION
This is where faith must have first place in our minds. We must read, study, and meditate on God's word and promises, regardless of how we might feel. We have a daily choice to make...

Do we believe God or not?

What, then, shall we say in response to this? If God is for us, who can be against us? He who did not spare his own Son, but gave him up for us all—how will he not also, along with him, graciously give us all things? Who will bring any charge against those whom God has chosen? It is God who justifies. Who is he that condemns? Christ Jesus, who died—more than that, who was raised to life—is at the right hand of God and is also interceding for us. Who shall separate us from the love of Christ? Shall trouble or hardship or persecution or famine or nakedness or danger or sword?

No, in all these things we are more than conquerors through him who loved us. Romans 8:31-35, 37 (NIV)

To him who overcomes, I will give the right to sit with me on my throne, just as I overcame and sat down with my Father on his throne. Revelation 3:21 (NIV)

WORSHIP/OBEDIENCE
Wow and wow again! Is our faith like a wave or a rock? It doesn't matter how we feel. We need to choose this day to believe that we are more than conquerors through Christ. God tells us that He is for us! Nothing can separate us from His love! We can believe God's promises.

Do you believe God or not?

October 30

When I was growing up, the night of October 30th was known as "mischief night." Kids went around soaping car windows and toilet-papering folk's homes. In most cases it was harmless fun, but very often someone took the mischief too far. What might have started out to be harmless fun ended up hurting someone or possibly damaging property.

ADORATION/EXPLANATION

Dear Lord, because of my adoration for you…I ask for help! Please show me today when and if my actions may become harmful to someone. Please let my speech and behavior be modeled after your example. Keep me aware of other people's feelings at my job, school, grocery store, or even in my own home.

Therefore each of you must put off falsehood and speak truthfully to his neighbor, for we are all members of one body. "In your anger do not sin"; Do not let the sun go down while you are still angry, and do not give the devil a foothold. He who has been stealing must steal no longer, but must work, doing something useful with his own hands, that he may have something to share with those in need.

Do not let any unwholesome talk come out of your mouths, but only what is helpful for building others up according to their needs, that it may benefit those who listen. And do not grieve the Holy Spirit of God, with whom you were sealed for the day of redemption. Get rid of all bitterness, rage and anger, brawling and slander, along with every form of malice. Be kind and compassionate to one another, forgiving each other, just as in Christ God forgave you. Ephesians 4:25-32 (NIV)

WORSHIP/OBEDIENCE

The definition of mischief basically means actions that annoy or irritate. As faithful followers of Christ, we cannot afford to act in ways that annoy, irritate, or harm, especially if our goal is to bring glory to God in our everyday lives. In our pursuit of having fun, please remind us Lord that we must take others feelings into consideration.

Lord, cause the very core of who I am to become a person of kindness, compassion and forgiveness, so that I can build others up for your glory!

October 31

Today is Halloween. Whether you like it, celebrate it, or agree with the custom of "trick or treating," it does not remove the fact that it is here. Stores have costumes for sale, masks, candy, decorations, and various other objects that let us know that Halloween has arrived.

ADORATION/EXPLANATION
If only we could stop putting on masks and start taking them off! What would happen if we removed our masks of fear, insecurity, low self-esteem, nervousness, worry and self-consciousness? Then we could really start living as imitators of Christ! How scary? How exciting!

Have nothing to do with godless myths and old wives' tales; rather, train yourself to be godly. For physical training is of some value, but godliness has value for all things, holding promise for both the present life and the life to come.

Don't let anyone look down on you because you are young, but set an example for the believers in speech, in life, in love, in faith and purity. 1 Timothy 4:7-8, 12 (NIV)

Come, everyone, and clap for joy! Shout triumphant praises to the Lord! Psalm 47:1 (TLB)

Be imitators of God, therefore, as dearly loved children and live a life of love, just as Christ loved us and gave himself up for us as a fragrant offering and sacrifice to God. Ephesians 5:1-2 (NIV)

WORSHIP/OBEDIENCE
Lord, you have created pumpkins, gourds, mums, candy, popcorn, and so many wonderful things for me. I will not see evil at every turn in this Halloween tradition, but instead look to you for a divine lesson. Help me to remove any false masks that I am hiding behind and step into the light of your love for me. I do not need to hide behind a costume of who I am, like a child dressing up in play-clothes. Instead, help me to live daily in obvious ways.

November 1

Cooler weather has arrived and clocks will soon be falling back an hour. It will start to get dark earlier in the evening and the street lights will be on by dinner time. My porch light and my driveway lanterns will be turned on at dusk. I am not afraid of the darker hour because I know that my home is well lit. The pathway to the door is discernable in the shining lights.

ADORATION/EXPLANATION

As children of God, we have the supreme privilege of always walking and living in His light. His whole persona is a lighthouse, so to speak, to my every day existence. The Bible guides my steps and the Holy Spirit guides my heart, soul, and mind. I must, therefore, make every effort to stay in the beams of that lighthouse. Watch where you walk!

For you were once darkness, but now you are light in the Lord. Live as children of light (for the fruit of the light consists in all goodness, righteousness and truth) and find out what pleases the Lord. Have nothing to do with the fruitless deeds of darkness, but rather expose them. For it is shameful to mention what the disobedient do in secret. But everything exposed by the light becomes visible, for it is light that makes everything visible.

Be careful, then, how you live—not as unwise but as wise, making the most of every opportunity, because the days are evil. Therefore do not be foolish, but understand what the Lord's will is. Ephesians 5:8-13, 15-17 (NIV)

Many are asking, "Who can show us any good?" Let the light of your face shine upon us, O Lord. Psalm 4:6 (NIV)

WORSHIP/OBEDIENCE

I want God's face to shine down upon me. Do you? I want to see clearly what to do and where I am supposed to go in order to please God with my life. I will strive to not be afraid of dark times during the course of my years because I know that the one true light will expose areas that I need to work on and be a beacon to my pathway each and every day. My only job is to stay in the line of His radiant beams…

Step into the light!

November 2

Taming the tongue—is there really such a thing? Can we actually tame our tongue? Should we even try? God has some clear words about our mouths and why we should practice to control them.

ADORATION/EXPLANATION
It is not really our tongue but what is in our hearts that is the problem. Our minds tend to focus on a thought or criticism or fault…and then it comes flowing out. Most of us spout out what's in our minds and hearts before we even think of the result that it may have, and sometimes doing so ends in dire consequences! Lord, guard my words today!

We all stumble in many ways. If anyone is never at fault in what he says, he is a perfect man, able to keep his whole body in check. When we put bits into the mouths of horses to make them obey us, we can turn the whole animal. Or take ships as an example. Although they are so large and are driven by strong winds, they are steered by a very small rudder wherever the pilot wants to go. Likewise the tongue is a small part of the body, but it makes great boasts. Consider what a great forest is set on fire by a small spark. The tongue is also a fire, a world of evil among the parts of the body. It corrupts the whole person, sets the whole course of his life on fire, and is itself set on fire by hell.

With the tongue we praise our Lord and Father, and with it we curse men, who have been made in God's likeness. Out of the same mouth come praise and cursing. My brothers, this should not be. Can both fresh water and salt water flow from the same spring? James 3:2-6, 9-11 (NIV)

WORSHIP/OBEDIENCE
Obvious living means we must have self-control of our mouths. Better advice still is dwelling so much on God's Word that the thoughts in our hearts do not rush quickly to our lips to say hurtful, negative things. Pray today that the overflow of your heart is beautiful, encouraging words to someone in need.

How, when, where, about whom, and to whom we speak should be of great concern for us as faithful followers of Christ. The Bible clearly warns against gossip, slander, and all falsehood. Our first line of defense against issues with people in our daily walk should be to keeps our lips zipped!

ADORATION/EXPLANATION

Better advice still would be to compliment others freely. Look for opportunities to speak love, joy, and peace into someone's life. Build them up, encourage them, sing and pray!

When words are many, sin is not absent, but he who holds his tongue is wise. The tongue of the righteous is choice silver, but the heart of the wicked is of little value. The lips of the righteous nourish many, but fools die for lack of judgment. Proverbs 10:19-21 (NIV)

Do nothing out of selfish ambition or vain conceit, but in humility consider others better than yourselves. Each of you should look not only to your own interests, but also to the interest of others. Philippians 2:3-4 (NIV)

Listen, everyone! High and low, rich and poor, all around the world—listen to my words, for they are wise and filled with insight. Psalm 49:1-3 (TLB)

Let your conversation be always full of grace, seasoned with salt, so that you may know how to answer everyone. Colossians 4:6 (NIV)

WORSHIP/OBEDIENCE

We need to keep our lips tightly zipped if what we are about to say to someone will not imitate Christ's behavior. God desires us to pause, think, and pray before we speak. Are we preoccupied with ourselves—our activities, feelings, reputation, or ego? Do we improve the flavor of others, as salt does to our meal? What is motivating our speech?

Dear Lord, keep me from having lack of judgment in my speech
and help me to find words to nourish many.

Are we good listeners? Do we actually hear what people are saying? Do we acknowledge their thoughts, opinions, feelings, and requests? Sometimes we can get away with just nodding our heads and pretending to hear, but on other occasions, it is imperative that we really listen well.

ADORATION/EXPLANATION
Sometimes with little children, I have just nodded my head and tuned out most of their chatter and ramblings. Imagine if God did that with us!

But He doesn't, and that is the beautiful thing about our relationship with Him. He hears us, and also wants us to listen and hear Him!

Now then, my sons, listen to me; blessed are those who keep my ways. Listen to my instruction and be wise; do not ignore it. Blessed is the man who listens to me, watching daily at my doors, waiting at my doorway. For whoever finds me finds life and receives favor from the Lord. Proverbs 8:32- 35 (NIV)

So then, just as you received Christ Jesus as Lord, continue to live in him, rooted and built up in him, strengthened in the faith as you were taught, and overflowing with thankfulness. See to it that no one takes you captive through hollow and deceptive philosophy, which depends on human tradition and the basic principles of this world rather than on Christ. Colossians 2:6-8 (NIV)

I tell you the truth, whoever hears my word and believes him who sent me has eternal life and will not be condemned; he has crossed over from death to life. John 5:24 (NIV)

WORSHIP/OBEDIENCE
God does not tune us out…therefore we must be careful not to tune Him out! We cannot take this task lightly though. We need to make a conscious effort to listen, hear and discern the things that God is speaking to us in that still small voice in our souls.

Open my ears, Lord. I want to hear you. I really want to listen!

November 5

The march towards Thanksgiving has begun. Although leaves are still lazily drifting from the trees, the date reminds me that we are headed towards the first big holiday before the end of this year. There is a slight chill in the air and an anticipation of an upcoming celebration. Why wait until then to be thankful?

ADORATION/EXPLANATION

Lord…we need to say thanks! Remind us to say thanks! Thank you for my life. Thank you for my faith and for the fact that I reside in a country where I can freely live out my faith. You remind me in your word to be thankful always, in every season. I adore you and want to give you praise on every day of the year.

Shout for joy to the Lord, all the earth. Worship the Lord with gladness; come before him with joyful songs. Know that the Lord is God. It is he who made us, and we are his; we are his people, he sheep of his pasture. Enter his gates with thanksgiving and his courts with praise; give thanks to him and praise his name. For the Lord is good and his love endures forever; his faithfulness continues through all generations. Psalm 100 (NIV)

Therefore, since we are receiving a kingdom that cannot be shaken, let us be thankful, and so worship God acceptably with reverence and awe, for our "God is a consuming fire." Hebrews 12:28-29 (NIV)

Thanks be to God for his indescribable gift! 2 Corinthians 9:15 (NIV)

WORSHIP/OBEDIENCE

Winter, spring, summer, fall—we need to study God's word, listen, meditate, and observe through them all. What is God showing you? What is God providing for you?

Do not miss an opportunity to say, "Thank-you!"

Generosity seems to be a lost art nowadays. In this "me first" world, "I'm number one," "Go for the gusto," and "get all you can" attitude, stinginess seems to reign supreme. It should come as no surprise that the Bible gives some very contrary advice on this subject.

ADORATION/EXPLANATION

Jesus warned us that believers are not of this world. Although we live here and are *in* the world, we are not to act and live the same way as unbelievers. Stinginess and greed can have no place in the life of a believer. Yet, many so-called Christians are some of the stingiest folks around. There is no sign of generosity. We jealously guard everything to ourselves. This should NOT be!

Remember this: Whoever sows sparingly will also reap sparingly, and whoever sows generously will also reap generously. Each man should give what he has decided in his heart to give, not reluctantly or under compulsion, for God loves a cheerful giver. And God is able to make all grace abound to you, so that in all things at all times, having all that you need, you will abound in every good work. 2 Corinthians 9:6-8 (NIV)

And now, brothers, we want you to know about the grace that God has given the Macedonian churches. Out of the most severe trial, their overflowing joy and their extreme poverty welled up in rich generosity. For I testify that they gave as much as they were able, and even beyond their ability. Entirely on their own, 2 Corinthians 8:1-3 (NIV)

WORSHIP/OBEDIENCE

We should wish to be known as the Macedonian believers were known! What a reputation for joyful generosity! They understood God's generous grace toward them and gave extravagantly…entirely on their own. We should concentrate and prayerfully remind ourselves that we own nothing. Everything that we have is His, and His provisions know no end.

Because of that promise, we CAN be cheerful givers!

The Bible talks about being a cheerful giver. What about a cheerful worker, student, parent, or spouse? The definition of cheerful includes merry, sunny, dispelling gloom and, my favorite of the adjectives, <u>ungrudging obedience</u>. Is this a character trait that you possess? If not, why?

ADORATION/EXPLANATION
I want to be known as cheerful. If I ponder what God has done for my life, even for a few moments daily, how can I be anything but cheerful? Maybe I need to make a conscious stop in my tracks to look about and realize my blessing? Today I am going to purpose in my heart to dispel gloom wherever I go.

A word aptly spoken is like apples of gold in settings of silver. Proverbs 25:11 (NIV)

A happy heart makes the face cheerful, but heartache crushes the spirit.

All the days of the oppressed are wretched, but the cheerful heart has a continual feast.

A cheerful look brings joy to heart, and good news gives health to the bones. Proverbs 15:13, 15, 30 (NIV)

Be joyful always, pray continually; give thanks in all circumstances, for this is God's will for you in Christ Jesus. 1 Thessalonians 5:16-18 (NIV)

WORSHIP/OBEDIENCE
Anyone can be cheerful if all is going well, yet we should desire to have a cheerful heart, even when going through trials and storms. Our daily obedience needs to flow from us without any grudges or gripes attached. It is not a forced cheerfulness…but rather the result of an obedient daily life. We choose to cheerfully share what we have been given from above. We want God to recognize us as ungrudgingly obedient!

How holy can a person get? Is it attainable for you and me in our daily lives? Is it out of our reach? Do we have to give up everything fun to get there? Should we even try?

God's Word speaks to us about being holy because He is holy. We are to resist evil and pursue God's example for us in the life of Jesus.

ADORATION/EXPLANATION

The cleansing blood of Jesus on the cross and the sanctifying (setting apart for a purpose) work of the Holy Spirit in my life can enable me to gain self-control and pursue holiness in my daily living. In and of my own effort I am not such a holy being, far from ever being perfect; but with the life of Christ dwelling inside me, I can look to the Bible daily and pursue a life dedicated to holiness.

Therefore, prepare your minds for action; be self-controlled; set your hope fully on the grace to be given you when Jesus Christ is revealed. As obedient children, do not conform to the evil desires you had when you lived in ignorance. But just as he who called you is holy, so be holy in all you do; for it is written; "Be holy, because I am holy." 1 Peter 1:13-16 (NIV)

I put this in human terms because you are weak in your natural selves. Just as you used to offer the parts of your body in slavery to impurity and to ever-increasing wickedness, so now offer them in slavery to righteousness leading to holiness. Romans 6:19 (NIV)

You, however, are controlled not by the sinful nature but by the Spirit, if the Spirit of God lives in you. And if anyone does not have the Spirit of Christ, he does not belong to Christ. Romans 8:9 (NIV)

WORSHIP/OBEDIENCE

These verses help provide us with the encouragement that WE CAN, with the Holy Spirit's help, live a life that daily chooses to pursue holiness. By studying the life of Christ, we can learn some very obvious ways to display grace, self-control, and holiness.

Look around you…opportunities to live holy are right in front of you!

November 9

I love attending marriage ceremonies. The bride and groom demonstrate their undying love for each other in front of all who are in attendance. But after the wedding and the honeymoon, when all the struggles of life take over, they will have to work diligently to keep their relationship vital and preserve their love for each other. The marriage celebration is over, party finished, and real life has begun. Relationships take work!

ADORATION/EXPLANATION

God demonstrated His undying love for us by sending his Son to actually die. While we were still sinners, He loved us beyond compare. God's love never fades no matter what trial or storm appears, and no matter how we may fail to keep up our end of the relationship. We can glory in the fact of His never-ending love. Blessed assurance!

The Lord appeared to us in the past, saying: "I have loved you with an everlasting love; I have drawn you with loving kindness." Jeremiah 31:3 (NIV)

For God so loved the world that he gave his one and only Son, that whoever believes in him shall not perish but have eternal life. John 3:16 (NIV)

There is no fear in love. But perfect love drives out fear, because fear has to do with punishment. The one who fears is not made perfect in love. We love because he first loved us. I John 4:18-19 (NIV)

WORSHIP/OBEDIENCE

We have a perfect God who loves us with a perfect love. His love never fails, never gives up, never runs out. Therefore, we do not have to live in fear of punishment. Instead, we can gladly seek daily ways to show our devotion to Him and cultivate a vital relationship.

The honeymoon may be over…
but the genuine love connection can last forever!

He loves me, He loves me not, He loves me? Is this how we should live our daily existence as faithful followers of Christ? Definitely not! Yet many people wake up each day with this same question. "Do you love me today, God?"

ADORATION/EXPLANATION
God's love for us does not wax and wane like our human devotion tends to do. We experience love and give love on an up-and-down emotional basis. Human love tends to have conditions attached to it. We love only when we feel like it. We tend to be fickle people! God is not like that. He is NOT like us!

For God so loved the world that he gave his one and only son, that whoever believes in him shall not perish but have eternal life. John 3:16 (NIV)

For I am convinced that neither death nor life, neither angels or demons, neither the present nor the future, nor any powers, neither height nor depth, nor anything else in all creation, will be able to separate us from the love of God that is in Christ Jesus our Lord. Romans 8:38-39 (NIV)

How great is the love the Father has lavished on us, that we should be called children of God! And that is what we are! The reason the world does not know us is that it di not know him. 1 John 3:1 (NIV)

WORSHIP/OBEDIENCE
Are you convinced that God loves you today and every day? The Bible tells us that this is true. He gave us His very own Son to prove it! This fact can and should make your day a little easier. Forget about all the other trivial things that may happen in your schedule today and keep this thought in front of you. God's love is big enough to engulf the whole world, yet specific enough to include each of us individually! Get ahold of the fact that He cares for your personal life. Are you convinced? I am!

I am choosing to have a perpetual thanksgiving attitude within my heart. I want to be gracious and full of grace towards others, just as God is toward me. If I find this difficult in my daily living then I must meditate and reflect on scripture to remind myself of God's goodness to me. Believing that God is good is much more than just spouting the words. God really is good! Believe it today!

ADORATION/EXPLANATION

Because we are human, we tend to forget God's promises. We need to dedicate ourselves to reading and re-reading them daily so that we can behave in a more Christ-like way. We have an awesome God who epitomizes the character trait of "good!" He deserves our praise.

It is good to say thank you to the Lord, to sing praises to the God who is above all gods. Psalm 92:1 (TLB)

For the law was given through Moses; grace and truth came through Jesus Christ. John 1:7 (NIV)

For the grace of God has appeared that offers salvation to all people. It teaches us to say "No" to ungodliness and worldly passions, and to live self-controlled, upright and godly lives in this present age... Titus 2:11-12 (TLB)

So that, having been justified by his grace, we might become heirs having the hope of eternal life. This is a trustworthy saying. And I want you to stress these things, so that those who have trusted in God may be careful to devote themselves to doing what is good. These things are excellent and profitable for everyone. Titus 3:7-8 (NIV)

WORSHIP/OBEDIENCE

If we really concentrate on God's freely given grace and forgiveness to us, then how can we not freely give it to others? We do not want become forgetful. We should want to live in obvious ways today that are excellent and profitable for those who come into contact with us. We never cease striving to become hopelessly devoted to doing what is good.

We never know who we might meet today!

November 12

The ancient Israelites used to sing as they were traveling. It made the journey easier and it was also their time of singing praises to God as they ambled along. In the Old Testament, Psalm 84 was most likely sung by pilgrims as they traveled to one of the annual festivals in Jerusalem.

ADORATION/EXPLANATION

Many beautiful pictures fill this psalm and speak of the spring season of the year and in the believer's heart, yet the devotion expressed here is rarely seen in Christians today—Christians who have the benefit of knowing Jesus and a clearer picture of God's plan of salvation through Him. Why is this? Do we sing often in adoration of our Lord?

How lovely is your temple, O Lord of the armies of heaven. I long, yes, faint with longing to be able to enter your courtyard and come near to the living God. Even the sparrows and swallows are welcome to come and nest among your altars and there have their young, O Lord of heaven's armies, my King and my God! How happy are those who can live in your Temple, singing your praises.

Happy are those who are strong in the Lord, who want above all else to follow your steps. When they walk through the Valley of Weeping it will become a place of springs where pools of blessing and refreshment collect after rains!

A single day spent in your Temple is better than a thousand anywhere else! I would rather be a doorman of the Temple of my God than live in palaces of wickedness. For Jehovah God is our Light and our Protector. He gives us grace and glory. No good thing will he withhold from those who walk along his paths. Psalm 84:1-6, 10-11 (TLB)

WORSHIP/OBEDIENCE

Verse ten needs to become the conviction of our hearts. Better is a single day in the presence of God, than a thousand days anywhere else! Can we honestly say that? Today, let's choose to walk in God's presence.

Appreciate the world around you and give Him praise for the many awesome blessings that you see throughout your day. It may even cause you to sing!

November 13

What is your name? What are you called by? When others hear your name mentioned, what thoughts are conjured in their minds? If this is a scary thought for you, God says that it should not be so! As a Christian, you should be known as a "Christ follower." How closely are you following?

ADORATION/EXPLANATION

My adoration for God should be lived out in my daily existence. It is not a show to put on for others, but a genuine character quality that can shine through in every situation. Although we cannot worry about everything others may say or think about us, God does say that as believers, we are responsible for our lives and speech. People should recognize us by our actions, speech, and lives!

***

And he humbled himself even further, going so far as actually to die a criminal's death on a cross. Yet it was because of this that God raised him up to the heights of heaven and gave him a name which is above every other name. Philippians 2:8-9 (TLB)

A good name is more desirable than great riches; to be esteemed is better than silver or gold.

One who loves a pure heart and who speaks with grace will have the king for a friend. Proverbs 22:1, 11 (NIV)

Lift your eyes and look to the heavens: Who created all these? He who brings out the starry host one by one, and calls them each by name. Because of his great power and mighty strength, not one of them is missing. Isaiah 40:26 (NIV)

WORSHIP/OBEDIENCE

He knows our names! God knows exactly who we are! If He cannot miss knowing even one star in the heavens, how much more will He have each one of our names on His lips? And if this is true of God, then how much more important is it for us to keep our names and reputations as a loving example for Him?

Lord, I am willing.

***

November 14

Are you afraid for God to call on you, for Him to use you, to want you as a friend, become familiar with you intimately, desire your whole heart and soul? Some people are. I am not! God knows your name. He knows your address. He knows where to find you. So stop running!

ADORATION/EXPLANATION

Believing that God knows my name and my every thought convinces me that I cannot hide anything from Him. He will lovingly search for me as His child. He continues to search until He finds me. I cannot hide from Him! Do we hear Him calling our names? If not, perhaps we should listen a bit more carefully. He may be trying to get your attention!

He determines the number of the stars and calls them each by name. Psalm 147:4 (NIV)

If we had forgotten the name of our God or spread out our hands to a foreign god, would not God have discovered it, since he knows the secrets of the heart? Psalm 44:20-21 (NIV)

Whoever acknowledges me before men, I will also acknowledge him before my Father in heaven. Matthew 10:32 (NIV)

WORSHIP/OBEDIENCE

God knows your name. Yes, you! What a beautiful comforting thought!

He wants to call on you. He wants to have a relationship with you.

All you have to do is acknowledge Him and make the time. And if the God of the universe has enough time to set aside for each of us, don't we think we can spare a few minutes as well? What a beneficial conversation that will be.

Jesus knows me…and still loves me. Wow!

November 15

What is reverent fear? Do we actually need to fear God? Is fear the only emotion that God desires from us? Do we truly realize that He alone deserves our reverence as the one true creator God? He is the great "I AM," the beginning and the end, the writer of the universe. This concept alone should stir up reverential feelings in our hearts.

ADORATION/EXPLANATION
These may be tough questions for some people, but it is necessary in our daily walk to fully appreciate what it is to fear God. Without first giving deep respect and reverence to the Lord, it will be difficult to wholeheartedly allow Him to conform us to the image of Christ.

Dwell on the fact of who He is… meditate…ponder!

Since you call on a father who judges each man's work impartially, live your lives as strangers here in reverent fear. 1 Peter 1:17 (NIV)

Therefore, since we are receiving a kingdom that cannot be shaken, let us be thankful, and so worship God acceptably with reverence and awe, for our "God is a consuming fire." Hebrews 12:28-29 (NIV)

The angel of the Lord encamps around those who fear him, and he delivers them. Taste and see that the Lord is good; how blessed is the man who takes refuge in him! O, fear the Lord, you his saints, for those who fear him lack nothing. Psalm 34:7-9 (NIV)

WORSHIP/OBEDIENCE
We are not to be afraid of God, but live in wondrous awe of our heavenly Father. In doing so, we will be drawn to serve Him obediently in our everyday, ordinary walk through life. We can joyfully obey Him because of who He is. Will God find us faithful?

Reverent fear leads to true worship!

November 16

Awe and fear of the Lord is expressed by faithfully walking in His ways, by loving Him, and by serving Him gladly all of our days.

Wait, gladly…? Are you kidding me?

Why would our service have to be done gladly? Aren't awe, reverence, fear, and serving enough for God?

ADORATION/EXPLANATION

Nope. God speaks many times on having joy, being cheerful, and serving with gladness and praise. When we truly realize who we are serving, we will not be able to keep from being glad!

I will be glad and rejoice in your love, for you saw my affliction and knew the anguish of my soul. Psalm 31:7 (NIV)

Clap your hands, all you nations; shout to God with cries of joy. Psalm 47:1 (NIV)

Create in me a pure heart, O God, and renew a steadfast spirit within me.

Do not cast me from your presence or take your Holy Spirit from me. Restore to me the joy of your salvation and grant me a willing spirit, to sustain me. Psalm 51:10-12 (NIV)

Blessed are you when people insult you, persecute you and falsely say all kinds of evil against you because of me. Rejoice and be glad, because great is your reward in heaven, Matthew 5:11-12a (NIV)

WORSHIP/OBEDIENCE

This is definitely a chance to "live the obvious" for God. My obedience requires no questions, no complaints and no grumbling attitudes. Rejoice and be glad!

Serve the Lord with gladness. Okay, we can decide to do that. But what about serving others? Or is serving one another and serving God basically the same thing?

By serving others with the correct attitude and motivation, are we also serving God?

Absolutely!

ADORATION/EXPLANATION

To <u>serve</u> is basically "minister to, attend to, care for, help, support, and encourage someone." And I would like to add that it does not mean only to those that you love and are easy to serve! Actually, it is usually the opposite. We are to serve the body of Christ, and many times these are some very unloveable parts in that body!

You, my brothers and sisters, were called to be free. But do not use your freedom to indulge the flesh; rather, serve one another humbly in love. Galatians 5:13 (NIV)

Whatever you do, work at it with all your heart, as working for the Lord, not for men, since you know that you will receive an inheritance from the Lord as a reward. It is the Lord Christ you are serving. Colossians 3:23-24 (NIV)

Do everything without complaining or arguing, Philippians 2:14 (NIV)

WORSHIP/OBEDIENCE

Yikes…do everything without complaining? You really mean everything?

Lord, I come to you in prayer. This is a tough task! When I truly decide that I want to serve You, then serving others will begin to show itself in me as a natural outcome. I will hear Your commands to be helpful, compassionate, forgiving, hospitable, and loving. Living obviously will mean that I will do it without a grumble or complaint! But I need your help. Amen.

Are there some days that you are so busy that you do not have time for anything else but your "busyness?" On days like this, we rush about, going from one thing to the next. We've all felt the hectic crunch of a schedule! And once in a while this is fine, but if we function like this on a daily basis, our busyness may make us miss out on something that God wants to show us.

ADORATION/EXPLANATION

Our life's greatest priority is to take time to reflect on God's word each day and learn what He would have us do. Even church work, ministry, or other Christian service must not keep us too busy for God. We need to pause so that we can hear His orders before rushing off to do His work!

As Jesus and his disciples were on their way, he came to a village where a woman named Martha opened her home to him. She had a sister called Mary, who sat at the Lord's feet listening to what he said. But Martha was distracted by all the preparations that had to be made. She came to him and asked, "Lord, don't you care that my sister has left me to do the work by myself? Tell her to help me!"

"Martha, Martha," the Lord answered, "you are worried and upset about many things, but only one thing is needed. Mary has chosen what is better, and it will not be taken away from her." Luke 10:38-41 (NIV)

We hear that some among you are idle and disruptive. They are not busy; they are busybodies. Such people we command and urge in the Lord Jesus Christ to settle down and earn the food they eat. And as for you, brothers, never tire of doing what is right. 2 Thessalonians 3:11-13 (NIV)

WORSHIP/OBEDIENCE

In the story from Luke, nothing was wrong with Martha's hospitality. Actually, we are told to be hospitable. But her priorities, sometimes like our own, were out of order. She was so concerned with the tasks at hand, that she missed the greater privilege of sitting at Jesus' feet. And even worse, she was grumbling and complaining!

God, show me how to manage my time so that I can meditate on You.

The weather is slowly dropping into the cooler temperatures. The wind is blowing the last of the leaves off of the trees. Here in the northeast, we are wearing jackets and sweatshirts outside on most days. Today is especially blustery, and as I look out of the windows I am reminded of God's breath. One exhale from His mouth could send great gusts across my yard, the mountains, or the sea!

ADORATION/EXPLANATION

We so often forget to dwell on the fact that God breathed and we came into existence. How awesome is He! Today, let's meditate on the mighty God that we serve. Breathe on us, breath of God!

The Lord God formed the man from the dust of the ground and breathed into his nostrils the breath of life, and man became a living being. Genesis 2:7 (NIV)

Jesus appears to his disciples after his death: On the evening of that first day of the week, when the disciples were together, with the doors locked for fear of the Jewish leaders, Jesus came and stood among them and said, "Peace be with you!" After he said this, he showed them his hands and side. The disciples were overjoyed when they saw the Lord. Again Jesus said, "Peace be with you! As the Father has sent me, I am sending you." And with that he breathed on them and said, "Receive the Holy Spirit." John 20:19-22 (NIV)

WORSHIP/OBEDIENCE

The word for breath and Spirit are the same in this passage. Whenever you see the wind at work in nature, make an effort to think of God's spirit that dwells in you—that beautiful entity of God that is not only swooping down on earth, but right into our very lives each and every day!

"Sweet Holy Spirit, Sweet heavenly dove...." Abide in me!

Are we foolish at times? According to God, if we believe the wisdom of this world over His wisdom, we are deemed foolish. God's wisdom appears foolish to the world or to unbelievers in the fact that they do not understand it, and it may often times even offend their senses. They believe it to be irrational or not realistic.

ADORATION/EXPLANATION

Paul tells the Corinthian people that they were better off believing God's so-called foolishness than the so-called wisdom of the world. God's word is a supernatural puzzle, complete with someone dying on the cross for our sins. This is where we trust God's grace, mercy, and wisdom by faith!

Where is the wise person? Where is the teacher of the law? Where is the philosopher of this age? Has not God made foolish the wisdom of the world? For since in the wisdom of God the world through its wisdom did not know him, God was pleased through the foolishness of what was preached to save those who believe.

For the foolishness of God is wiser than man's wisdom, and the weakness of God is stronger than human strength.

The man without the Spirit does not accept the things that come from the Spirit of God, for they are foolishness to him, and he cannot understand them, because they are spiritually discerned.

Do not deceive yourselves. If any one of you thinks he is wise by the standards of this age, he should become a "fool" so that he may become wise. For the wisdom of this world is foolishness in God's sight. 1 Corinthians 1:20-21, 25; 2:14; 3:18-19 (NIV)

WORSHIP/OBEDIENCE

I will honor God by refusing to allow myself to be deceived by the intelligence and wisdom of this age. Looks can be deceiving! This is your brain on the world's wisdom: foolishness! This is your brain on God's wisdom: trust, faith, spiritual understanding! He is God. We are not!

Any questions?

Today I am thankful that I can rest in my own foolishness. What? Who would admit that they are satisfied with being foolish? No one! But the Bible says that all the knowledge in this world will never make us smart enough, savvy enough, or clever enough to rely totally on our own wisdom. So don't stress over what you don't know. No, just rest on God!

ADORATION/EXPLANATION
The apostle Paul (who was quite the intellectual, by the way) was willing to be considered foolish for God. He did not boast about his own abilities but gave credit to the Holy Spirit working in his life.

For the foolishness of God is wiser than man's wisdom, and the weakness of God is stronger than mans strength. 1 Corinthians 1:25 (NIV)

When I came to you, brothers, I did not come with eloquence or superior wisdom as I proclaimed to you the testimony about God. For I resolved to know nothing while I was with you except Jesus Christ and him crucified. I came to you in weakness and fear, and with much trembling. My message and my preaching were not with wise and persuasive words, but with a demonstration of the Spirit's power, so that your faith might not rest on men's wisdom, but on God's power. 1 Corinthians 2:1-5 (NIV)

However, it is written: "No eye has seen, no ear has heard, no mind has conceived what God has prepared for those who love him" 1 Corinthians 2:9 (NIV)

WORSHIP/OBEDIENCE
"Resting, resting, sweetly resting..."—what a relief it is, not having to know everything at once! God has prepared so many things for us to learn. Each day is a new opportunity to gain another nugget of truth for our life.

Wow! Know that TRUE wisdom comes from God!

November 22

I am thankful that my parents did not allow me to be a willful, grouchy, stubborn young girl. I had to learn to look others in the eyes, compliment them, and to make polite conversation. If I was in a foul mood, the only thing that I could do was to march upstairs to my bedroom. If I disobeyed, I was punished. I had to eat whatever was cooked for me with thankfulness to the one who cooked it. The list goes on!

ADORATION/EXPLANATION
Sound like a tough life? Sometimes it was. Did I always want to obey all those lessons and directives? Nope. Am I a better woman because of those enforced rules? You bet!

Listen, my son (daughter), to your father's instruction and do not forsake your mother's teaching. They will be a garland to grace your head and a chain to adorn your neck. Proverbs 1:8-9 (NIV)

Above all else, guard your heart, for it is the wellspring of life. Put away perversity from your mouth; keep corrupt talk far from your lips. Let your eyes look straight ahead, fix your gaze directly before you. Make level paths for your feet and take only ways that are firm. Do not swerve to the right or the left; keep your foot from evil. Proverbs 4:23-27 (NIV)

Train a child in the way he should go, and when he is old he will not turn from it. Proverbs 22:6 (NIV)

WORSHIP/OBEDIENCE
My parents obeyed God's word on how to raise their children. They made me live out God's good path, even when I didn't want to! Was it difficult for them at times? Yes—have you ever tried to discipline a grouchy teenager? But have I departed from those teachings? No!

Thank you, God, for molding me into a mighty woman, ready and able to live for Christ! Thank you for my parent's love and commitment.

This morning I looked up at the sky and saw a contrail. Do you know what a contrail is? It is the streaks of smoke (aka water vapor) left in the sky by an airplane at high altitude. It shows the path that the plane has taken, and it remains for a long while after the aircraft has passed.

ADORATION/EXPLANATION

If we each left a contrail behind us wherever we went, what would it be? What would it look like? Would people be able to identify us by our contrail? Would anyone see enough of a difference to know that we'd been there? Are we forging a path…?

For it is God's will that by doing good you should silence the ignorant talk of foolish men. 1 Peter 2:15 (NIV)

But thanks be to God, who always leads us in triumphal procession in Christ and through us spreads everywhere the fragrance of the knowledge of him. For we are to God the aroma of Christ among those who are being saved and those who are perishing. 2 Corinthians 2:14-15 (NIV)

This is how we know what love is: Jesus Christ laid down his life for us. And we ought to lay down our lives for our brothers. If anyone has material possessions and sees his brother in need but has no pity on him, how can the love of God be in him? Dear children, let us not love with words or tongue but with actions and truth. 1 John 3:16-18 (NIV)

WORSHIP/OBEDIENCE

Actions and truth! This is a lesson that requires some fervent prayer if we are to really live it out.

Dear Lord, I want to leave a beautiful contrail for you in my daily existence. Show me obvious ways today to love others, not just in words or tongue but with actions and truth. Let me see and pursue opportunities to leave an impression of YOU wherever I go!

November 24

What does it mean to have etiquette? Basically it is using manners for day-to-day commonplace behaviors and obligations that help us get along with one another. Did you know that there is a Christian version to etiquette?

ADORATION/EXPLANATION
As believers in Christ, etiquette should be important, though I'm not necessarily talking about keeping your elbows off the table at dinner. God also has a version of etiquette. He calls it fruit! The fruit of the Spirit is behaviors or traits that develop in us as we seek to follow God's word in our daily life. When we allow Christ-like etiquette to develop in our lives, we can be comfortable among princes or paupers! His fruit never goes out of season.

Therefore, as God's chosen people, holy and dearly loved, clothe yourselves with compassion, kindness, humility, gentleness and patience. Bear with each other and forgive whatever grievances you may have against one another. Forgive as the Lord forgave you. And over all these virtues put on love, which binds them all together in perfect unity. Colossians 3:12-14 (NIV)

But the fruit of the Spirit is love, joy, peace, patience, kindness, goodness, faithfulness, gentleness and self-control. Against such there is no law. Galatians 5:22-23 (NIV)

Show proper respect to everyone: Love the brotherhood of believers, fear God, honor the king. 1 Peter 2:17 (NIV)

WORSHIP/OBEDIENCE
God's version of etiquette is the best charm course that we could ever sign up for! The most beautiful fact about this course is that we have a whole lifetime to let God produce this fruit in us. He is NOT a forceful gardener, though, and He will only work on the branches that stay connected to Him!

The big question is…will we allow Him to teach us, mold us, and prune us?

Can we fool or trick God? No, I'd hope not. At least, I don't think so…

Where do you stand? On whose word do you base your belief? Most people would say a resounding "NO" to being able to fool God, yet the way they live is contrary to this. In life's busyness, we cannot afford to forget that God cannot be fooled by you or anyone. No amount of pretty, eloquent words can pull the wool over our God's eyes!

ADORATION/EXPLANATION

Lord, do not let me forget that you are God. You are so far above my ways that I cannot always comprehend you, and yet you are so clear in Your Word that I can gain understanding by studying it. I want a God that cannot be fooled! I want to be honest before you! I trust you! Amen.

Do not deceive yourselves. If any one of you thinks he is wise by the standards of this age, he should become a "fool" so that he may become wise. For the wisdom of the world is foolishness in God's sight. As it is written: "He catches the wise in their craftiness…" 1 Corinthians 3:18-19 (NIV)

Do not be deceived: God cannot be mocked. A man reaps what he sows. The one who sows to please his sinful nature, from that nature will reap destruction; the one who sows to please the Spirit, from the Spirit will reap eternal life. Let us not become weary in doing good, for at the proper time we will reap a harvest if we do not give up. Galatians 6:7-9 (NIV)

WORSHIP/OBEDIENCE

I do not want to be deceived… and I do not want to live in a deceiving way towards others. God hears my heart's true motives and not just what my lips utter out loud. He is not fooled by craftiness! I want to live honestly before Him!

Today, I choose to believe God!

Thankfulness—is it a word of gratitude or an attitude of my heart? Is it expressing all that we have to be thankful for, or is it rather the *not* expressing what we wish we had? We do not just want to utter words for others to hear, but for our hearts to really recognize the greatness of God's power and provisions in our lives.

ADORATION/EXPLANATION

The result of this heart change is pure contentment. This real, authentic contentment will culminate in an over abundance of thanksgiving in the form of words and praise, glory and honor for our Lord. So, do we believe God is able to handle all of our needs or not?

Rejoice in the Lord always, I will say again: Rejoice! Philippians 4:4 (NIV)

To him who is able to keep you from falling and to present you before his glorious presence without fault and with great joy— Jude 1:24 (NIV)

Then he said to them, "Watch out! Be on your guard against all kinds of greed; a man's life does not consist in the abundance of his possessions." Luke 12:15 (NIV)

Let us come before him with thanksgiving and extol him with music and song. Psalm 95:2 (NIV)

WORSHIP/OBEDIENCE

My obvious act of obedience and worship to what I read in the Bible is to bow my head in a simple, heart-felt prayer.

Lord, You are able, you are able. I know you are able! You are not only able but promise to provide my needs in each situation that I face today. Let me demonstrate with my whole voice, attitude, and heart that my trust is in you! Amen.

Contentment …what exactly is it? Are you content? What if this is as good as life is going to get for us? Will our faith in God be enough to keep us persevering through this life on earth? It was for the apostle Paul. But I'm thinking (just as you probably are), that I am not as strong as the apostle Paul!

ADORATION/EXPLANATION
Paul was a human being just like you and me, a major sinner saved by God's wonderful grace! What made him special was that he chose to listen to God and be led by Him!

I am not saying this because I am in need, for I have learned to be content whatever the circumstances. I know what it is to be in need, and I know what it is to have plenty. I have learned the secret of being content in any and every situation, whether well fed or hungry, whether living in plenty or in want. I can do everything through him who gives me strength. Philippians 4:11-13 (NIV)

But godliness with contentment is great gain. For we brought nothing into the world, and we can take nothing out of it. 1 Timothy 6:6-7 (NIV)

Give thanks in all circumstances, for this is God's will for you in Christ Jesus. Thessalonians 5:18 (NIV)

WORSHIP/OBEDIENCE
Simply speaking, contentment is being satisfied or choosing to be okay with our circumstances. This was Paul's secret. He chose to be satisfied because he knew that he could do all and handle all things through Christ.

Was this easy? No, not at all! Much of his life was spent in prison.

The secret is learning to rely on God's strength in us, and not our own.

Let's CHOOSE to be satisfied! Pass on the secret!

November 28

If *God's* wants for your life don't agree with *your* wants, which wants have to go? Here's another question: do you really believe that God is sovereign, is your creator, and is the one true master of the universe? Do you really believe that he knows the best and wants the best for you? Your answer to these questions will determine which wants will have to be cut loose from your life!

ADORATION/EXPLANATION

Surrender is tough. Giving up things in life is not easy! But we do not have to understand or agree with it before we obey God. He wants to reveal areas in our lives that need to change. It is only as we study His word in those areas and then obey that He will slowly, slowly, maybe even VERY slowly, make His way clear!

Being confident of this, that he who began a good work in you will carry it on to completion until the day of Christ Jesus. Philippians 1:6 (NIV)

Trust in the Lord with all your heart and lean not on your own understanding; in all your ways acknowledge him, and he will make your paths straight. Proverbs 3:5-6 (NIV)

Submit yourselves, then, to God. Resist the devil, and he will flee from you. James 4:7 (NIV)

In his heart a man plans his course, but the Lord determines his steps. Proverbs 16:9 (NIV)

WORSHIP/OBEDIENCE

There's a popular hymn that says, "I surrender all. I surrender all. All to thee my blessed Savior, I surrender all!" Do we really?

Help us start surrendering today, Lord!

Kind words, pleasant words, beautiful words, wonderful words! Who would not enjoy being around the person filled with these? If we are to be faithful followers of Christ, then we obviously need to practice this kind of conversation.

ADORATION/EXPLANATION:
Do I have a choice? Is there an option, an escape route, an exemption clause that can free me from my obligation to speak this way? Sorry…there is not! Actually, as we grow in our relationship to God we will desire to live and speak in this way. It is beneficial not only to the hearer, but also to us!

A man finds joy in giving an apt reply—and how good is a timely word! Proverbs 15:23 (NIV)

Pleasant words are a honeycomb, sweet to the soul and healing to the bones. Proverbs 16:24 (NIV)

He who guards his mouth and his tongue keeps himself from calamity. Proverbs 21:23 (NIV)

Make it your ambition to lead a quiet life: You should mind your own business and work with your hands, just as we told you, so that your daily life may win the respect of outsiders and so that you will not be dependent on anybody. 1 Thessalonians 4:11-12 (NIV)

If anyone considers himself religious and yet does not keep a tight rein on his tongue, he deceives himself and his religion is worthless. James 1:26 (NIV)

 Don't grumble against each other, brothers, or you will be judged. James 5:9a (NIV)

WORSHIP/OBEDIENCE
God leaves no questions as to how we are to speak. 'Nuff said!

How do we conduct ourselves? Our conduct is our mode or standard of personal behavior. As Christians, our conduct should be based on the principals of scripture. Observers should be able to see a pattern or predictable path to our lives if they choose to spend enough time with us.

ADORATION/EXPLANATION

Our awesome God is mighty, powerful and predictable. He can be counted on! He is trust worthy! As the sun rises and sets…so is our God!

Dear God, stay with me, ever guiding my life, words, thoughts, and actions. Let my conduct lead people to look to you for answers. Let my personal standard of operating speak volumes that "This is not me….it is ALL Christ in me!"

Even a child is known by his actions, by whether his conduct is pure and right. Proverbs 20:11 (NIV)

And whatever you do, whether in word or deed, do it all in the name of the Lord Jesus, giving thanks to God the Father through him. Colossians 3:17 (NIV)

Whatever happens, conduct yourselves in a manner worthy of the gospel of Christ. Then, whether I come and see you or only hear about you in my absence, I will know that you stand firm in one spirit, contending as one man for the faith of the gospel Philippians 1:27 (NIV)

WORSHIP/OBEDIENCE

So you mean to tell me that whatever happens, I am to conduct myself in the way that Christ would want? Yes! Obviously this leaves no room for excuses on our part. We need to be aware, awake, and on the lookout in each and every situation that takes place. No matter how difficult, we must <u>choose</u> to live in a manner worthy of our relationship with Christ!

Many thoughts, ideas, and concepts in the Bible are repeated over and over again. Is this repetition because we are forgetful creatures? Perhaps, but more than likely it's because they are important concepts that warrant repeating so that we will not forget them.

ADORATION/EXPLANATION

The Bible is not a one-time novel, meant to be read and then put away on a shelf. It is meant for constant reading, studying, discussion, and meditation. Then it's meant to be re-read, studied some more, and put into practice! Then read again, thought about more, and studied anew! PHEW!

Finally, my brothers, rejoice in the Lord! It is no trouble for me to write the same things to you again, and it is a safeguard for you.

But whatever was to my profit I now consider loss for the sake of Christ. What is more, I consider everything a loss compared to the surpassing greatness of knowing Christ Jesus my Lord, for whose sake I have lost all things. I consider them rubbish, that I may gain Christ. Philippians 3:1, 7- 8 (NIV)

Good and upright is the Lord; therefore he instructs sinners in his ways. He guides the humble in what is right and teaches them his way. All the ways of the Lord are loving and faithful for those who keep the demands of his covenant. Psalm 25:8-10 (NIV)

WORSHIP/OBEDIENCE

I will choose to read and ponder the advice and wisdom in the Bible. It is a wealth of knowledge at my finger-tips that I will not take for granted.

Dear God, thank you for your gift of the Bible. Thank you that we have the freedom to read and re-read it every day. This is a privilege that we sometimes take for granted in our busy schedules. Thank you for taking delight in telling us the same things over and over again so that we may meditate and digest them fully! Help us to humbly listen and learn!

Anyone can look godly in church. Have you noticed this? Dressed nice, on our best behavior, singing, praying, worshipping…of course these are all just superficial things, but they do look good to anyone observing. So what would happen if you were turned inside out? What would you look like?

ADORATION/EXPLANATION

God can see right through these superficial traits and directly into our hearts. This can be a wonderful or a frightening thought. We need to be just as concerned with the condition of our hearts as we are with what is observed on the outside. There should not be one heart for church and one for during the week. We cannot have a two-faced heart!

But the Lord said to Samuel, "Do not consider his appearance nor his height, for I have rejected him. The Lord does not look at the things man looks at. Man looks at the outward appearance, but the Lord looks at the heart." 1 Samuel 16:7 (NIV)

"And you, my son Solomon, acknowledge the God of your father, and serve him with wholehearted devotion and with a willing mind, for the Lord searches every heart and understands every motive behind the thoughts. If you seek him, he will be found by you; but if you forsake him, he will reject you forever." 1 Chronicles 28:9 (NIV)

Teach me your way, O Lord, and I will walk in your truth; give me an undivided heart, that I may fear your name. Psalm 86:11 (NIV)

WORSHIP/OBEDIENCE

If King David's advice to his son Solomon (the wisest man on earth) was to have a whole heart with devotion and motives, then we should heed that advice as well. We should choose this day, whether it be in church or in our everyday lives, to have an undivided heart!

Let the one, true face of my heart shine out brightly today!

December 3

Everybody needs hope! What would be our purpose of living if there were no hope for better times, hope for better finances, better relationships, or even just hope for a brighter tomorrow?

During this month, we're going to reflect on all the things that we as humans want and need. As we move towards Christmas day, we can also reflect on how these things were sent special delivery, directly to us, and packaged in a manger!

ADORATION/EXPLANATION
God, sometimes in the busyness of my life, I tend to forget that YOU are my true source of hope. You never change. You never shift. You never give up on me!

Do you not know? Have you not heard? The Lord is the everlasting God, the Creator of the ends of the earth. He will not grow tired or weary, and his understanding no one can fathom. He gives strength to the weary and increases the power of the weak. Even youths grow tired and weary, and young men stumble and fall; but those who hope in the Lord will renew their strength. They will soar on wings like eagles; they will run and not grow weary, they will walk and not be faint. Isaiah 40:28-31 (NIV)

We have this hope as an anchor for the soul, firm and secure. It enters the inner sanctuary behind the curtain, where Jesus, who went before us, has entered on our behalf. Hebrews 6:19-20a (NIV)

Find rest, O my soul, in God alone; my hope comes from him. He alone is my rock and my salvation; he is my fortress, I will not be shaken. Psalm 62:5-6 (NIV)

WORSHIP/OBEDIENCE
Yes, everybody needs hope. We have this hope in our lives, but it's not found in our own strength. It is resting, relying, trusting, and believing in Jesus and His finished work on the cross for all of us.

My HOPE is in you Lord...I will not be shaken.

We all need help at some time or another in our life. When I was younger, I wanted to be independent and tried to accomplish many things without help. However, as I matured, I came to realize that life can be difficult and everyone needs help at times.

This is not a sign of weakness! It is actually the mark of a faithful follower of God.

ADORATION/EXPLANATION

The more time we spend reading God's word, the more we learn that we need His help to live our lives. We need this assistance not only after we have exhausted our own efforts as a last resort, but also in everyday life, from the minute we rise to the close of the day.

God is our refuge and our strength, an ever-present help in trouble. Therefore we will not fear, though the earth give way and the mountains fall into the heart of the sea, Psalm 46:1-2 (NIV)

So do not fear, for I am with you; do not be dismayed, for I am your God. I will strengthen you and help you; I will uphold you with my righteous right hand. Isaiah 41:10 (NIV)

In the same way, the Spirit helps us in our weakness. We do not know what we ought to pray for, but the Spirit himself intercedes for us with groans that words cannot express. Romans 8:26 (NIV)

WORSHIP/OBEDIENCE

Everybody needs help! What a beautiful description in Romans of how the Spirit is there for us, even when the actual words of what we need may escape our lips. God beseeches us to ask for help and He takes joy in giving it.

Lord, I need your help today. Amen.

December 5

Everyone wants courage. Even the cowardly lion in the Wizard of Oz desired courage. How would you describe this trait, though? Is it already in us? Can someone bestow it on us like a title?

ADORATION/EXPLANATION

Basically, having courage is the opposite of being cowardly. Having a strong spirit in the face of opposition, standing firm, being tenacious, and perseverance are all character qualities of a faithful Christian.

"Be strong and courageous. Do not be afraid or terrified because of them, for the Lord your God goes with you; he will never leave you nor forsake you." Deuteronomy 31:6 (NIV)

Be on your guard; stand firm in the faith; be men of courage; be strong. 1 Corinthians 16:13 (NIV)

"Be strong and courageous, because you will lead these people to inherit the land I swore to their forefathers to give them. Be strong and very courageous. Be careful to obey all the law my servant Moses gave you; do not turn from it to the right or to the left, that you may be successful wherever you go. Do not let this Book of the Law depart from your mouth; meditate on it day and night, so you may be careful to do everything written in it. Then you will be prosperous and successful. Have I not commanded you? Be strong and courageous. Do not be terrified; do not be discouraged, for the Lord your God will be with you wherever you go." Joshua 1:6-9 (NIV)

WORSHIP/OBEDIENCE

When God says, "*Be* strong and courageous," that is a charge to action! It is not a suggestion or an idea up for discussion. Our courage must lie in the fact that if God commands it, we can do it! No matter how hard the opposition is, He is with us wherever we go!

December 6

Everyone needs compassion. As faithful followers of Christ, it is obvious that we should be compassionate. Just as God demonstrates compassion and caring towards us, we in turn need to channel this to others that we come in contact with each day.

ADORATION/EXPLANATION

God loves us so much that He cannot help but have a sympathetic, caring desire to alleviate our struggles. If He chooses not to totally remove our trials, He promises to be gracious and compassionate to us during them, if we will only remember to call on Him.

They refused to listen and failed to remember the miracles you performed among them. They became stiff-necked and in their rebellion appointed a leader in order to return to their slavery. But you are a forgiving God, gracious and compassionate, slow to anger and abounding in love. Therefore you did not desert them, Nehemiah 9:17 (NIV)

When he saw the crowds, he had compassion on them, because they were harassed and helpless, like sheep without a shepherd. Matthew 9:36 (NIV)

Because of the Lord's great love we are not consumed, for his compassions never fail. Lamentations 3:22 (NIV)

Finally, all of you, live in harmony with one another; be sympathetic, love as brothers, be compassionate and humble. 1 Peter 3:8 (NIV)

WORSHIP/OBEDIENCE

*Dear Lord, teach me today to have the same heart of compassion
for others that you have demonstrated toward me.*

December 7

Riches, wealth, money, good fortune—everyone wants them, don't they? After all, who would choose to be poor if they had the choice? But God's word speaks directly about this topic. Material things are very uncertain and our hope is not to be based on them. Instead, we should focus on the spiritual blessings from God that do not fade over time.

ADORATION/EXPLANATION
If you have a relationship with Christ, you are considered rich by God's standards. We are heirs and adopted children into a glorious inheritance that is waiting for us in heaven. It may not be the riches that this world tells us that we should strive for, but oh, they are so much better!

Command those who are rich in this present world not to be arrogant nor to put their hope in wealth, which is so uncertain, but to put their hope in God, who richly provides us with everything for our enjoyment. Command them to do good, to be rich in good deeds, and to be generous and willing to share. In this way they will lay up treasure for themselves as a firm foundation for the coming age, so that they may take hold of the life that is truly life. 1 Timothy 6:17-19 (NIV)

Whoever loves money never has money enough; whoever loves wealth is never satisfied with his income. This too is meaningless. Ecclesiastes 5:10 (NIV)

People who want to get rich fall into temptation and a trap and into many foolish and harmful desires that plunge men into ruin and destruction. For the love of money is a root of all kinds of evil. Some people, eager for money, have wandered from the faith and pierced themselves with many griefs. 1 Timothy 6:9-10 (NIV)

WORSHIP/OBEDIENCE
Whatever financial circumstance we may find ourselves in, we need to choose to be content. We need to choose to work hard, pay our bills, and serve God with our money! Simple, isn't it?

"Tell me the truth!" All of us want to know the truth—or do we? Do we really desire to know the truth about everything, or would that just mean we are now responsible to act accordingly? So, think about it. Do you desire to know TRUTH?

ADORATION/EXPLANATION

Do you know the King of Truth? I know Him well. As a matter of fact, I have a personal relationship with the only "true life" story that will really affect my life. I have also read the back cover, and I LOVE the ending!

Yet a time is coming and has now come when the true worshipers will worship the Father in spirit and truth, for they are the kind of worshipers the Father seeks. John 4:23 (NIV)

"Then you will know the truth, and the truth will set you free." John 8:32 (NIV)

Thomas said to him, "Lord, we don't know where you are going, so how can we know the way?" Jesus answered, "I am the way and the truth and the life. No one comes to the Father except through me. If you really knew me, you would know my Father as well. From now on, you do know him and have seen hm." John 14:5-6 (NIV)

All your words are true; all your righteous laws are eternal. Psalm 119:160 (NIV)

WORSHIP/OBEDIENCE

You are getting ready to celebrate Christ's birthday in a couple of weeks. How familiar are you with the King of Truth himself? He has given us His word, the Holy Bible, to read, search out, and to discover for ourselves all the great life changing precepts. Do you really want to know the TRUTH?

God has NOT stopped speaking, and He is as good as His word!

December 9

Everyone likes bread. Okay, maybe not bread, but pasta, rolls, cake, cookies, etc. Personally, I love bread—Italian, wheat, rye, French bread, bagels, biscuits, and rolls...complete with butter! Most of us will have a lot of it during this holiday season. But if bread was all there was, and I did not have the promise of turkey, ham or better things to come, would I be satisfied? Most likely not!

ADORATION/EXPLANATION
In Jesus' time on earth, bread was not a side nor afterthought to a meal as it is now. In fact, bread was their basic life-sustaining food. It carried a special significance. People relied on it! People depended on it!

He humbled you, causing you to hunger and then feeding you with manna, which neither you nor your fathers had known, to teach you that man does not live on bread alone but on every word that comes from the mouth of the Lord. Deuteronomy 8:3 (NIV)

Then Jesus declared, "I am the bread of life. He who comes to me will never go hungry, and he who believes in me will never be thirsty. But as I told you, you have seen me and still you do not believe."

"I tell you the truth, he who believes has everlasting life. I am the bread of life."

"I am the living bread that came down from heaven. If anyone eats of this bread, he will live forever. This bread is my flesh, which I will give for the life of the world." John 6:35-36, 47-48, 51 (NIV)

WORSHIP/OBEDIENCE
Wow...what proclamations! My holiday bread and butter fantasies pale in significance compared to Jesus' bold claims about His bread.

Lord, I desire this kind of bread for my life. I believe your words and trust that I have everlasting life. Thank you for giving your bread of life to the world!

Presents!!! Yes, those wonderful, thoughtful, awesome gifts that are picked perfectly with us in mind. Everyone wants cool presents! No one wants a thoughtless gift picked at the last moment, at the final hour, no wrapping, maybe even handed to us in a paper bag. Thoughtless presents are not always appreciated. Oh, the gift may be nice, in and of itself, but the intent of the giver is often displayed in the presentation.

ADORATION/EXPLANATION

It is really wonderful that God didn't wait until the last second to run out and get a gift for us. He reasoned and sought out a way to bring all men to Him, and He did it with the gift of Christ's birth in Bethlehem!

For the wages of sin is death, but the gift of God is eternal life in Christ Jesus our Lord. Romans 6:23 (NIV)

For it is by grace you have been saved, through faith---and this not from yourselves, it is the gift of God— Ephesians 2:8 (NIV)

"Ask and it will be given to you; seek and you will find; knock and the door will be opened to you. For everyone who asks receives; he who seeks finds; and to him who knocks, the door will be opened." Matthew 7:7-8 (NIV)

"I give them eternal life, and they shall never perish; no one can snatch them out of my hand." John 10:28 (NIV)

WORSHIP/OBEDIENCE

Yes, everyone likes cool presents! But when I really understand the awesome gift that is available for all of us, the one God sent as a special delivery on Christmas day, all I can do is utter a solemn, "Thank you." And again, "Thank you." And again… "THANK YOU!"

Who doesn't want a wonderful, physically fit body? If I could just ask for a better body for Christmas—stronger, leaner, less weight, more muscle tone, maybe even able to leap tall buildings in a single bound—I think I would! Anyone who claims that they wouldn't like a better physical body is usually not telling the truth. Keeping a lean physique is great, but it takes a lot of work and many people don't want or have time to do the maintenance. That is why we would take it as a free gift if it were offered!

ADORATION/EXPLANATION
God is really more interested in "soul building" though, and this requires much more discipline than "body building." He wants us to desire a beautifully shaped, stronger, leaner, loving, and honorable soul!

Love the Lord your God with all your heart and with all your soul and with all your strength. These commandments that I give to you today are to be upon your hearts. Impress them on your children. Talk about them when you sit at home and when you walk along the road, when you lie down and when you get up. Deuteronomy 6:5-7 (NIV)

"But be very careful to keep the commandment and the law that Moses the servant of the Lord gave you; to love the Lord your God, to walk in all his ways, to obey his commands, to hold fast to him and to serve him with all your heart and all your soul." Joshua 22:5 (NIV)

Praise the Lord, O my soul; all my inmost being, praise his holy name. Psalm 103:1 (NIV)

WORSHIP/OBEDIENCE
"Soul building" is the continual pursuit to love God, follow His instructions, meditate on and obey His words, one day at a time. Applying these Bible verses to our lives daily is like a personal exercise program for our hearts and souls. It may seem tough, but it pays big dividends later. Just like our bodies, our souls are a work in progress.

Choose the trainer of your spirit well!

December 12

Function versus dysfunction? Which one would you choose if you had the choice? Of course, everyone wants and desires something that functions well, especially if it is their family. Yet many, many families in our world today have some kind of dysfunction. Divorce, bitterness, anger, abuse, prison time, adultery, gluttony, selfishness, silence, name-calling, addictions, guilt, or just plain disinterest and lack of love are only a few of the issues plaguing families these days.

ADORATION/EXPLANATION

Many people learn to live with dysfunction in order to survive everyday life, but that was never God's perfect plan for us. He is not a God of dysfunction, but a totally opposite God of functioning love. In a world that struggles, we can be sure to find a constant, steadfast anchor to hold onto, no matter what is not functioning around us!

I love you, O Lord, my strength. The Lord is my rock, my fortress and my deliverer; my God is my rock, in whom I take refuge. He is my shield and the horn of my salvation, my stronghold. I call to the Lord, who is worthy of praise, and I am saved from my enemies. Psalm 18:1-3 (NIV)

Keep me safe, O God, for in you I take refuge. I said to the Lord, "You are my Lord; apart from you I have no good thing." Psalm 16:1-2 (NIV)

The name of the Lord is a strong tower; the righteous run to it and are safe. Proverbs 18:10 (NIV)

WORSHIP/OBEDIENCE

A well-functioning car, cell phone, job, computer, relationship, or everyday life is a desire of all of us, but only one thing remains constant and truly functioning today, yesterday, tomorrow, and forever—God! We can worship and obey His commands with confidence because He remains constant and true.

Run to Him and stay safe!

Everyone wants a good attitude. No, let me rephrase that: everyone wants to be around someone with a good attitude, someone who is positive, pleasant, and cheerful, who sees the proverbial glass as always half full and not half empty! All of us should desire to live this way daily so that others will want to be around us. But is it really possible to always have a good attitude about life on our own? What if I am a negative person by nature? What if I tend to be melancholy, withdrawn, skeptical, critical, or grouchy?

ADORATION/EXPLANATION

A truly correct and right attitude toward life only comes from the presence of Christ in daily living. So I will pose the question again: what if I am negative, depressed, shy, critical, skeptical, or grouchy by nature?

The answer is simply this: <u>allow</u> God's word to influence you. Consciously choose to focus on the attitude that Jesus had with people.

Your attitude should be the same as that of Christ Jesus: Who, being in very nature God, did not consider equality with God something to be grasped, but made himself nothing, taking the very nature of a servant, being made in human likeness. Philippians 2:5-7 (NIV)

Therefore, since Christ suffered in his body, arm yourselves also with the same attitude, because he who has suffered in his body is done with sin. As a result, he does not live the rest of his earthly life for evil human desires, but rather for the will of God. 1 Peter 4:1- 2 (NIV)

For the word of God is living and active. Sharper than any double-edged sword, it penetrates even to dividing soul and spirit, joints and marrow; it judges the thoughts and attitudes of the heart. Hebrews 4:12 (NIV)

WORSHIP/OBEDIENCE

Many of our behaviors and attitudes can be blamed on our natural human nature, but these lame excuses will never fly in front of the God who tells us in His word how much power, strength, courage, and hope He has blessed us with. Impatience, anger, rudeness and negativity need to go!

Allow God's sharp sword to cut away any wrong attitudes today!

December 14

Everyone loves peace. If you ask them, most people will say that they want peace.

What does it look like, sound like, or feel like? Peace on earth, peace of mind, peace treaty, peace pipe, peace and quiet, and at Christmas, we talk and sing about the Prince of Peace. Yes, everyone does love peace, but does anyone really pursue it?

ADORATION/EXPLANATION

God's version of peace comes only as a result of His Holy Spirit living within our hearts, minds, and souls. It is an inner calm, stillness of life, and tranquility of soul, even amidst life's trials and troubles. It is especially evident when we are not in control or can clearly see the future. God's peace passes all rational understanding!

For to us a child is born, to us a son is given, and the government will be on his shoulders. And he will be called Wonderful Counselor, Mighty God, Everlasting Father, Prince of Peace. Isaiah 9:6 (NIV)

Turn from evil and do good; seek peace and pursue it. Psalm 34:14 (NIV)

You will keep in perfect peace him whose mind is steadfast, because he trusts in you. Isaiah 26:3 (NIV)

"Do not let your hearts be troubled. Trust in God, trust also in me."

"Peace I leave with you; my peace I give you. I do not give to you as the world gives. Do not let your hearts be troubled and do not be afraid." John 14:1, 27 (NIV)

WORSHIP/OBEDIENCE

Of course we want peace and peacefulness! Who doesn't? Our obvious daily behavior needs to make God our top priority. Top dog…so to speak over all of our concerns, because we recognize that He is ultimately in charge! Everyone wants peace, but not many want the Prince of Peace. Jesus needs to be Prince of our jobs, our homes, our relationships, our trials, our burdens, and our daily lives!

Keep the Prince. Keep Peace!

December 15

We are all drawn to shiny, sparkling objects—shining cars, bicycles, hair, faces, water, fruit, glass, leaves, gems, jewelry, shiny dishes, bottles, gold, silver, sun, and stars!

At Christmas time, we love shiny wrapping paper, bows, and ornaments best. Commercials advertise shiny jewelry and shiny new cars! These shining objects just seem to stand out and call for our attention.

ADORATION/EXPLANATION
Our eyes are certainly drawn to shiny objects, but the real question that we should ask ourselves daily is, "Am I so drawn to Christ that others can see Him shining in me?"

Do everything without complaining or arguing, so that you may become blameless and pure, children of God without fault in a crooked and depraved generation, in which you SHINE like stars in the universe. Philippians 2:14-15 (NIV)

Your beauty should not come from outward adornment, such as braided hair and the wearing of gold jewelry and fine clothes. Instead, it should be that of your inner self, the unfading beauty of a gentle and quiet spirit, which is of great worth in God's sight. 1 Peter 3:3-4 (NIV)

"Arise, shine, for your light has come, and the glory of the Lord rises upon you." Isaiah 60:1 (NIV)

WORSHIP/OBEDIENCE
I am still going through my normal habits of showering, dressing stylishly, and doing my hair and make-up. God is not saying that we should not desire to look our best on the outside. Instead, we need to concentrate our real energy on our inner beauty. It is a new day, a new opportunity, a new adventure, and an exciting new privilege to look for ways to let God's beautiful light shine through our lives like stars in the universe.

Rise and shine, my friend! The glory of the Lord rises upon you!

Joy, joy, joy! Who doesn't desire joy? I did not say laughter or the giggles; I did not say funny, hysterical or happy; I said "joy!" True, pure, wonderful, not based on circumstances—JOY! It is the one quality that produces a satisfaction of spirit and a magnetic personality in us!

ADORATION/EXPLANATION

I love to laugh. I think many things are hysterical and comical and funny. I even believe that God loves humor. But when the Bible talks about joy, it is talking about something totally different. True godly joy comes from within. It cannot be pursued. It comes as a result of Christ living, breathing, and working in our daily lives.

❦

You will go out in joy and be led forth in peace, the mountains and the hills will burst into song before you, and all the trees of the field will clap their hands. Isaiah 55:12 (NIV)

"This day is sacred to our Lord. Do not grieve, for the joy of the Lord is your strength." Nehemiah 8:10b (NIV)

But the angel said to them, "Do not be afraid. I bring you good news of great joy that will be for all the people. Today in the town of David a Savior has been born to you; he is Christ the Lord. Luke 2:10-11 (NIV)

I have told you this so that you will be filled with my joy. Yes, your cup of joy will overflow! John 15:11 (TLB)

WORSHIP/OBEDIENCE

Our celebration of the birth of True Joy is coming in nine more days. Once we accept the news that a Savior has been born to us, we can continue to keep a joyful fountain continually over-flowing in our lives, regardless of what is happening around us! Do not be afraid! Accept His joy!

❦

December 17

Who hasn't seen a sign? Billboards, posters, street signs, traffic signs, store signs, pool signs, restaurant signs, peace signs, and even toxic waste signs! But just seeing a sign isn't really the point, now is it? Unless a sign is obeyed and the directions on it followed, it will be of no use. In fact, failing to heed the warning could actually become very dangerous, perhaps even deadly.

ADORATION/EXPLANATION

God has placed signs all throughout nature, in our lives, and in His word. Nature, people, circumstances, situations and so called coincidences are right in front of our faces! Just because we do not always see these signs, does not mean that God has not placed them there. More often the problem is that we are too busy or too distracted with our own pursuits to pay attention, even when a sign is directly in front of our face!

"This will be a sign to you: "You will find a baby wrapped in cloths and lying in a manger." Suddenly a great company of the heavenly host appeared with the angel, praising God and saying, "Glory to God in the highest, and on earth peace to men on whom his favor rests."

When the angels had left them and gone into heaven, the shepherds said to one another, "Let's go to Bethlehem and see this thing that has happened, which the Lord has told us about." So they hurried off and found Mary and Joseph, and the baby, who was lying in the manger. When they had seen him, they spread the word concerning what had been told them about this child, and all who heard it were amazed at what the shepherds said to them. Luke 2:12-18 (NIV)

WORSHIP/OBEDIENCE

The shepherds saw the sign! More impressive is that, not only did they see the sign, but they obeyed it. Better yet, not only did they obey, they hurried! They ran (not walked) to see this thing that God had told them about! After that, they spread the word and everyone was amazed! Signs, signs…do you see them? Are you looking?

Open my eyes, Lord!

December 18

Wouldn't everyone want to get rid of things that cause worry in their life? I know I would! If I could receive one special present this holiday season, it would be to totally eradicate worry in my life. Actually, it is not really the worry itself, but what conditions and problems that it causes in my physical, mental, and spiritual being.

ADORATION/EXPLANATION

Excessive worry can cause headaches, stomach-aches, jitters, crying, depression, allergies, nervousness, heart problems, rise in blood pressure, loss or gain of appetite, hair loss, skin issues, sleepiness or sleeplessness, just to name a few. God never claims or promises to take our worry away, though. Instead, He beseeches us to cast it on to Him! Let it go, again, and again and again!

"Therefore I tell you, do not worry about your life, what you will eat or drink; or about your body, what you will wear. Is not life more important than food, and the body more important than clothes?"

"Who of you by worrying can add a single hour to his life?"

"But seek first his kingdom and his righteousness, and all these things will be given to you as well. Therefore do not worry about tomorrow, for tomorrow will worry about itself. Each day has enough trouble of its own." Matthew 6:25, 27, 33-34 (NIV)

WORSHIP/OBEDIENCE

The Greeks describe worry as something that tears a person in two, like a garment coming apart at the seams. Have you ever felt like this? The Anglo-Saxon word for worry describes a power gripping a man by the throat, as a wolf would seize a sheep and strangle the vitality out of it! So basically, worry is an action that twists or strangles the neck or spirit. If left unchecked, worry can choke the physical, mental, and spiritual life out of us. DON'T LET IT! Instead, choke out worry by handing it over to your Heavenly Father. Then, hand it over again, and tomorrow, give it back again!

Whatever your worry may happen to be about, God can handle the situation!

December 19

There are always many commercials on television at this time of year for diamonds. They advertise diamond necklaces, bracelets, rings, and earrings. The media makes us think, "Who doesn't love diamonds?" Aren't they supposed to be a girl's best friend?

ADORATION/EXPLANATION

The Bible can be compared to a diamond mine. Some of the jewels are lying right on top of the soil because they have been stirred up. They are easy to spot and pick up. Others are to be found only after a lot of digging, searching and polishing. They look like lumps of coal at the start, but after much digging, forging and then polishing, they demonstrate their true value. The most precious gems take much work! Hence the term "mining" for diamonds! These are generally the most valuable.

***

The Lord their God will save them on that day as the flock of his people. They will sparkle in his land like jewels in a crown. Zechariah 9:16 (NIV)

I rejoice in your promise like one who finds a great spoil. Psalm 119:162 (NIV)

I delight greatly in the Lord; my soul rejoices in my God. For he has clothed me with garments of salvation and arrayed me in a robe of righteousness, as a bridegroom adorns his head like a priest, and a bride adorns herself with her jewels. Isaiah 61:10 (NIV)

How blessed is the man who finds wisdom, and the man who gains understanding. She is more precious than jewels; and nothing you desire compares with her. Proverbs 3:13, 15 (NASB)

WORSHIP/OBEDIENCE

These are the kind of diamonds and jewels that we should desire. God's Word can withstand the most careful digging and examination. In fact, many of the treasures of scripture can be found only after long, careful mining! This very process can open up new insights into God's truth that may have been previously overlooked. Open your Bible.

What are you waiting for? Start digging!

***

December 20

Got wisdom? Who wouldn't love to skip all the hardships and life lessons, and jump right to acquiring wisdom? It would sure save a lot of time and trouble if we were just born with it. We have to remember though, that knowledge, intelligence, and factual information alone is NOT God's version of wisdom.

ADORATION/EXPLANATION

Asking wiser older, more mature friends for advice in certain situations is a great start, but we must not forget to ask and seek the One who is the source of all wisdom too. The coupling of good judgment with information, facts, godly principles, and truth will steer you toward growing in wisdom.

And he said to man, "The fear of the Lord—that is wisdom, and to shun evil is understanding." Job 28:28 (NIV)

For the Lord gives wisdom, and from his mouth comes knowledge and understanding. He holds victory in store for the upright, he is a shield to those whose walk is blameless, for he guards the course of the just and protects the way of the faithful ones. Psalm 2:6-8 (NIV)

If any of you lacks wisdom, he should ask God, who gives generously to all without finding fault, and it will be given to him. James 1:5 (NIV)

WORSHIP/OBEDIENCE

Whenever you pray and ask God for insight, picture yourself as a little kid, standing beside an all-wise Father, listening for His voice to help and direct you. He WILL give you wisdom if you seek it, so go ahead and ask for God's common knowledge for your daily plans. After you ask, make sure that you are listening carefully for the answer. It may come in an obvious form that you are not expecting.

Look alive and live alert! What are you waiting for?

I love hearing music. Who doesn't love hearing music? Well, maybe a few grouchy, overly-tired people, or maybe certain types of loud head-banging, heavy metal music. On the whole, most folks love some sort of music and, especially around Christmastime, have it playing daily. Stores, offices, schools, homes, churches, and carolers can be heard playing or singing music throughout this month! Tis' the season!

ADORATION/EXPLANATION

Music is a mood-altering gift from God. It can result in toe tapping, finger snapping, clapping, smiling, head bobbing, marching, dancing, singing, and praising. It can soothe the soul, rock us to sleep, and lift our spirits!

Most importantly, it can point us to God!

"Hear this, you kings! Listen, you rulers! I will sing to the Lord, I will sing; I will make music to the Lord, the God of Israel. Judges 5:3 (NIV)

Shout for joy to the Lord, all the earth, burst into jubilant song with music; Psalm 98:4 (NIV)

Speak to one another with psalms, hymns and spiritual songs. Sing and make music in your heart to the Lord, always giving thanks to God the Father for everything, in the name of our Lord Jesus Christ. Ephesians 5:19-20 (NIV)

Remember what Christ taught and let his words enrich your lives and make you wise; teach them to each other and sing them out in psalms and hymns and spiritual songs, singing to the Lord with thankful hearts. Colossians 3:16 (TLB)

WORSHIP/OBEDIENCE

God tells us in His word to speak to each other with music. Can you imagine being mad, grouchy, bitter, mean, or rude if it was put to a beautiful melody? Maybe that is why we have been given this beautiful sound! So go ahead—soothe your soul, rock and roll, lift your spirits, praise God and most of all, minister to others!

December 22

Have you ever gone into someone's home and felt welcome the minute you arrived, comfortable and at home? The surroundings made you feel pleasant and accepted. You were not afraid to sit on the furniture, relax and be yourself. Is it the house itself, the furniture, or the people?

ADORATION/EXPLANATION
This is hospitality. It is not a characteristic of houses, furniture or inanimate objects; but it is a biblical trait of godly people. Hospitality says, "What's mine is yours! Sit and enjoy." It is the very attitude of graciousness and love that teaches us that our material possessions have come from God, so therefore, we should use them to make others feel welcome and comfortable. We can share and not be selfish. We can never run out of hospitality!

Rather he must be hospitable, one who loves what is good, who is self-controlled, upright, holy and disciplined. Titus 1:8 (NIV)

Offer hospitality to one another without grumbling. Each one should use whatever gift he has received to serve others, faithfully administering God's grace in its various forms. 1 Peter 4:9-10 (NIV)

Be joyful in hope, patient in affliction, faithful in prayer. Share with God's people who are in need. Practice hospitality. Romans 12:12-13 (NIV)

WORSHIP/OBEDIENCE
Isn't it amazing how God mentions hospitality right alongside such various admirable traits such as self-control, uprightness, holiness, and discipline? Hospitality takes practice. It is an attitude of the heart.

Give someone the gift of your hospitality.

Invite someone for lunch, for tea, or for dinner. Get practicing!

December 23

In two days most of us will celebrate the birth of Jesus Christ. The beauty of this is that we can have every gift that God deems important for our lives. God knew best what we needed and it may not come in the form of any of our previous desires for wealth, sparkly things, bread or physically fit bodies. Instead He may bring: hope, help, courage, compassion, truth, functioning lives, good attitudes, peace, joy, worry free living, wisdom, music in our heart, and hospitality. This can all be ours by just believing, celebrating, and accepting our Savior's birth. This free gift to us came down on Christmas day!

ADORATION/EXPLANATION
It is Christ's birthday, yet we can claim and obtain all these gifts? What a celebration! I should be jumping for joy, right? Yet many people have forgotten one very important fact about gift giving. You must reach out and take hold of the gift and then, in order to appreciate what you have been given, you must unwrap it!

The next day John saw Jesus coming toward him and said, "Look, the lamb of God, who takes away the sin of the world!" John 1:29 (NIV)

In reply Jesus declared, "I tell you the truth, no one can see the kingdom of God unless he is born again." John 3:3 (NIV)

"For God so loved the world that he gave his one and only Son, that whoever believes in him shall not perish but have eternal life. For God did not send his Son into the world to condemn the world, but to save the world through him. Whoever believes in him is not condemned, but whoever does not believe stands condemned already because he has not believed in the name of god's one and only son." John 3:16-18 (NIV)

WORSHIP/OBEDIENCE
I have accepted my present and I love it! What are you waiting for?

Come on—start tearing off the wrapping paper! This is going to be the best Christmas ever!

Today is Christmas Eve. This is probably the most wonderful day and night of the year for most girls and boys because it is filled with hopes, dreams, expectations, and excitement! As adults, we sometimes lose that sense of wonder and excitement, exchanging it for hurry, stress, and worry. Finances, hardships, sickness, and strained relationships push out the reality of God's beautiful son.

ADORATION/EXPLANATION

This is the day before Christmas, the day before the most celebrated birthday on earth, the day before the event that can make the greatest impact on your life, if only you let it. Do NOT let this day be taken lightly. Regain your joy, your sense of wonder, and excitement!

In the sixth month, God sent the angel Gabriel to Nazareth, a town in Galilee, to a virgin pledged to be married to a man named Joseph, a descendant of David. The virgin's name was Mary. The angel went to her and said, "Greetings, you who are highly favored! The Lord is with you." Mary was greatly troubled at his words and wondered what kind of greeting this might be. But the angel said to her, "Do not be afraid, Mary, you have found favor with God. You will be with child and give birth to a son, and you are to give him the name Jesus. He will be great and will be called the Son of the Most High. The Lord God will give him the throne of Jacob forever; his kingdom will never end."

"How will this be," Mary asked the angel, "since I am a virgin?"

The angel answered, "The Holy Spirit will come upon you, and the power of the Most High will overshadow you. So the holy one to be born will be called the Son of God." Luke 1:26-35 (NIV)

WORSHIP/OBEDIENCE

"Joy to the world..." "Oh come let us adore Him, oh come let us adore Him..." Why not just go ahead and read Christmas day's page in this book right now? You know that you will be too excited and busy to read tomorrow anyway! I'm just stating the obvious!

December 25

Merry Christmas!

What long expected joy…

What long awaited joy…

Christmas day is here! Jesus our Savior has been born to us!

ADORATION/EXPLANATION
The Old Testament prophets foretold in scripture that the Messiah would be a descendant of King David's royal family line. How could his very own people not recognize him?

So Joseph also went up from the town of Nazareth in Galilee to Judea, to Bethlehem the town of David, because he belonged to the house and line of David. He went there to register with Mary, who was pledged to be married to him and was expecting a child. While they were there, the time came for the baby to be born, and she gave birth to her firstborn, a son. She wrapped him in cloths and placed him in a manger, because there was no room for them in the inn.

And there were shepherds living out in the fields nearby, keeping watch over their flocks at night. An angel of the Lord appeared to them, and the glory og the Lord shone around them, and they were terrified. But the angel said to them, "Do not be afraid. I bring you good news of great joy that will be for all the people. Today in the town of David a Savior has been born to you; he is Christ the Lord." Luke 2:4-11 (NIV)

WORSHIP/OBEDIENCE
How did lowly shepherds recognize the Messiah, yet most of His very own people did not? His birth was foretold. His lineage was prophesied about in Scripture. Why do so many still not recognize him today?

Do you? Do you live like you recognize Him?

Oh come let us adore Him, oh come let us adore Him…
Christ the Lord!

December 26

Whew! Another Christmas passed. The Christmas season can be exhausting for many people. Instead of reveling in the joy of the birth of our Savior, they are now contemplating how to return and exchange an unwanted gift. I prefer to relax, rest, and enjoy the lights, music, and leftovers of a beautiful celebration.

ADORATION/EXPLANATION

Hard work, lack of sleep, and preparation can make you tired. A good night's sleep can usually remedy this, but if you are finding that Christianity exhausts you, then you are prepping and practicing for something instead of living in a daily relationship with God. Burdens, crises, and sometimes even being zealous in our service can exhaust and fatigue us. Jesus needed rest and so do we.

"Come to me, all you who are weary and burdened, and I will give you rest. Take my yoke upon you and learn from me, for I am gentle and humble in heart, and you will find rest for your souls. Matthew 11:28-29 (NIV)

He who dwells in the shelter of the Most High will rest in the shadow of the Almighty. I will say of the Lord, "He is my refuge and my fortress, my God, in whom I trust." Psalm 91:1-2 (NIV)

Therefore, my beloved brethren, be steadfast, immovable, always abounding in the work of the Lord, knowing that your toil is not in vain in the Lord. 1 Corinthians 15:58 (NASB)

WORSHIP/OBEDIENCE

If you are tired, you can go on a vacation, but your soul may not be restored. Your mind may still be weary. Check yourself to see if you are striving, prepping, and working in your own efforts to live a Christian life. Your daily walk with the Lord can restore you, give you energy, and invigorate you. Are you weary?

Get into the yoke alongside Jesus. Let Him do the pulling!

As we approach the turning of the calendar and the arrival of a new year, we need to be living an alert, vigilant life! Jesus told his disciples when he left that he would also return. As faithful followers of Christ, we need to live each day with an effort to glorify God while we are alive on this earth. Why? Because this is not all there is! This is not the end of our story. This is NOT our final home!

ADORATION/EXPLANATION

God has not revealed the exact time of Christ's return, but He has told us the various signs to watch for. In scripture, Jesus said that certain events would signal the nearness of His coming. There will be wars, famines, earthquakes, false teachers leading many astray, persecution to believers, lawlessness, and out-of-control crime, just to name a few. The Bible describes these events as birth pangs or pains. The birth pangs let us know to be ready and expecting because they only signal the beginning!

Jesus answered: "Watch out that no one deceives you. For many will come in my name, claiming, "I am the Christ, and will deceive many. You will hear of wars and rumors of wars, but see to it that you are not alarmed. Such things must happen, but the end is still to come. Nation will rise against nation, and kingdom against kingdom. There will be famines and earthquakes in various places. All these are the beginning of birth pains."

"No one knows about this day or hour, not even the angels in heaven, or the Son, but only the Father." Matthew 24:4-8, 36 (NIV)

WORSHIP/OBEDIENCE

Scared? Alarmed? You don't have to be. As a matter of fact, Jesus tells us just the opposite. "See to it that you are not alarmed," is what we are told. Fear and alarm about the end times can paralyze people. What good is that? Our salvation is guaranteed if only we believe. We can live secure and confident with Christ. God gives us a daily living guide in the Bible so that we can live joyfully and fruitfully while we are looking for His imminent return.

December 28

Most of us have all used the phrase, "hindsight is 20/20" at some time or another. It is only in looking back at God's activity in our lives that we realize the supreme wisdom that He has. How He has worked out many things for the best that we did not understand at the time of their happening.

ADORATION/EXPLANATION
Rarely does God do something exactly as we think He will. Many times we try to second-guess God and His plans for our lives, and therein lies the issue. We forget that they are God's plans and not our own; we forget that our lives are *His* lives, not our own! When Christians get frustrated, it is usually because God didn't act in the way that we thought He should! Things might even get worse before they get better, and we often question whether or not what is happening is God's will.

Lord, you have been our dwelling place throughout all generations. Before the mountains were born or you brought forth the earth and the world, from everlasting to everlasting you are God. You turn men back to dust, saying, "Return to dust, o sons of men." For a thousand years in your sight are like a day that has just gone by, or like a watch in the night. Psalm 90:1-4 (NIV)

"Obey the laws of the Lord your God. Walk in his ways and fear him." Deuteronomy 8:6 (TLB)

"For my thoughts are not your thoughts, neither are your ways my ways," declares the Lord. "As the heavens are higher than the earth, so are my ways higher than your ways and my thoughts than your thoughts." Isaiah 55:8-9 (NIV)

WORSHIP/OBEDIENCE
God does not eliminate our common sense, but instead gives us wisdom to understand and accept His ways. That is one of the beautiful benefits of spending time daily in the Bible. As we look forward to what God may do in the coming year, we need to be careful NOT to try and predict or orchestrate what He will do next. If we do, we may find ourselves completely off the mark!

News Flash…His ways are NOT our ways!

December 29

Have you ever noticed how many keys a janitor or custodian wears on a chain at his waist? He or she has access to many restricted areas that most people cannot get into. As a young girl, all those keys that I saw jingling at someone's side always impressed me. I wanted to have all that access. Or at least I wanted to have all those keys!

ADORATION/EXPLANATION

If you are a true believer in Christ, you have all the keys to the Kingdom of heaven. Our relationship to Jesus opens the doors of heaven and gives us direct access to the Father. I do not need a human intercessor for I have an unobstructed path of conversation and time with God. That pathway was made open by the person of Jesus Christ. Wow!

"I will give you the keys of the kingdom of heaven; whatever you bind on earth will be bound in heaven, and whatever you loose on earth will be loosed in heaven." Matthew 16:19 (NIV)

Once, having been asked by the Pharisees when the kingdom of God would come, Jesus replied, "The kingdom of God does not come with your careful observation, nor will people say, "Here it is," or "There it is," because the kingdom of God is within you." Luke 17:20-21 (NIV)

Jesus said, "My kingdom is not of this world." John 18:36a (NIV)

WORSHIP/OBEDIENCE

When we recognize that Jesus is Christ, our Savior who died on the cross for our sins, only then can we enter into a unique and personal relationship with Him. This relationship of faith gives us all the resources we need to face any circumstance. The key is actually Christ himself. He has given us the keys to living for God here on earth and the key to our heavenly kingdom when we pass from this earth into everlasting life. The Bible gives us the information about Christ's life and his example for us. I have the keys…do you?

Yesterday we talked about the keys to the kingdom. There are no keys without Christ, and there is no belief in Christ without accepting the cross. Our keys to God's kingdom come with beneficial resources for our lives, but there is no genuine Christianity without a cross. You cannot be a disciple of Jesus without taking up your cross.

ADORATION/EXPLANATION

Bearing a cross can be painful and forever change your life. Jesus understood that His father's plan for Him would lead Him to Calvary. He understood, yet still asked that God would take it away if He could. Why? Jesus lived in a human form just as we do and did not want the pain and agony of death on a cross. The difference between Jesus and us lies in the fact that when God did not choose to remove the cross from his life, He still willing accepted the decision and obeyed.

***

"I tell you the truth," Jesus said to them, "no one who has left home or wife or brothers or parents or children for the sake of the kingdom of God will fail to receive many times as much in this age and, in the age to come, eternal life." Luke 18:29-30 (NIV)

Then he said to them all: "If anyone would come after me, he must deny himself and take up his cross daily and follow me. For whoever wants to save his life will lose it, but whoever loses his life for me will save it. What good is it for a man to gain the whole world, and yet lose or forfeit his very self?" Luke 9:23-25 (NIV)

WORSHIP/OBEDIENCE

Condemned criminals were forced to carry their crosses. Unlike the others however, who were brought to this place of death unwillingly, Christ voluntarily gave up His life. When Jesus spoke the words in Luke 9, the listeners were probably shocked and startled. Take up a cross? Why? Are we condemned criminals? God is asking us to deny our self-centeredness and commit our lives wholeheartedly to Him, to take up His example and obediently make his priorities our priorities!

***

Tonight is New Year's Eve! For some it will be a party lasting long past midnight, for others it will hold excitement and hope about the upcoming New Year. Yet for many, it will hold great trepidation about the future. Not a healthy cautiousness, but a paralyzing worry over what is to come. They will quietly go to bed and try not to think about the up-coming year. They are filled with fear...

ADORATION/EXPLANATION

The Bible encourages believers to fear God. This fear is another way of giving God reverence and respect. According to the Psalmist, it is the "beginning of wisdom," and it teaches us that we can look expectantly (and not fearfully) toward our future. Troubles may come and troubles may go—after all, no one can see into a crystal ball to what lies ahead—but we do have a Savior who sees, knows, and walks side by side with us along the way.

The fear of the Lord is the beginning of knowledge, but fools despise wisdom and discipline. Proverbs 1:7 (NIV)

For the Lord gives wisdom, and from his mouth come knowledge and understanding. He holds victory in store for the upright, he is a shield to those whose walk is blameless, for he guards the course of the just and protects the way of his faithful ones. Proverbs 2:6-8 (NIV)

For God did not give us a spirit of timidity, but a spirit of power, of love and of self-discipline. 2 Timothy 1:7 (NIV)

And out of justice, peace. Quietness and confidence will reign forever more. Isaiah 32:17 (TLB)

WORSHIP/OBEDIENCE

Fear and timidity cause us to stop and question what God has clearly told us to do in His word. We do not know what lies ahead of us, so we become apprehensive and fearful. Fear is not an excuse to fail to obey God in your daily living in this upcoming year. You have been given a spirit of power, love, and self-discipline. Always remember, Christ has set you free!

CPSIA information can be obtained at www.ICGtesting.com
Printed in the USA
BVOW08s2236280914

368535BV00001B/1/P

9 781937 660314